BELLWOOD PUBLIC LIBRARY

Bellwood, Ill.

Phone Li 7-7393

H o u r s

Monday – Thursday

9:30-9:00 P.M.

Friday

9:30-6:00 P.M.

Saturday

9:30-4:00 P.M.

A Reader's Guide to Science Fiction

A Reader's Guide to Science Fiction

By
Baird Searles,
Martin Last,
Beth Meacham,
and
Michael Franklin

With a foreword by
Samuel R. Delany

Facts On File, Inc.
119 W. 57 Street, New York, N.Y. 10019

A Reader's Guide to Science Fiction

Published in hardcover by Facts On File, Inc., in 1980, by arrangement with Avon Books.

Originally published in paperback by Avon Books in 1979.

Index prepared by Marjorie Bank, Susan Ginzburg and Kurt L. Roth.

ISBN 0-87196-473-2

Printed in the United States of America

10   9   8   7   6   5   4   3   2   1

This book is dedicated specifically to Alice K. Turner and Rafe Blasi, without whom the Science Fiction Shop would not be what it is today, and generally to all our intelligent, friendly, and honest customers who so far outnumber the other kinds.

Contents

Foreword

by Samuel R. Delany

On the upper left-hand shelf of my library, there are, by measure-ment, thirty-one inches devoted to books about science fiction. They range from computer assisted word-analysis of texts by Isaac Asimov to divigations on imagery in early Zelazny. Some are written by well-known academics, printed in hardcovers and bearing the names of respected university presses. Some are lavish over-sized affairs, interleaved with reproductions of surreal art and old magazine covers. Still others, written by enthusiastic kids (most of theirs, mimeographed and stapled pam-phlets), are simply determined to have a say about much loved (or hated) books. There's everything in between—two even by me.

Though all these books are more or less fascinating (and, yes, some are fascinatingly bad), very few of them are generally useful—useful to the general reader who wants to know, "What do I read *now?*"

Who is this general reader? It can be the reader who has just heard that there *is* such a thing as science fiction, that some other readers are excited about it, and who wants to try some out—only to walk into a bookstore and find that the largest wall of face-out paperbacks in the shop is full of bizarre pictures, odd-sounding titles, and hundreds of completely unknown authors: "Science Fiction," says the sign at the shelf-top.

"All right, what *do* I do now?"

Or it can be the reader who used to read science fiction back when there were maybe ten-to-twenty s-f titles available in paperback over the course of the year and the monthly magazines provided the bulk of the stories anyway; a reader who ceased to read for a while, but who has somehow gotten an inkling that something exciting has been going on in the genre recently, but who has to deal with the fact that over four-teen percent of *all* the fiction published in the United States this year was science fiction—that's over five hundred new titles and even more reprints of old ones!

"*Now* what am I supposed to do?"

Or it could be you: You've read some science fiction—a little or a lot—and you've liked it—a lot or a little.

"Okay, what *are* we supposed to do now?"

Get hold of a copy of this book and keep it where you can put your hands on it: that's the best thing I can think of. This book *is* useful...

One reason most of the books on my shelf are not generally useful is because they are almost all organized around something we might call the "historical model," or: "Start at the beginning and go on till you come to the end." Despite the fact that deciding just what *is* the beginning of anything is a hopelessly complicated task (and always turns out to be a decision pretty well determined by the use you want to put your end-points to), this model is also a very hard one to learn things from, especially if it's a real-world phenomenon—and nothing is realer than the prevalence of science fiction on bookstore racks and library shelves today. The easiest way to learn anything, in matters written, say poetry or drama, is to start with what's going on *now*.

What's going on now is always the easiest thing to understand because, if nothing else, it is written in the most immediate language—the language we speak today. Only then do you start working your way back, a little at a time, to what was written yesterday; and then you go back to what was written just before that. You see the changes, but you see them happening slowly. You learn their directions, their nuances; you learn them as you would a natural language—by exposure. You get comfortable with them through repeated contact. In this way, you can work your way back to Aeschylus and Archilochus if you like. What's more, by the time you reach them, Aeschylus and Archilochus will make a good deal of sense, and you will have negotiated the changes in the genres in a reasonable way, i.e., a little bit at a time, seeing how each changed in each little way from the stuff you've already experienced. Also, by the time you get there, many things you've read well back along your trip will make even more sense than they did when you first read them; you will be able to see the highlights cast by the works written before and after them. But if you start right out with Aeschylus and Archilochus—just becaue they come at the "beginning"—they are probably going to be Greek to you in more ways than one. The change from modern conventions of thought and language is simply too great for one to just jump in and splash around without a fair amount of preparation. By the same token, if you do get caught up in those early works without really knowing where you and they are, when you finally *do* turn to look at contemporary work, *that's* not going to make much sense either, because it's so different from the things you've been struggling with.

The same applies to science fiction: you'll suffer the same confusions if you start with, say, the cumbersome 16th- and 17th-century texts of Kepler or Bacon that a number of the more academically oriented writers on my shelf wish to use, for their particular ends, as the origins of science fiction.

The book at hand gives you a tool with which to negotiate the sea of paperbacks facing you from the s-f racks of your nearest bookstore, or the recently published hardcovers in your local library. It will leave you free to map out your own useful, creative, and illuminating path back into and through the various "golden ages" of the genre, a path littered with wonder and paved with the marvelous. But whether your journey goes toward the future of the genre, or into the genre's past glories, I can think of no better beginning preparation than a few hours with this book. That's why it's useful. When you've read the introduction by the authors following these pages, you'll learn how they came by such useful knowledge.

A closing thought: I can think of a distressing number of the least useful academic writings on science fiction where, if the writers had had a book like this, they might have been a good deal better. Writing seriously about science fiction is a comparatively recent enterprise—compared, say, to writing seriously about the fall of Rome, Provencal poetry, Shakespeare, and the Bible. The academics who write about science fiction have to take a great deal of flack, both from their fellow academics who wonder why they bother in the first place, and then from folks like me who want them to do it differently. All in all, they're a rather courageous bunch, and it's as a tribute to their courage that I have my thirty-one inch shelf up there in the first place. But there is a tradition of reader response to science fiction—printed and considered response—that is comparatively old. It is older than the discovery of Game Theory, older than the knowledge of viral bacteriophages, older than the decipherment of the dance code of the honey bee. It is based on science fiction readers wanting to communicate with other readers about what they are reading now; and it manifests itself in hundreds of fanzines (amateur magazines about science fiction), hundreds of science fiction conventions each year, probably thousands of local science fiction clubs—and *more* hundreds of fanzines! It's a tradition that, *if* academics

do not at least take intelligent cognizance of, they will simply not be talking about the totality of the science fiction experience. This book comes
very much out of that tradition; the tradition of people who read science
fiction and talk about it to other interested people, who will be reading
it now and today.

Use it for reference, for browsing, for stimulation—or just plain fun.
And have a good read.

—Samuel R. Delany
New York, 1978

Introduction

How and Why
To Use This Book
Plus a Brief Introduction
to Its Authors

More than five years ago, The Science Fiction Shop opened its door; through it since then have passed tens of thousands of science fiction buyers, from the most knowledgeable collectors to the most timid newcomers to the genre. Because of this, those associated with the Shop rapidly got to know what other people wanted to know. This book is that knowledge transferred to paper, the product of thousands of questions.

It's possible that the most erudite of science fiction scholars might find something new here, but this volume is really aimed at a range of readers that will cover those just trying to find their way around the vast amount of literature, through those who have been reading s-f for some time, but who might want to expand their horizons without the time and expense of the trial and error method.

Not that we have anything against the trial and error method. It can indeed run into time and money, but it will often incorporate serendipity, the fortuitous finding of a book or author one might never have come across save by accident. But we hope that this book might even make serendipity easier, that by dipping into, browsing in, or reading through it, the questing reader will get a concrete idea of what lies behind most of the covers that so intimidatingly line the science fiction shelves of his bookshop. (A more concrete idea, certainly, than what the usual paperback blurb might give. Never has "Don't judge a book by its cover" been more meaningful.)

And due to the history of science fiction as the stepchild of literature, that escapist stuff that only perpetual adolescents read, very few librarians or booksellers really know much about it. (A situation that, in time, will be corrected by the rising of a generation that may or may not be perpetually adolescent, but that knows its science fiction.)

"Which author(s) should I try first (or next)?" Turn to the next chapter, "If You Like Heinlein, Will You Love Van Vogt?" Here you will find a listing of over two hundred science fiction authors of the past and present. Dip into it. Even if you're hard to please, you're bound to soon find a writer who sounds tempting. We have tried, as is explained more fully in the introduction to that chapter, to convey the quality of each author without critical dissection. Now if you already have an idea of which authors you like, check them out in the listing. You may find mentioned novels or stories you might not have known about *or* in many cases, there will be a parenthetical notation following the author's profile that suggests others, that for one reason or another, might appeal in the same way.

"What are the other books in the_____series?" Science fiction is series prone. You'll find a listing of the components of most current series in the "Last and First Books" chapter.

"What are the major awards and who are the award winners in science fiction?" If you go on the perfectly valid theory that an award winner must have *something* going for it, check the winners in the chapter "The Space Academy Awards."

"What would be a good basic reading list to give me an idea of the history and various kinds of science fiction?" See our "5 Parsec Shelf" chapter; we think it's more than good, but we're prejudiced.

And finally, if you're curious as to where all this came from and "Exactly what *is* science fiction, anyhow?" there's a painless history of it all as a final bonus.

We sincerely hope you will find it all useful. We're pretty sure you will.

Who *are* "we," anyhow? Well, as is obvious, we have been associated with The Science Fiction Shop through all or most of its history. The Shop was Baird's idea: he has been a reader of science fiction since 1945, and has had reviews in *The New York Times, The Village Voice, Publishers Weekly* and other arcane places, as well as the first sustaining science fiction review program on radio. He currently reviews films for *The Magazine of Fantasy and Science Fiction* and books for Isaac Asimov's *SF Magazine*.

Martin has also been associated with the Shop since its beginning, and is now Baird's partner in the enterprise. A published poet and art critic, he was editor-in-chief of *The Science Fiction Review Monthly*. His particular interests in the field now are the contemporary stylists, Ballard, Delany, et al.

Michael and Beth both grew up with science fiction, and cut their eye teeth on the excellent science fiction juveniles of the 1950s, such as those of Robert A. Heinlein. (Michael had a good start because his father was a dedicated aficianado.) Beth has co-authored a book before this one, (*Nightshade,* with Tappan King); her particular field of interest within the genre is the rising number of female writers. Michael is an aspiring comedy writer and is particularly knowledgeable about the more traditional contemporary s-f authors.

That's the us of "we." We hope that our combined knowledge of science fiction will help you find many authors and books you might have missed otherwise. After all, half the fun of loving something is the joy of being able to share it, and we love science fiction.

Authors' Note: Only a time machine could solve the problem of the important works and major authors that will emerge after this book goes to press. Not having such a gadget, we only hope that writers *and* readers will understand.

Part One

If You Like Heinlein, Will You Love Van Vogt? 200 Authors and Their Major Works

You will find here, in the central and largest section of the *Reader's Guide*, articles on almost all the science fiction writers currently working, and many from the past whose writings have remained available. ("Classic" is a tricky word, particularly used in conjunction with any sort of literature; let's just say these older works have endured for various reasons.)

At The Science Fiction Shop, one of the routines we're quite used to is the customer who says (usually apologetically, like the prodigal returned), "I haven't read any science fiction in 10 (or 15 or 20) years. Can you suggest something?" Other variations are "I've only read books by Larry Niven and Zenna Henderson. Who writes like they do?" (!) and, most challenging of all, "I've never read any science fiction. Where should I start?"

In the articles on the many authors you will find here, there is a minimum of material that is biographical, bibliographical, encyclopedic, or referential. What we want to do is to give you a good solid idea of what the author's *work* is like; his own particular flavor, as it were. Nor are these pieces critical; one man's masterpiece is another man's yawn. We have tried to point out the positive elements in each author's output; what qualities the potential reader will find there and *not* what is "good" or "bad" (science fiction, thank God, has not gotten to the hit or flop syndrome ordained by a Critical Establishment; authors are popular because the readers like them, peculiarly enough).

We have also in many cases suggested that if you like author A, you might find author B interesting. These are purely subjective judgements; no one author writes just like another (though there are those who try very hard—enough said about *them*).

One terrible frustration for us in writing this section is the knowledge that some of the books mentioned are not available currently ("in print" or "out of print" is publisher's parlance for available or not available). What titles *are* in print changes almost daily; paperbacks in particular can go out of print within months of publication. However, publishers are realizing that science fiction, in a peculiar way, is almost timeless, and often doesn't date as quickly as "mainstream" literature. Therefore, more and more science fiction works remain in print longer, and more and more of the older works are being brought back. So if a particular book mentioned here is reported as out of print by your (hopefully knowledgeable) bookseller, keep asking. There's a good chance it will return.

So here, in a nutshell, are hundreds of the authors you might have wondered about, individually or collectively. May we introduce you to Mr. Ballard, Mr. Niven, Ms. Bradley, and all their wild, wonderful, and varied kin?

MARK ADLARD came to the attention of readers with the publication of his trilogy called overall "T-city," consisting of *Interface, Voltface,* and *Multiface.* These novels deal with a vast corporation of immense power and the people who run it, and run afoul of it. The world, or at least the world of T-city, seems entirely built from something called Stahlex, an all-purpose plastic from which virtually everything needed can be fashioned.

The ambiance of T-city is one of leisure, boredom, outre pleasures, and internecine business dealings, with the wants and needs of its people provided for. This situation, of course, leads to mass neurosis, revolution and pandemonium. The Stahlex corporates, who control the social structures of T-city, decide that the cure to this chaos and unrest is to put everyone back to work...work as such has been for the most part obviated by the high degree of automation and cybernetics.

In book 3, *Multiface,* the people are contentedly working, occupying their time and minds with dehumanizing and pointless activity, as numbing as was the monotony of the past.

Although there is considerable plot and narration in the T-city trilogy, and much interpersonal goings-on, the work's thematics are elsewhere. Adlard writes caveats, ugly predictions of an ugly world of the future with his material firmly rooted in the social and corporate potentials for horror we find in the world of today. No work, or body of work, in s-f has so thoroughly developed the ramifications of future mega-corporation activities, controls and interferences with the social order, and the author's dire visions are chilling.

(If you like Adlard's work, try that of Mack Reynolds.)

ALAN BURT AKERS is known for one extended work, the Dray Prescott Series, and as lengthy series go, Akers' goes well.

Antares is a double sun in the constellation Scorpio, and the planet Kregen orbits Antares. Kregen is the epicenter of a vast, intergalactic struggle which uses as pawns the humanoid types found in the many states on the planet. Earthman Dray Prescott has worked for the battling powers, and his courage and intelligence have won him a degree of personal freedom and a sound place in the Empire. Duplicity, disruption, strange monsters threatening the Empire, a princess loved by Prescott, deceptive schemes, quasi-humans and peculiar aliens complicate life as Prescott performs the required fantasy-hero wonders. Akers' power to maintain the level of adventure and the reasonable quality of writing provide a very long and event-rich series, one that seems prepared to continue ad infinitum.

(If you like Akers, certainly the adventure series of Edgar Rice Burroughs, Lin Carter, and John Norman might appeal, as well as Jack Vance's "Planet of Adventure" series.)

BRIAN ALDISS, along with his peer and friend J. G. Ballard, writes and thinks with enormous sophistication and wonderfully casual erudition. And, like Ballard, Aldiss indicates his respect for his reader by assuming that said reader knows quite a lot about quite a lot. No condescension; no parenthetical explanations.

Aldiss has written many novels, published handfuls of short stories, and contributed much analytical non-fiction. His novels deal with a wide range of material: *Non-stop (Starship)* is a tale of mutants and disorder. *Cryptozoic* tells of a man who moves through layers of time (time travel is a frequent device explored in Aldiss' fiction) discovering the truths and terrors of the human condition. *Hothouse*, or *The Long Afternoon of Earth*, is put together from a five part idea. Earth no longer rotates and the hemisphere that faces the sun is overgrown with sometimes sentient flora, rather less than friendly to mankind, or what is left of it. Man's ever diminishing supply of himself, his eventual extinction, is unassuaged when he is given a chance to go off-planet to seed a new world. He stays with his dying Earth. In *Report on Probability A* watchers watch watchers watching watchers; comparative and related phenomena are explored and reality and illusion become indistinguishable. *The Dark Light Years* is about a race of repulsive but cultured and intelligent aliens whose social behavior is curious and fascinating. *Barefoot in the Head* tells of the aftereffects of an acid (LSD) war in which the Middle East has virtually stoned all of Britain and Europe. Colin Charteris tries to sort out the dippy chaos only to find himself the focus of the messianic desperation of the people. He is hailed and appointed, and eventually Charteris believes in what is happening to him. Aldiss expertly communicates the disorientations of mind, lapses of order and expectation, and oblique humour involved. *Barefoot* is a most contemporary novel.

Frankenstein Unbound and *The Malacia Tapestry* are time travel novels which explore the past from alternate points of view; the former has been called a love letter to Mary Shelley. Aldiss' short fictions are contained in such collections as *Airs of Earth, The Saliva Tree, Galaxies Like Grains of Sand* and *Who Can Replace a Man?*

Brian Aldiss uses most of the familiar themes and conventions of the genre, but because of his enormous ability for deviant extrapolation and his always modern equivocation his fictions are fresh and invigorating.

(If you like Brian Aldiss, you might try John Brunner or T. J. Bass.)

POUL ANDERSON published his first short story in 1947, one year before he received a degree in physics. The lure of the typewriter was apparently stronger than the lure of the laboratory, and Anderson has made a successful career out of writing science fiction.

Anderson has written nearly forty novels (and scores of short stories), but tends to return to the same theme again and again, each book or story exploring a different aspect of whatever trouble he has gotten his hero into. Anderson's style is a blend of hard science (remember the physics), swashbuckling adventure, and Scandinavian mythology. Anderson is also the originator of most of the military tactics used in s-f; his battles are the most exciting around.

Like all s-f writers, Anderson has taken a stab at time travel, notably in *There Will Be Time*. Jack Havig is able to travel in time, not with any device, but simply by willing a time shift. Jack doesn't like all that he sees in the future, so he sets out to change things; he twists the past but finds the future even less palatable, and himself irrevocably outside it. When read with the Time Patrol stories (*The Corridors of Time* and

Guardians of Time) There Will be Time gives the reader a logical and consistent temporal theory.

Exploring and colonizing new planets is a primary theme in s-f; indeed all s-f is about exploring our universe. In *Tau Zero,* a work of great maturity and realism, Anderson creates a portrait of interstellar exploration at sub-light speed. Because of an accident, the ship is unable to brake and cannot stop at its destination. Anderson deftly weaves his plot around interpersonal relationships, the psychic shock of relativity, and the physical ambience of a starship. *Tau Zero* is a hard science novel, but transcends the problems that such books usually have with characterization.

After Doomsday exemplifies the post-catastrophe novel, dealing with a search through space for human survivors after the Earth is blown up.

The High Crusade is a story of borrowed technology; a spaceship, you see, landed on Earth in about 1200 A.D., the aliens intending to invade. A group of knights defeated them in battle, and then set out in the spacecraft to carry their Crusade to the stars. They succeeded in establishing an empire, but could never find their way back to Earth. The novel opens with a Terran contact team trying to understand why this new found culture is so much like ancient Earth history. *High Crusade* is a witty and internally consistent story. If it isn't true, it ought to be.

Anderson's novels are solid, inovative s-f, though they sometimes lack the vision and scope of other writers. It is in his series that Anderson's range and talent is fully revealed; but his series require a word or three of explanation.

Anderson has limned out a "future history," and has written of it in fifteen novels and many short stories. However (and this is where it gets confusing), the history revolves around two characters in two disparate time periods. The first is Trader Nicholas Van Rijn, chief activist of the Polesotechnic League, a loosely confederated organization of interplanetary merchants. The second is Dominic Flandry, a secret agent of the much, much later Galactic Imperium. One could, and many do, say that these are two separate series—but Flandry occasionally refers to Van Rijn much as we would refer to Alexander the Great.

Van Rijn is the very epitome of a crafty merchant, a capitalist with no apologies, yet he has a heart of gold and the soul of a buccaneer. Van Rijn is always running up against faceless corporate entities and monopolists, meanwhile meeting and trading with aliens of all kinds.

Flandry is the unsung hero of the twilight Empire, secret agent extraordinary, who sees himself fighting a losing battle against the decline of humanity. Flandry's adventures are exciting and varied, and sometimes verge on being actual mysteries.

Because Anderson has had so much time to work out their worlds, times, and personalities, Van Rijn and Flandry are very real people. They are quirky, they have pasts, they worry about the future, they grow and age.

Finally, one cannot ignore Poul Anderson's fantasies; based on Norse legend, they are epic sagas full of high romance, heroism, and humanity. *The Broken Sword* is a classic retelling of the changeling myth, and *Three Hearts and Three Lions* is the story of a man caught up in a heroic cycle. These are only two of the fantasies Anderson has written; all are a pleasure to read.

(If you like Poul Anderson, we suggest Gordon Dickson, Arthur C. Clarke, Larry Niven, Jack Williamson, Isaac Asimov, James Blish, or Hal Clement.)

PIERS ANTHONY is one of those authors who can perform magic with the ordinary; he manages to take what at first glance seems to be a fairly pedestrian plot and make of it something rather special.

Omnivore, for instance, is basically the story of three human explorers of a strange fungoid-populated planet and the super-secret semi-clone agent attempting to discern what they discovered there. Where Anthony's skill comes into play is in the colorfully detailed descriptions of the planet, Nacre, its inhabitants and ecology, and in the careful development of the characters involved. The further adventures of the explorers are followed in the novels *Orn* and *Ox.*

Anthony concocts an unusual blend of high adventure and rich characterization in *The Battle Circle* trilogy. Set in a post-catastrophe world where a benevolent scientific elite keeps the rest of the populace in ignorant barbarism and nomadic wandering, the three novels, *Sos, Var,* and *Neq,* detail intriguing cultures, beliefs and characters, often in violent and well described conflict.

Prostho Plus is a novel that in other hands might have been just plain silly, but Anthony makes this farce about the kidnapping and education of one Dr. Dillingham, a forty-one year old dentist from Earth, by an exotic array of aliens, a loving satire of space opera, soap opera, and pretensions.

Macroscope is Piers Anthony's most widely known work and seems almost like two novels rolled into one. The first portion of the book is straight science fiction, dealing with the discovery and potential of the Macroscope, possibly a literal doorway to unknown universes, and conveyor of a message that drives men mad. The use of this machine takes the four protagonists into the second portion of the novel, where astrological symbolism and alien races weave a thread of sexual and emotional change through the lives of the quartet.

Weaving with words is an apt analogy for his *Cluster Series*, a magnificent tapestry with intergalactic war and fascinating speculation on development in the use of Kirlian auras merely the basic fabric. Set in this background are carefully picked out threads of thoughtful creation; detailed sexual, emotional, and societal examinations of the various alien and humanoid species that compose the membership of the Milky Way and Andromeda galaxies, romantic interludes between friends and/or enemies, and a complex and rational use of Tarot cards and readings. Related closely to this series is the *Planet Tarot* trilogy, a novel in three volumes chronicling the founding of the church of Tarot and the life of its founder, Brother Paul.

Anthony is a craftsman, and, like a skilled furniture builder who can make a chair much more than a place to sit, makes a book more than words to read. Don't be misled by plot summary of any of his works; even if it sounds like you may have read it before by another author, Anthony will give you something extra.

(The work of Alan Dean Foster or Andrew Offutt might appeal to you if you like Piers Anthony.)

CHRISTOPHER ANVIL is the pseudonym of Harry C. Crosby, Jr. Should we wonder if his chosen surname is indicative of the ironic character of his Pandora stories, out of which grew the novel, *Pandora's Planet?* Though the stories were popular in the late '50s, the novel didn't appear until recently. It is, indeed, an ironic romp having to do with the surrender of the forces of Earth (military forces, that is, not *the force* force) to those of Centran. As placation, Earth exports all of its finer ideas and processes: credit, socio-religious fanaticism, totalitarianism, dietary trends, Karl Marx, and all of the other whimsies of modern life. The galactic empire of the Centrans, at first delighted with these new notions, finds itself less conqueror than conquered as it is undermined by the bounty.

Warlord's World is space opera in its modern but unadulterated form, yet in it Anvil deliberately plays for laughs—not a convention of the sub-genre. It all has to do with a space cop who is more than cuckolded by a conniving princess who has attracted him with a call for help.

(If the adventure novels of Anvil appeal, you might try those of Jerry Pournelle.)

ISAAC ASIMOV has written books on practically everything except animal husbandry, and we could have missed that one in the crowd. He is known around the science fiction world as "the good doctor," not because he's a whiz at setting bones, but because his output indicates a doctorate in anything doctoratable. Though he is now well enough known beyond s-f to have done TV commercials, he keeps his ties there and can frequently be seen and heard (well across the room) at conventions.

His science fiction writing alone would be a career in itself for any less prolific writer. He was one of the three giants to emerge from the golden age of s-f magazines (the others are Heinlein and Clarke); his stories appeared with amazing (not to mention astonishing and astounding) regularity in the pulps of the '40s.

Asimov's science fiction is perhaps epitomal of the classics of the '40s; it is very much concerned with ideas. His characters are on hand to keep the plot moving and not much else (though in the "Mule" of the Foundation stories, he did create one of science fiction's most memorable antiheroes; there are few if any true villains in his works). But his concepts are a marvelous mixture drawn from both the "hard" and "soft" sciences. His great Foundation trilogy (*Foundation, Foundation and Empire, Second Foundation*—originally published in magazines as a series of short stories and novelettes) is rightly considered by many as the peak work of the Golden Age. It concerns a Galactic Empire of the far future, soon to collapse from decadence within and barbarians from without. The "psycho-historians" of the age have developed history into a hard science, with the high probability ability to foresee major events. To prevent an age-long Dark Age, a Foundation is set up to help mankind recivilize itself, and a mysterious Second Foundation is also established in case the first fails. The suspense involves the history of mankind; will the Foundations succeed, given the emergence of random variables such as a powerful mutant dictator (the aforementioned Mule)? The background technology of the Galactic Empire is "nuts-'n-bolts" s-f at its best, but the conceptual excitement here comes from extrapolations in sociology and history.

The classic short story "Nightfall" is about a civilization existing on a planet so astronomically situated that darkness comes only once every 2000 years; when that occurs, the social system collapses.

The *The End of Eternity*, Asimov sees the time continuum in terms of space. The various eras, by means of time travel, maintain diplomatic and trade relations with each other, and reality is rigidly maintained by an organization of which the hero is a member.

And mention must be made of Asimov's robot stories (collected in *I, Robot* and *The Rest of the Robots)* in which his Three Laws of Robotics, which neatly and simply prevent the intelligent robot from being a menace to man or mankind, are a prime example of the axiom adopted by the entire science fiction writing community simply because it must be so.

There are numerous other novels (*Caves of Steel* and *The Naked Sun* are rousing detective novels of the future, featuring a robot investigator) and even more short stories, gathered into many collections.

(If you like Asimov, we suggest Heinlein, the science fictional Leiber, Anderson, and Le Guin.)

J. G. BALLARD stands oddly and enigmatically apart from the main-stream of science fiction. Although his early work, particularly his first four novels, continued an especially British theme (the "disaster" novel), they had the quality of being internalized; most s-f tends to be militantly externalized. These novels, along with several collections of highly styled and much praised short stories, established Ballard quickly in the forefront of a new generation of British writers, many of whom were major movers in the avant-garde magazine *New Worlds*.

Ballard's first novel, *The Wind From Nowhere,* tells of an increasingly inexorable wind which is reducing the world to randomly distributed rubble. What is fascinating is the oblique glimpse into the psyches of the novel's actors as they cope with collapse. In *The Drought* the north-ern latitudes (Ballard's novels, with one exception, all take place in England) are parched, as the rains cease and the seas recede. One man, a non-hero, and a clutch of perhaps emblematic others work their way to-ward the sea, only to return, finally, to a smoking, ravaged, dry London. In *The Drowned World* there is too much water, and in *The Crystal World,* the finest of the four, the world is crystalizing. Passages from this book describing the fantastic vision of man, animal, and flora becoming pure abstract crystal are writing at its lapidary best.

A group of compressed fictions, highly experimental in both attempt and result, came to form *The Atrocity Exhibition,* and traditional s-f threw Ballard out of the club. This astonishing work, with its objectively depicted violence and its masterfully honed prose, utilized, among other inventive devices, real people: JFK, Elizabeth Taylor, and Ronald Reagan move in these inner landscapes. Ballard had begun to attract the attention of outside readers, and by most traditional definitions was no longer an s-f writer.

Perhaps Ballard's quintessential work is a collection of stories, alike in locus and character, and written over some ten years, called *Vermilion Sands.* Vermilion Sands is a kind of future Palm Springs, inhabited by artists of various persuasions, and dilettantes. It is a civilized world of flyers who sculpt the clouds, sculptures with organic qualities, plants that sing, and a poetess whose mad poems fly in the night on printout tapes. Ballard says that Vermilion Sands is where he would be happy to live.

A direct outgrowth of *The Atrocity Exhibition, Crash* explores in poetically clinical detail the tantalizing relationship between the disorganized violence of an auto crash and the also disorganized allure of sex. Again there are "real" people here, including the author himself, though at a remove. *Concrete Island* is a kind of diary, detailing the physical metaphors of its protagonist's own *gestalt* when he finds himself isolated in the midst of the city's webbing of roads and flyovers after he crashes into a disused and forgotten area. He is surrounded by indifferent traffic, alone and unseen, and finally he finds himself less and less interested in escaping. In *High Rise* Ballard postulates the physical and moral decay, the return to barbarism of the tenants of a high rise living complex in London. Here, as in all of Ballard's work, there are no heroes, no villains. Only people shaped and reshaped by the structures they, as society, continually construct and demolish.

Ballard has always written lean and often puzzling short stories, of which there are several collections (*The Terminal Beach, Chronopolis*) and here, as in the novels, the event never exists for itself. Narrative is inner and is always mirrored by the somehow surreal landscapes Ballard's sparely elegant prose manufactures.

Not for the reader seeking entertaining adventure, Ballard's work usually makes a memorable and haunting impact on the serious s-f explorer.

(Ballard fanciers might explore the works of Samuel R. Delany, John Christopher, John Crowley, Marta Randall, Jack Vance, or John Wyndham.)

T. J. BASS didn't miss a Nebula by much in 1974 with his remarkable novel *The Godwhale*. Bass envisions a world devastated and bereft of all sentient life except human, with only rudimentary plant forms remaining; a world in which humans live underground in colonies or hives, while others manage to live in the seas enclosed in bubbles. . . Bass calls them Benthic, things that live in great deeps. One Larry Dever, whose body is in suspension awaiting a medical technology advanced enough to put it back together again, employs a cyborg-whale, a wondrous blend of robot, whale, and computer—in fact, the title character—to work for the ultimate good. That good is the eventual regeneration of the Earth's biology. Bass brings a fascinating and considerable knowledge into his story; the complexity of the biological detail, as extrapolated, is convincing and entertaining.

In an earlier novel, *Half Past Human,* a kind of rehearsal for *The Godwhale,* Bass' powers of invention present four-toed humans of a far future who live in hives in unimaginable numbers; and five-toed ones who live above, but they are hunted and harvested by a sort of pre-Godwhale in the form of a spaceship which (who?) plants them on other planets with Earth-like conditions. The complexities of human biology and genetics, the arcane bio-physics Bass involves in his novel all but swallow its thin plot, but detail is thorough and credible.

Though the two novels have obvious and subtle connections, they are not interdependent.

(We suggest Aldiss if you like Bass.)

BARRINGTON J. BAYLEY. Ideas are the playthings of science fiction; Bayley is a skillful player. He works with theories of the related concepts of probability and time, and juggles them into a good story while he's at it. *The Grand Wheel* is the story of a gambler, in a future where "randomatics," the mathematics of chance, has been developed to the point where chance has essentially vanished. Cheyne Scarnes, anxious to get into the Grand Wheel, descendant of organized gambling, parlays his stake into a gamble for the human race and the entire universe.

To Bayley, time is a malleable thing. In *The Fall of Chronopolis,* it is a wave with plateaus, or islands, of "now"; in *Collision Course* there are two separate civilizations on Earth, each with its origin in the far future of the other.

If playing with time and chance appeal to you, obviously so will Bayley's work.

(Keith Laumer and Robert Heinlein also play amusingly with time.)

GREGORY BENFORD's first novel to gain significant attention was *In the Ocean of Night*, a complex and subtle tale of near-future man confronting the inevitably existential questions and decisions about contact with extraterrestrial intelligences. The subject is hardly a new one for s-f writers, but several recent novelists have brought a new sensibility to it. In Benford's book what is believed to be a comet speeds toward Earth with an at least partial collision seen as inevitable. An astronaut, a fully realized *person*, is dispatched to plant charges on the dangerous debris and destroy it. When he discovers, in scenes of gathering intensity, that the supposed comet is, in fact, an ancient derelict spaceship from an unknown, uncomputerized elsewhere, he rebels and refuses to demolish this invaluable relic of a civilization he is convinced was far superior to his own. When later another alien ship enters Earth's purview, this time giving off clear indications of life and intelligence, Walmsly, the astronaut, looks with near messianic expectation to its arrival.

Gregory Benford won a Nebula Award, with Gordon Eklund, for the novella "If the Stars Were Gods," later expanded by the two writers into a full-length novel. Benford's earlier book, *Deeper Than Darkness,* has been rewritten and is now called *The Stars in Shroud.* It is a serious and provocative novel dealing with the threat of the Quarn, distant aliens, to move into Earth's sphere by systematically spreading a psychic disease among the populations of Earth's far-flung empire, and the nefarious and always short-sighted quarrels among Earth's shapers and movers as to how to deal with the mounting incursion.

Benford's work is a tasteful and powerful mesh of technology as a poetic blended with good thoughtful storytelling.

(If excellent writing and fine s-f such as Benford's attracts you, then look at the work of Michael Bishop, Samuel Delany, or Tom Disch.)

ALFRED BESTER. It comes as a surprise to many readers to be told that Alfred Bester has been publishing science fiction since 1939, even though he is accepted as one of the classic authors in the field. This is in a sense, an acknowledgment of one of his outstanding attributes, the quality that can best be described as sophistication. One of the curious facts about the history of s-f is that until very recently its major writers have been academics and/or provincials. Bester's two novels of the '50s were urbane (in the literal sense of the word); science fiction was ready for this then, and both *The Demolished Man* and *The Stars My Destination* were immediate hits. They have remained so to this day; because they were in a sense ahead of their time, they have not dated even in the small degree that good s-f sometimes does.

To further define this one-man stylistic revolution, Bester's work (which would seem to owe a good deal to the hard driving Chandler mystery school) moves enormously fast; not with the simplistic speed of the action-adventure pulp fiction, but at a narrative pace that is also immensely detailed, giving the reader a lot about his characters and milieu, but never stopping for long-winded explanations of how things worked.

The Demolished Man is indeed a murder mystery, featuring a detective hero. But both he and the reader know who the killer is; the question for the detective is *how* the murder was accomplished (which the reader *does* know) and how to pin it on the killer. What makes all this so difficult is that the murder is the first to be committed in nearly a century in a future that has a large population of telepaths (among whom is our detective hero). Bester's evocation of the intra-telepath society is extraordinary.

The Stars My Destination is one of the most indescribable novels in a generally indescribable field. In this Bester future, teleportation ("jaunting") is as common as telepathy is in that of *The Demolished Man,* and the society built around it is as believable. The plot has been compared to that of *The Count of Monte Cristo;* it contains such memorable characters as the blind albino heiress who "sees" in the infrared, not to mention the Neanderthalesque hero, Gully Foyle, whose name, unlike most science-fictional characters', seems to be one that no reader forgets. Among the many dizzying high points of the book is a "trip" sequence that long predates the psychedelic '60s. *The Stars My Destination* is one of those few books that is almost universally regarded as a classic in the field.

Typically, Bester's career has been atypical. He began, back in 1939, by winning an amateur short story contest in *Thrilling Wonder Stories* (yes, there was a magazine called that, and a good one, too) which should be encouraging to all would-be writers. And then, soon after the sensational *Stars My,* he ceased publishing s-f for almost two decades (which makes his continuing popularity the more remarkable—most inactive writers sink into oblivion more often than not). He returned in the mid-'70s with *The Computer Connection*. Given the circumstances, it would have had to have been a miraculous work to live up to the standards Bester himself had set. Many readers thought it did not, missing the tightly though intricately-knit plotting of the earlier novels. Nevertheless, the breakneck speed, unceasingly inventive concepts, and pyrotechnical play with words were still there in this slightly mad story about an Amer-indian genius and a super-computer who wants to take over.

There are also a number of short stories, gathered into several collections (*Starlight*). Among his works, you will find the Bester of all possible worlds.

(If you like Bester's work, try that of Fritz Leiber, Michael Moorcock, Lloyd Biggle and/or Thomas Scortia.)

LLOYD BIGGLE, JR., is a *rare avis*, a science fiction author who is interested in, and knows, the arts, an area that science fiction has often handled in rather embarrassingly provincial terms. Biggle is a musicologist; music plays a major role in much of his work.

In *The Still, Small Voice of Trumpets*, Jef Forson of the Cultural Survey is assigned to find why the attempts of the Interplanetary Relations Bureau to democratize the planet Gurnil aren't working. (A worldwide democracy is necessary for admission to the Federation of Independent Worlds.) The plot is somewhat along the lines of the typical extra-competent intelligence agent story, but Biggle's attention to the details of culture (in the broad and narrow senses of the word) makes his societies come to life. And his solution to the problem is as beautiful as the title of the book.

World Menders is another novel about the Cultural Survey force. *The Light That Never Was* is an unlikely blend of science fiction, mystery, and aesthetics, and *The Metallic Muse*, as its title implies, is a collection of short stories treading the line between the scientific and the artistic.

In another direction, Biggle has written three novels concerning Jan Darzek, future private eye. *All the Colors of Darkness*, *Watchers of the Dark*, and *This Darkening Universe*, all concern Darzek's adventures with various aliens.

With his concern for the arts, and his connections with the secret agent/murder mystery genre, Biggle brings a slightly different flavor to science fiction

(If his work appeals to you, you might try Alfred Bester or William Rotsler.)

EANDO BINDER was actually two writers: Earl Andrew Binder and his more talented younger brother Otto Oscar. ("E" AND "O," get it?) Imaginative workhorses of the late thirties, the Binders were a cut above their contemporaries with their ingenious plot twists and relatively human protagonists.

Their prime achievement was the creation of *Adam Link,* one of the first successful attempts to explore the human feelings of a sentient robot.

Otto struck out on his own in the '40s, editing short-lived s-f magazines and writing an occasional novel, but earning his bread and butter with above-average scripts for comic book characters. Several serials by the Brothers Binder were collected and to some extent updated in the '60s. These melodramatic future-histories, among them *Lords of Creation* and *Enslaved Brains,* deal with a favorite theme of Otto's, the struggle of humanity against loathsome dictatorial overlords.

(If you like the Binders, we suggest "Doc" Smith and the *Jay Score* stories of Eric Frank Russell.)

MICHAEL BISHOP's first short stories began to appear in the early/ middle '70s in genre magazines, and these, and in particular his novella "Death and Designation Among the Asadi," immediately drew highly favorable response. The novella, an alien encounter piece, treated an oft-treated subject in a way that made the whole idea seem new, and when his first novel, *A Funeral for the Eyes of Fire* appeared, it became apparent that a new practitioner of the arts would bring a considerable intelligence to bear on his material. (Both *Funeral* and *Asadi* have been rewritten and expanded.)

In *Funeral* two brothers involve themselves in interplanetary politics and sociology. When they encounter the aliens of the world they have come to push around, they find their mission increasingly blurred. The more they attempt to accomplish their end the more they become enmeshed, actually and psychologically, in the local problem. The novel is complex and involving, and though imperfectly structured, it was an auspicious first. Bishop's novels all seem to be further explorations, and extrapolations, of locales and social orders first dealt with in short stories. Thus, *And Strange at Ecbatan the Trees* (retitled *Beneath the*

Shattered Moons in paperback) and *A Little Knowledge* suffered their birth pangs in earlier stories.

Ecbatan concerns a pivotal "spy" who involves himself in a symbolic society of two genetically engineered groups who live under constant threat, real and imagined. Character is explored more than event, though event shapes character. War, duplicity, and strong personal ties weave the elements of the narrative into an often violent, often compassionate tale. *A Little Knowledge* takes place in a future Atlanta (Bishop's archetypal city) and penetratingly explores socio-religious structures and alien incursions; the author's knowledge and understanding of religious thought and his powers of extrapolation, provide the book's heart. It is challenging and complex, as is *Stolen Faces,* a sombre, chilling novel of disease and personal disaster, on a cold tundra-like world. Here, again, Bishop uses his remarkable knowledge in many areas to enrich and support his vision, this time with linguistic and sociological references to meso-American history.

Bishop is the sort of whom it is often said "He's a writer's writer"; highly literate, immensely imaginative and absolutely convincing, his stories and novels have an ever-increasing readership.

(If you like Bishop's work, try that of Naomi Mitchison, Chad Oliver, and Richard Cowper.)

JAMES BLISH writes technical s-f; he works out his scientific advances carefully and logically. Then he slips over into social and moral implications and turns out a cracking good adventure. He wrote a number of excellent short stories, several minor novels, and about a jillion *Star Trek* novelizations. Weightier and of more concern though are two series which demonstrate both Blish's scientific imagination and his philosophical concerns.

The *Cities in Flight* series of four novels are extrapolation at its exciting best. Given two inventions—the "spin-dizzy," which nullifies gravitational forces (no need to build a spaceship; just take Manhattan Island and fly away), and effective immortality—Blish creates a galaxy full of itinerant cities. *Cities in Flight* is rich in cultural detail, human foibles and triumphs, and is lots of fun.

On the philosophical side are a group of three novels and a novella, considered by many to be Blish's most important work. He called the series "After Such Knowledge," and in it he wrestles with a proposition: is the unceasing quest for knowledge a sin?

The first book is *Doctor Mirabilis;* it is not s-f at all but an excellent historical novel on the life of Roger Bacon. The second part is made up of a novel and the novella *Black Easter* and its direct sequel, *The Day After Judgement.* In these books a munitions manufacturer hires a black magician to release all the demons in Hell for one night. The results are predictably disastrous. There is a remarkable sequence in *Day After Judgement* where the United States military command computer processes the data and announces that Armageddon has occurred.

The final book is a novel called *A Case of Conscience.* The protagonist is a Jesuit priest who is also a biologist. He is sent on a survey mission to a distant planet where he is confronted by intelligent but non-human aliens; these aliens do not have the concept of sin.

All of Blish's work is carefully researched and accurate in detail. Plots are strong, and the writing style is unobtrusive, though certainly there. Readers who have a nodding acquaintance with philosophy and the classics will find a delightful added dimension, although it is certainly not necessary in order to appreciate Blish's work.

(Isaac Asimov and Poul Anderson might appeal to those who like Blish.)

BEN BOVA has been known for many years as a foremost editor of science fiction, particularly that of a technical bent. It is therefore not surprising that his fiction is usually hard-science extrapolation of the near future.

In *As On a Darkling Plain,* the human race is confronted with undeniably alien artifacts; the shock of the discovery drives men either to suicide or to exploration. Sydney Lee's choice is to explore, and he has adventures on many plantes both in and out of our own solar system. Since this book is a cobbling together of a group of short stories, it suffers in continuity, but makes it up by the richness of its imagery.

Multiple Man is an extraordinary s-f novel set in the present...or tomorrow, or yesterday. The milieu is Washington, D.C., and the lead character is the President of the United States. Three exact doubles of the President have been murdered, and there is no way to know that the present incumbent is the one elected. It's a great s-f mystery.

In *Millennium,* Bova indicts the stupidity of the military mentality. The cold war has heated up to the flash point as the year 2000 rolls around, and military/scientific installations on the Moon, both Russian and American, take a stand against war. Bova's evocation of life on the moon, and his grasp of the technology of war make *Millennium* a fast and believable story.

(If you like Bova, we suggest Hal Clement, John Brunner, or Arthur C. Clarke.)

JOHN BOYD was persuaded to turn to writing by the race riots in Watts. As might be expected of a young man of those times his work is basically satirical, ranging from broad to subtle.

His first novel, *The Last Starship From Earth,* is a humorous and sophisticated story of an alternate universe with, among other things, a Catholic Church headed by a computerized Pope.

Satire and sensuality share the stage in his story of sentient flowers, *The Pollinators of Eden,* and sex(?) again rears its lovely head in the novel *Sex And The High Command,* a broad slap at male chauvinism and a warning about carrying women's liberation too far.

Andromeda Gun, while not as "meaningful" as his other books, is really fun to read. Energy being G-7, exploring for sources of energy his race needs, encounters Johnny McCloud, amoral gunfighter, and enters into a symbiotic relationship with him, unbeknownst to the man. With tongue planted firmly in cheek, Boyd plays with the manners and mores of the American Old West, strange indeed when viewed from G-7's alien perspective.

Boyd is a skilled writer, and his satire is more sophisticated than the broad stuff commonly encountered in s-f.

(Harry Harrison's work might appeal to those who like that of Boyd.)

LEIGH BRACKETT. The female writers of science fiction could be counted on the fingers of one hand in the days of the pulp magazines. The first finger position could arguably be divided between C. L. Moore and Leigh Brackett. Ms. Brackett not only nobly continued the great romantic tradition of Edgar Rice Burroughs (though with infinitely more sophistication), but she managed to sneak into the Puritan pulps (which were rigorously moralistic despite their covers featuring scantily clad females) a sensuousness which the male writers of the period couldn't seem to achieve, both in descriptive ability and hints that the hero and heroine wanted more than for the former to save the latter from a bug-eyed monster.

A typical Brackett novel, and perhaps her best early work, is *The Sword of Rhiannon.* Here is a Mars straight from Burroughs, of canals and deserts and a dying civilization. But Burroughs' noble standards would never have let him characterize the inhabitants thus:

"Lean, lithe men and women passed him in the shadowy streets, silent as cats except for the chime and the whisper of the tiny bells the women wear, a sound as delicate as rain, distillate of all the sweet wickedness in the world."

Nor did he have any touch of the poetry implicit in that passage.

The hero, an Earthman, discovers an ancient Martian tomb, and in it, a force that throws him back to the ancient days of Mars, when it still had oceans and a brilliant civilization. He becomes a pawn in the great struggle between the humanoid Martians and the half-human Children of the Serpent, and what a struggle it is, involving the superhuman Quiru, the demon-god Rhiannon, the other half-human races of Mars, and the warrior princess, Ywain.

After too many years of inactivity in science fiction (devoted at least in part to a successful screen writing career), Brackett made a smashing comeback in the '70s with the Skaith trilogy, reviving a hero of former works, Eric John Stark, to go to the exotic planet of Skaith to persuade its diverse races to join the Galactic Union for its own preservation, if nothing else. Among them are the Fallarin, an imperfect avian race who control the winds; the Ssussminh, a true amphibian mutation; the Children of Skaith-Our-Mother, furred inhabitants of the Northern regions, and lots of other wonderfully conceived species who help and hinder Stark in his mission. (Not to mention the villainous Antarean, Pankawr-Che, who...oh, you get the idea...)

Brackett's works are adventurous world-creating at its best, both in the novels and the too few short stories. (If you can find it, check out an unlikely collaboration with Ray Bradbury, of all people, called "Lorelei of the Red Mist." The title says it all, and its *not* in *The Martian Chronicles.)*

(If you like Brackett, we suggest Moore, Merritt, Burroughs, and some Kuttner.)

RAY BRADBURY is a bit of a problem. While to many people outside the field of science fiction, his is one of the first names that comes to mind when science fiction is mentioned, many aficionados will argue as to whether he's a science fiction writer at all. While his many short stories are for the most part fantasies, mood pieces, or plain old horror stories (particularly his earlier ones), those of the late '40s that were gathered into *The Martian Chronicles* do take place for the most part on Mars, were published in science fiction magazines of the period, and use the stuff of science fiction imaginatively and poetically.

The Martian Chronicles do not make a whole greater than their parts; the links between them are tenuous at best. Perhaps the most powerful of them is ". . . And the Moon Be Still As Bright," whose protagonist is the one sensitive soul on the first expedition to Mars, who watches his companions pollute and destroy the remnants of the Martian civilization. This was a disturbing antidote to the astronaut-as-hero theme which had reigned as s-f until then.

Many of the short stories in the other collections also play in this stylized way with science fiction, and the thrust is often against technology (perhaps this sub-genre could be called anti-science fiction). The only one of his few novels that even ventures this far into the field is the famous *Fahrenheit 451*, a dour look at a book burning future written during the McCarthy days of U.S. politics. (One rare edition was bound in asbestos).

In recent years, Bradbury has devoted his time mostly to poetry, and to adapting many of his works for the stage.

MARION ZIMMER BRADLEY is, in a kind of human microcosm, a history of modern science fiction. Her chatty and enthusiastic letters can be found in the letter columns of the magazines of the '40s under the name of Marion "Astra" Zimmer. Her short stories began to appear in the magazines of the '50s. Her first novels appeared in the '60s in book form in the old Ace "Double" series which, despite their eccentric format (two short novels back-to-back and up-side-down, each with a "front" cover) and sleazy appearance, introduced a number of major authors to (paperback) book publication. Among them was Bradley's first Darkover novel—Darkover, a created world to which she was to devote most of her output from then on, forming a series that might well be used to define the s-f of the 1960s and 1970s as the Foundation series defines s-f of the '40s.

The earliest Darkover novels (for instance, *The Bloody Sun* and *Star of Danger*) are pure action adventure space opera, but they served as an excellent base for Bradley's writing to mature as science fiction matured, and the later novels (say, *The Heritage of Hastur* and *The Shattered Chain*) show her concern with adult themes (homosexuality, women's rights) without losing their speculative glamour, or being overloaded with message.

What is the magic of Darkover? Part of it is literally magic; Bradley has been highly influenced by Tolkein, and while the Darkover books have a strongly science fictional base, the world of Darkover is a fey world. Settled by castaway humans from a lost spaceship, the Darkovers are for generations out of contact with the expanding Terran Empire, and strongly influenced by indigenous races who are psi-oriented. Strange powers and forces are developed by this orphan strain of humanity, and when finally they are discovered by the technologically inclined parent race, the culture clash is inevitable.

Each Darkover book is a chapter in the history of Darkover; some overlap, with a major character in one, turning up younger or older, as a minor character in another. *Darkover Landfall* is the story of the initial crash landing, but it needn't be read first; in fact, it is better to become acquainted with the Darkovan culture in one or two of the other books, and then have the joy of discovering sources in *Landfall*. There is no suggested order of reading for this series; it is a mosaic whose pieces can be enjoyed in any combination.

Bradley's other works also have the same verve and imagination, if not on so epic a scale. *Hunters of the Red Moon,* for instance, is a thriller about a vast hunting preserve, stocked by intelligent races from all over the Galaxy. But *who* are the hunters?

Displaying a bit of everything that makes and has made science fiction "the thinking man's escapism," Bradley is deservedly on her way to being one of the most popular writers in the field in this decade.

(Bradley's mixture of s-f and fantasy is really only matched in the few works of Sterling Lanier.)

FREDRIC BROWN is one of the really funny writers in science fiction. Mostly a writer of short and very short stories, his trademark is the twist ending, sometimes a twisted twist ending. One of his most talked-about stories, rarely credited to him, is "Answer," the one-page kicker about hooking all the computers in all the galaxies in series, and then asking if there is a God. The reply? "Now there is." He would have a place in s-f if only because he is the reputed author of the following short story, reprinted here *in toto:*

"After the last atomic war, Earth was dead; nothing grew, nothing lived. The last man sat in a room. There was a knock on the door..."

Happily, Brown was not content to rest on that slim credential. It does, however, serve to illustrate Brown's literary virtues: inventiveness, brevity, and dry wit. Brown's humor runs from the macabre, in such pieces as "Etaoin Shrdlu," about a linotype machine with a will of its own, to the sublime, as in "Politeness," a stumper for Emily Post.

He spent his literary career with one foot in detective fiction, one foot in the mainstream, and one foot in s-f (perfectly possible for an s-f writer!).

Brown's well received first novel was *What Mad Universe,* a complex detective story about an alternate world in which science fiction is fact and Buck Rogers types are the heros of straight adventure stories. Our detective, erst-while editor of a science fiction pulp magazine in *our* universe, has a double who is the editor of a fiction magazine *there,* and the Arcs are invading Mars, and the streets are deadly at night, and it can get very confusing. It's a grand mixture of lunacy and satire on s-f readers and writers.

Martians Go Home takes the pop cliche about science fiction, little green men, and carries it to mad extremes. Earth is invaded by little green men. They don't *do* anything, but they watch. Every embarrassing little thing. And make remarks. And nothing will make them go away, though everything is tried, including, in one of s-f's great phrases, "heavy water, holy water, and Flit." (One of the most memorable of science fiction illustrations is Kelly Freas' of one of Brown's little green men, framed in a keyhole, used for the cover of the original magazine publication and on a later paperback edition.)

Brown's serious side is represented by the wonderfully titled and beautiful novel *The Lights in the Sky are Stars,* the poignant story of one Max Andrews, once kept out of space due to an accident, who now fights bureaucracy and alcoholism to see a flight to Jupiter lift off and the human exploration of space continued. The characterization is rich and mature, and today's reader can easily empathize with Andrew's desire, and his frustration at being on the edge of space and yet denied entrance.

Fredric Brown's work is an oasis in a field where humor is too much lacking, or sophomoric when present. And then there's *The Lights in the Sky are Stars.*

(If you like Brown's work, we suggest Goulart, Tenn, Sheckley, Pohl, and/or Kornbluth.)

JOHN BRUNNER is one of those prolific British authors, unusual, but by no means unique, in that he began writing and selling s-f at age seventeen. Brunner's specialty is psychological fiction, liberally laced with science. His plots are labyrinthine; he attempts to show the reader each force at work in the worlds he envisions. His books are often topical, extrapolating our present-day concern with ecological disaster, nuclear war, overpopulation, and political manipulation. But unlike many topical writers, Brunner begins his story at the point most writers would consider the happy (or unhappy) ending.

Among Brunner's many books are *Stand on Zanzibar*, *The Sheep Look Up*, and *The Jagged Orbit*. These are dystopias, where war, population, and pollution have run wild, after a brief flirtation with control. Brunner's solutions are alternately bleak and hopeful.

Age of Miracles is the story of an Earth that has been invaded—not by tentacled aliens with designs on humanity, but by a faceless and nameless culture which has no more concern for human beings than we have for an ant-hill in the path of a super-highway. In *The Whole Man*, which is a departure from Brunner's general pessimism, the UN has finally taken over the government of the world with the aid of humans with psi powers.

The Squares of the City is one of the strangest s-f novels ever written, excellent though it be. The plot is based on a chess game played in 1892 between Steinitz and Tchigorin, a game well known to chess aficionados. The setting is a small South American country and the game is being played by the country's dictator and his loyal opposition...using citizens of the country as chess pieces. The s-f element is the way in which the people/pieces are manipulated into making their moves. *Squares* is frightening, believable, skillfully written, and one of those s-f novels that benefits from re-reading.

(If you like Brunner, we suggest James Gunn, Frank Herbert, Brian Aldiss, and Robert Silverberg.)

EDWARD BRYANT. Colorado dwelling, s-f writer's workshop frequenting, fan-turned-writer Ed Bryant has published a collection of stories, *Among the Dead*, a novelization of Harlan Ellison's Starlost teleplay, *Phoenix Without Ashes*, and a quasi-novel composed of vignettes with a common setting, *Cinnabar*. Cinnabar is a place on an ocean adjacent to a desert. Vermilion Sands, invented by J. G. Ballard (who see), is just such a place, and Bryant makes his obeisance to it in the introduction. Bryant peoples his story with ''characters' who are as elusive as their doings, and, for that matter, as elusive as the city of Cinnibar itself. Bryant uses filmic techniques in the presentation of these vaguely related pieces: cutaways, freeze frames, intercutting, etc. The quaint personalities of Bryant's mythic place interact with very contemporary and trendy dialogue, adding substance to the gathering of the pieces and the coming together of the characters. Toward the end, Bryant deals with plot and tries to tie up the loosely sewn garment, but the elements tend to wander off, leaving *Cinnabar* phantomic and evasive.

(If you like the stories of Ed Bryant see the writing of Harlan Ellison, Spider Robinson, and William Rotsler.)

ALGIS BUDRYS, novelist, short story writer, editor, genre critic and officer in the Lithuanian army, produces pragmatic, realistic, literary adventures such as *Michaelmas,* whose titular protagonist masquerades as a mere TV reporter while in fact, with the limitless aid of a secret and highly sophisticated computer, he controls, governs the whole world. Michaelmas' computer is called Domino, a convincingly near-sentient collection of technologies; a computer with as much real character as Budrys gives Michaelmas, and Budrys is something of a master at character, especially in a field where carefully reasoned and created character is a recent manifestation of a move toward more literary values. An astronaut who should by all rights be dead from a trial rocket shot that goes wrong, reappears alive, causing Michaelmas and Domino to involve themselves in a situation that smacks of duplicity and dangerous international implications.

The theme of dubious identity is also explored in the earlier *Who?* A one-of-a-kind physicist who is working on a project vital to national security is horrendously injured in a lab accident, and the Russians who have recovered him reconstruct him bionically. Failing to get information from him he is returned to the U.S., only to be doubted and ostracized. *Rogue Moon* is a fascinating and intriguing mystery about an ostensibly alien building on the moon, and the devastating effect it has on the lives of those sent to explore it. *Amsirs and the Iron Thorn,* a superior and intelligent space opera, contains some excellent characterizations of diverse synthetic beings.

Budry's reputation as a writer of craftsmanlike short stories is reinforced by several fine collections: *Budrys' Inferno* and *The Unexpected Dimension.*

(If you like Budrys, try the work of Piers Anthony.)

KENNETH BULMER. A British writer who has been producing novels regularly for years, Bulmer seems essentially unread. Though his books range over the usual spectra of s-f and fantasy themes, providing a goodly variety of adventures both in space and on earth, his audience remains small.

In *To Outrun Doomsday*, a down-and-out space jockey finds himself on a mysterious world wherein the people are lavished with meaningless plenty—jewels, couture, arms—and denied essentials—food, housing—by their eccentric deity. In *Stained Glass World* Bulmer deals with so contemporary a theme as drugs (not that s-f hasn't been inventive and imaginative in that area before), postulating a future society of class polarity, the top luxuriously drugged on the "joy juice" they extract from the bottom of society, that is. An earlier novel *City Under the Sea* combines effective, if dated, notions of future ocean use with a plot of trivial huggermugger. And more recently, *On the Symb-socket Circuit* is an amusing, hyper-paced romp about migrants who travel from world to world living it up and roistering, until one of them becomes involved in a moral dilemma—a planet needs saving and only he can do it.

In all, Bulmer spins what can only be called action-packed stories, stories that are often rich with inventive ideas, but pedestrain in plot; it's a sort of latterday pulp idiom.

(Those who find Bulmer fun to read might think the same of Harry Harrison.)

EDGAR RICE BURROUGHS was not merely the author of the Tarzan books. He is universally acknowledged as the grand-daddy of American science fiction.

In the early days of this century, when a growing literacy moved the population to demand more and more popular reading matter, magazines of adventure fiction proliferated. A few of the stories contained therein were about weird adventures on other planets. Burroughs, who had tried his hand at a number of careers without notable success, decided that he could write these as well as any of the hack authors who did so, and turned out something called "Under the Moons of Mars" which *Argosy All-Story* published in 1912. Burroughs had submitted it to be published under the *nom-de-pun* of Normal Bean (to indicate that he was a "normal being" and not some occultist nut); the magazine typoed that into Norman Bean, so Burroughs published under his own euphonious name after that.

And what a great deal was published under that name! (His writing career continued until his death in 1950.) And what a lot of science fiction readers got their start with his romances.

Romances they were—in the old sense of the word. Scientific romances really; Burroughs used the popular scientific theories of the day for his speculation and, well, if they're scientific nonsense now, his tales simply slide gracefully into being fantasy rather than s-f, and are still delightful.

Not to everybody, of course. One must have grown up on them or have a certain historical perspective to read them. The writing is naive. The morality is deplorable by our standards today—John Carter of Mars is willing to send 10,000 warriors to their deaths to save the virtue of Dejah Thoris—which she thinks is the only right thing to do. Coincidence is rife to the point where it is a way of life; if there's a hero, a heroine, a villain, and a sabre toothed tiger all within an area of a thousand square miles, they will invariably end up in the same place at the same time.

And, yet, for ERB fans, who cares! He has created wonderful worlds, most notably in his three major s-f series: the books about Mars (Barsoom); the books about Venus (Amtor); the books about Pellucidar (Pellucidar).

Burroughs' Mars set a pattern for decades to come. A dying world of dead sea bottoms, ancient abandoned cities, canals, and artificially maintained atmosphere, it is home to numerous races, red, white, black, tan, and yellow (lemon yellow—no pastels for ERB). Not to forget the six-armed green men. Brave warriors. Beautiful women (who are oviparous). Villainous villains. A hundred exotic cultures and a thousand fearsome beasties. That's Barsoom.

His Venus, on the other hand, is a world steaming with hot seas and gigantic forests, which has (you guessed it) brave warriors, beautiful women (non-oviparous), villainous villains, etc.

Pellucidar has all those, and a few other things to boot. It is the interior surface of our own hollow Earth, lit by the molten center matter which has coalesced into a pseudosun. This leads to two interesting concepts. The horizon goes *up* (a source of despair to anyone who has tried to illustrated the Pellucidar stories). And time is totally relative, due to the lack of moving heavenly bodies. . .which was a pretty sophisticated idea for the early part of the century. Pellucidar is flora'd, fauna'd, and peopled by examples of life forms from every period of terrestrial history, which have wandered down by various routes from the earth's surface.

All this is great fun and games for today's readers with the right tolerance for yesterday's literature. But even those who find Burroughs unreadable cannot deny that he set the pattern for American science fiction to which almost everything written today can be traced.

(If you like Burroughs, we suggest the works of Lin Carter, Leigh Brackett, Alan Bert Akers, and Ray Cummings.)

F. M. BUSBY, in a comparatively short time and with a comparatively few novels, has established a firm reputation in science fiction. He is a perfect example of a modern trend in the field of taking themes and concepts that are well established, perhaps even over-used, and by scrupulous attention to detail and characterization making them components in novels that can only be described as solid.

Rissa Kerguelen, for instance (initially published in hard cover as two volumes, *Rissa Kerguelen* and *The Long View),* is fairly unoriginal in plot. Young woman flees repressive, regimented Earth for far-flung, more individualistic and free worlds, marries space pirate, initiates and carries through action to defeat dictatorial regime back home. But no plot precis can convey the complex character of Rissa and her friends and enemies; the curious results of the relativity of time in space travel which results in seventy-five years of objective events transpiring in the twenty-eight years of her life that are covered in the book (the "long view" of the second part); and such details as the leader(s) of the resistance on Earth, a "family" of female clones becoming more and more unstable with each duplication.

In another novel of two books, *Cage A Man* and *Proud Enemy,* Busby again uses a plot of well worn parts. Human is captured by aliens, escapes aliens, leads expedition to conquer aliens. But again it is the details that elevate the books to something special: the curious motives of the extraterrestrial Demu, the relationship between the human hero and other non-human races imprisoned with him, and the difficult task of creating a love interest between the human and an alien female.

In these novels and many short stories, with intelligent and skillful writing, Busby has brought a new level of what can be called "realism" to science fiction.

(If you like Busby, by all means try Heinlein if you haven't, and also Sydney van Scyoc.)

JOHN W. CAMPBELL accomplished something allowed to few men; he remade, single handedly and single mindedly, the entire field of endeavor in which he worked, in this case of course, science fiction. This astounding feat was achieved primarily through his talent as editor of the magazine *Astounding Science Fiction,* later *Analog.* The story of this is told elsewhere, but for the historically minded reader, the seeds of what happened can be found in Campbell's fiction, the writing of which he abandoned when he took up his editorial duties.

In 1930, when Campbell's first story was published, magazine science fiction, though a relatively young field, had already developed a pervading formula, to which Campbell wrote. It was best typified by the galumphing-about-the-galaxy novels of E. E. Smith; Campbell mastered the formula with gusto, injected it with a great deal of technical justification for the various devices that he came up with, and almost immediately became popular with readers for novels such as *The Mightiest Machine,* in which a trio of future geniuses devise an interstellar ship that can use the power of the Sun ("the mightiest machine") or any star that happens to be in the vicinity. Off they go on a test run, hit a space warp, and get thrown into some other area of space and smack into a space war between descendants of the refugees from ancient Mu and....(Another three novelettes, published under the name of *The Incredible Planet,* are used to get them home.)

Finding the formula restrictive to what he thought the potential of science fiction to be, Campbell began publishing a series of very different stories under the name of Don A. Stuart, and soon found himself, in Lester del Rey's felicitous phrase, "the two most popular writers of science fiction." The Stuart stories are what Campbell thought science fiction should be, and in them can be found foreshadowings of the stellar stable of writers—Heinlein, van Vogt, del Rey, Asimov to name a few—that he developed as an editor.

They (the stories) are as widely divergent as: "Forgetfulness" in which an alien race discovers that the decadent human race of the far future is not what it seems; "The Machine" in which the treasured science fictional concept of a mechanistic paradise of the future is Not A Good Thing; and "Who Goes There?" a hair-raising suspense story of an Antarctic expedition that discovers and defrosts a really nasty alien that can physically assume the shape of any other being (this became the movie *The Thing,* brilliant in its own right, but a far cry from its original source material).

The "Don A. Stuart" stories are of more than historical interest to today's readers, and can be found in the two collections *Who Goes There?*

and *Cloak of Aesir,* The fiction Campbell wrote under his own name, however, might be a little hard to take for a modern reader who is not a confirmed space opera addict.

(For those who like Campbell the writer, certainly sample Murray Leinster and George O. Smith.)

TERRY CARR is well known in the s-f field as a virtually peerless editor, but has there ever been a real editor who could resist writing? His first novel (there were a couple of more or less aborted early ones; they don't count), *Cirque,* is an imagistic, brief and tender look at xenophobia. In a far future remote city there is a vast, perhaps bottomless pit into which all of the city's refuse, detritus, and eeuch has been dumped forever. Then a great, white, many-appendaged, wooly and fabulous monster appears in the pit: are there more, are they menacing? When the monster finally does appear in public (at a religious service!) the people find that rather than horror and fear, they feel love and care. The monster obliges by turning (mirabile dictu!) into a floral piece of proportionate hugeness.

Like Carr's short story collection, *The Light At the End of the Universe, Cirque* is literate, conscientious, and gentle, its allegory plain and painless.

(Those who like Carr's work might check out that of another excellent editor, Damon Knight.)

ANGELA CARTER. Several odd and wonderful novels had established a certain reputation for Angela Carter before she published her first s-f work, *Heroes and Villains.* Like her earlier books it is erotic, linguistically bejewelled, bizarre, and spellbinding. In it, society is sundered by ruin and disorder; two groups endure. A girl—from the remains of order, culture, and civilization, sees her brother murdered in a raid by disorder, chaos, and barbarism; but her life is drab and boring. The barbarians seem exciting. She leaves order, etc. and joins disorder, etc. Carter deals with the ambiguous situation she establishes, and the equally ambiguous locus and time of her novel with a deftness remarkable in a first-time s-f writer.

War of Dreams (original, and better, title: *The Infernal Desire Machines of Doctor Hoffman*) and *The Passion of New Eve* are far from the usual s-f fare. Often outrageously bizarre, intellectually delicious, and neo-surrealist in plot and point, they are both quite literally, indescribable. A recounting of their narratives would profit nothing because in Carter's work the story is in the words, not the other way around. She is a writer of very special talents for the reader of very special discernments.

(If you appreciate Carter's special talents, you might sample the work of another highly original Englishwoman, Jane Gaskell.)

LIN CARTER is probably best known as a knowledgeable editor and essayist on fantasy. But he has also been called a "born story teller" and his nostalgically styled novels are unabashed pastiches of the authors of the early days of science fiction, particularly Edgar Rice Burroughs.

Carter also writes a good deal of that sub-genre of fantasy called "sword and sorcery," which again is reminiscent of Burroughs, with his fondness for swords and sometimes none-too-solid scientific premises. Carter's "World's End" and Thongor series are more fantasy than s-f, but his Callisto novels are sheer mock-ERB, taking place on that moon of Jupiter, and with his hero, Jandar, facing countless dangers for the beautiful princess Darloona. Carter himself shows up there as "Lankar of Callisto" in one volume.

The "Green Star" series falls somewhere between the two; the Terrestrial hero travels by a kind of astral projection to the world of the Green Star, and his spirit then inhabits the bodies of various adventure-prone inhabitants.

(If you like Carter, you might try the great originals: Burroughs, Merritt, and Brackett.)

JACK CHALKER was already known in the field of science fiction as a specialty publisher of esoteric and often intriguing items that no commercial publisher would touch when suddenly he switched hats and wrote some novels that readily found commercial publication. What he lacks in technical polish is made up for by what seem to be inexhaustible imaginative concepts.

The wonderfully titled *Midnight at the Well of Souls* is a dandy example, a combination of the all-in-the-same-boat and everything-but-the-kitchen-sink school of plot development. A miscellaneous group of passengers and the skipper of an interstellar scow get sucked into a "well" manufactured by a long dead race. They find themselves (and, of course, their destinies) on an artifical world made up of 1,560 hexagons each inhabited by a different intelligent species. The various chases and quests through these areas result in a new environment every few chapters, reminding the reader of the nuttily never-ending communities with which L. Frank Baum filled Oz. (In fact, one Chalker character, taking a guess at what's over the next hill, comes up with the Emerald City.)

If Chalker's prolific imagination doesn't fail him, he stands a good chance of becoming very popular with the non-stop action s-f readers.

(If you like Chalker, you might like Zelazny and Farmer.)

A. BERTRAM CHANDLER was a ship's captain in the Australian merchant marine, writing s-f on the side; he gives us the said merchant marine mysteriously catapulted into space. There is a maxim that a writer should write about what he knows, and the dedicated young, steely-eyed lieutenant has a time honored place aboard a spaceship. So, of course, does the experienced captain suffering under the burden of command. And yet, and yet...somewhere in the background is a noise that sounds suspiciously like waves lapping at the gunwales.

Most of Chandler's work is encompassed in his Rimworlds stories. These deal with the fleet of the somewhat rebellious colonies at the galactic rim. The fleet is crewed and captained by refugees from the Imperial merchant fleet (what else?). A novel, *Road to the Rim,* is an episodic account of one old salt's conversion from company man to rim-runner. This is seen and told from the viewpoint of a young commissioned officer on his way to his first command. Chandler's future concept is undeniably interesting, and he may well be right about the structure of an interstellar merchant fleet.

Chandler is not what could be called a great stylist. He *is* a romp, and his gutsy, old-tar's point of view is worth having, if only to balance out all the scientists and militarists writing in the '50s.

(If you like A. Bertram Chandler, try the books of E. E. "Doc" Smith.)

C. J. CHERRYH has an uncanny ability to plunge the reader into the heart of an alien culture. She unfolds her tales with skill and restraint, and without the convenient device of the handy history book (in standard Terran, of course) or a friendly psychologist to explain the structure of the society to the hero. If you like to play with cultures and languages, then you will enjoy Cherryh.

Her first book *Gate of Ivrel,* is s-f fantasy at its best. An outcast barbarian links up with a mythic sorceress to destroy an evil wizard. This is a fairly standard plot, but Cherryh develops it, through riddles and myth, into something quite different. The barbarian is an inhabitant of a primitive, feudal world, and the sorceress is a cop in the service of an interstellar empire; no one involved is entirely human. The book is strangely reminiscent of Poul Anderson's *Three Hearts and Three Lions,* a different tune played on the same instrument. *Gate of Ivrel* earned Cherryh the praise of the s-f world, and the 1977 Campbell Award for the most promising new writer.

Brothers of Earth deals with a human soldier, cast away on a planet inhabited by humanoid aliens. The hero, Kurt Morgan, is a moving viewpoint, exploring the culture and gradually becoming a part of it.

In *Hunter of Worlds* Cherryh returns to the totally alien theme. The world is a great space vessel, inhabited by the *Iduve*, its slaves and dependents. Here the reader is completely immersed in the language, customs, and structures of this race without a hint of explanation. You are forced to adapt right along with the lead character, who has been taken captive by the Iduve captain, Chimele. *Hunter of Worlds* is a stunning display of a dedication to the art of world building. Cherryh has created—presumably for this book only—a language, three cultures, many races, a set of ethics, and a new technology.

(If you like C. J. Cherryh, we suggest you try Poul Anderson or Ursula K. LeGuin.)

ROBERT CHILSON is a comparative newcomer to science fiction, but his several novels show a wide range of subject matter. They also never lack for action, with hairbreadth escapes and interstellar chases.

In the provocatively titled *The Shores of Kansas,* the hero travels back to the Mesozoic Age, a background that is expertly delineated, to hunt dinosaurs with gun and camera. *As the Curtain Falls* is set on Earth in the farthest of futures, when civilization is more than a million years old. The seas have dried up, and the world is littered with the remnants of myriad past cultures of mankind. The plot is a classic quest across a moribund landscape, but far from being drearily dramatic, the novel is almost tongue-in-cheek, with every now and then little in-joke references to classic works of science fiction and fantasy that are great fun to try and catch.

The Star-Crowned Kings is also set in the future, this one about a galaxy of many worlds settled by humanity, but ruled by a group of mutated humans with superior psi powers. The hero thinks he is of ordinary stock, but discovers he has Starling (as the mutants are called) powers, and is involved in a great chase across space, hunted by both sides.

Chilson's books so far have shown enough talent and variety to make him one of the younger authors to keep an eye on.

(If you like Chilson, we suggest you try Vance.)

JOHN CHRISTOPHER (the pen name of Christopher Samuel Youd) was one of the several British authors who suddenly achieved prominence in the late '50s by killing off humanity and/or destroying the Earth in a myriad of fascinating ways.

Christopher's variations involved a blight that destroyed all cereals and grains (*No Blade of Grass*), a new Ice Age *(The Long Winter)*, and multiple earthquakes *(The Ragged Edge)*. All of these were unnervingly realistic and harrowingly suspenseful.

In recent years Christopher has devoted his writing to several series and single novels ostensibly for "young adults." Crisply and excitingly written, they are ideal for introducing adolescents to well done science fiction, but are also excellent reading for adults. *The White Mountains* trilogy (which also includes *The City of Gold and Lead* and *The Pool of Fire)* is the adventure of a young man fighting against the alien Tripods who have achieved dominance over the Earth, and who plan to change its atmosphere to suit themselves, thereby destroying all life on the planet.

The Guardians shows the influence of H. G. Wells in a society of a hundred years hence that is divided between a mechanized mass of city dwellers and a landed elite. There are, of course, many problems simmering beneath the surface of this "Utopia." "The Prince in Waiting" series concerns a post-apocalypse future where the culture has returned to the medieval, but in a Heinleinesque touch, the religion of the state masks a new return to technology in a society where machines are officially taboo.

(If you like Christopher's adult novels, we suggest the early J. G. Ballard and John Wyndham.)

ARTHUR C. CLARKE is something of a maverick in the world of science fiction. One of the giants to emerge from the golden age of s-f magazines, he was one of the few Englishmen writing in the genre at that time to be published in the U.S., which may account for the special flavor of his fiction. As strongly based as Asimov in the hard sciences, his works display a philosophical humanism that is very English, and are much related to that of the greatest of science fictional philosophers, Olaf Stapledon.

Clarke's novels are seldom strongly plotted, though his best known work, *Childhood's End,* is a prime exception. And while superficially his characters might seem to be examples of the old science fiction convention of being simply mouthpieces for the author's concepts, they are generally more well rounded than the usual cardboard hero and heroine. (It is also of interest that there are no villains in Clarke's works.)

Clarke, like Asimov, has become well known beyond his science fiction work, both through his voluminous nonfiction writings which are mostly about space flight and its implications, and from co-scripting the movie that many think is the best s-f film every made, which is of course, *2001, A Space Odyssey.* The genesis of *2001* was in Clarke's short story, "The Sentinel"; he later made a novel from the screenplay which, unlike most such after-the-fact efforts, stands very nicely on its own merits.

Childhood's End became a campus cult book in the '60s. It starts with a twist—that mankind, in the near future, is "invaded" and ruled by a thoroughly beneficent race. A Utopic Earth is rapidly achieved, but what mankind doesn't know is that it is being prepared for a major step in racial evolution, which comes about in a finale that can only be described as Wagnerian.

The other major work from what could be called Clarke's early period, *The City and the Stars,* has a slightly unusual history. First published in 1948 as *Against the Fall of Night* in a magazine with the typical-for-the-time name of *Startling Stories* (with a wonderfully raunchy cover—busty lady, tentacled robot and all), it was Clarke's first novel. In 1956 it reappeared, totally rewritten and greatly expanded, as *The City and the Stars.* The curious part is that both versions have remained in print; the earlier version is ideal for younger science fiction readers.

The City and the Stars takes palace in an immeasurably far future. Mankind has conquered the stars, but returned to Earth to Diaspar, the last city, a ravishingly conceived technological Nirvana where, it seems, humanity will stagnate until the end of time. But the protagonist, Alvin, a young man of the city, wonders and questions, and eventually discovers *why* humankind has retreated from space, and also, that there is yet another human culture left on Earth, diametrically opposed to Diaspar. If the reader detects a resemblance to *Logan's Run* and others of that ilk, forget it. Diaspar is no mindless dictatorship; it is so wonderfully described an environment that many have felt that it just might be worth stagnation to live there.

Clarke's later novels, for the most part, have been extended tours of various speculative locales. This is not meant negatively. Clarke is probably the foremost of science fiction writers in the building of infinitely detailed future or alien worlds, and whether it is the underwater farms of *The Deep Range,* with whales as cattle and porpoises as herd dogs, or the strange wonders of the mile-long, extraterrestrial space ship Rama, in *Rendezvous with Rama,* or the optimistically described Earth of 2276 of *Imperial Earth,* the reader is kept turning pages to discover what new and imaginative details Clarke will reveal next.

Mention must be made of the short stories, also, which make up the numerous Clarke collections. Many conclude with a surprising twist; for instance, "Rescue Party" with its devastating last sentence, or "The Star," which caused a mild furor on publication, speculating as it does that the Star of Bethlehem was a nova that destroyed a rich and beautiful civilization.

The works of Arthur C. Clarke are certainly among the best places to start for the science fiction novice. Because of their clarity and richly imaginative extrapolations, they typify the "beyond-this-horizon" glamour for which so many people read science fiction.

(Those who enjoy Clarke's work might also look into that of Poul Anderson, Fred Hoyle, and Frederik Pohl.)

HAL CLEMENT. Reading a novel or short story written by Clement is much like taking a course in physics, chemistry, and astronomy. Clement is one of the most scientifically oriented of science fiction writers and goes to a great deal of trouble to explain the whys of any aliens or alien environments. In one of the finest novels of hard science fiction written, *Mission of Gravity,* Clement creates a world called Mesklin, with a gravity that varies from three Earth Gs at the equator to seven hundred Gs at the poles. Along with this strange environment come the Mesklinites, among the most likable of extraterrestrials. The plot concerns the trek of a band of Mesklinite traders from the equator to the pole to recover a rocket probe crashed there during gravity experiments performed by human scientists. *Star Light* finds the same band of Mesklinites working on still another strange planet. *Cycle of Fire* and *Close to Critical* have other fine examples of planets created with scientific accuracy. *Ice World* views our Earth through an alien's eyes, and for the first few chapters one wonders how any species could live on such a forsaken planet. *Needle* could almost be called a s-f detective story; it deals with an alien detective searching the Earth for an alien criminal (its sequel is *Through the Eye of the Needle*). Clement is the author of many short stories, some of which are collected in *Space Lash* and *Natives of Space*.

(If you like Hal Clement's work, you might try that of Poul Anderson, Larry Niven, Ben Bova, Fred Hoyle, and James White.)

STANTON A. COBLENTZ first began writing science fiction for *Amazing Stories* in the late 1920s. Unlike his fellow pulp artisans who concentrated on action, adventure, and a speedy pace, Coblentz was an early practitioner of the usage of s-f as satire; this was a pioneering approach in the American magazines, but certainly opened the way for the socially satirical trend of the '50s from such authors as Pohl, Kornbluth, and Brown, and which continues with Ellison and Moorcock.

The current reader's tolerance for the works of Coblentz rather depends on his tolerance for s-f that is long on message and short on science, spooned out with somewhat broad humor. In *The Blue Barbarians* he takes on business, in *Lord of Tranarica* dictatorship, in *Moon People* racism. In *Hidden World*, the inhabitants of Wu and Zu, two underground nations, make war on each other incessantly and brainlessly.

Coblentz has also had a successful career in poetry.

(Fred Pohl, Cyril Kornbluth, Fredric Brown, and Harlan Ellison are more recent writers who make use of satire.)

D. G. COMPTON is one of the English writers who, along with John Wyndham, John Christopher, and others has concerned himself with socio-ecological problems and the ever-present dangers of governmental paternalism and snoopery. His novels have treated the questions of man-pollution (*The Quality of Mercy*), penal servitude *(Farewell, Earth's Bliss)*, and bio-engineering *(Synthajoy)*. In *Synthajoy* Compton postulates a machine which records human psychological experience and introduces those experiences to others. The machine's inventor, a successful psychiatrist, is murdered by his own invention working through his wife. In this novel, as in Compton's more recent work, characterization is strong and people, rather than technical wonders, are the actors.

The Unsleeping Eye (The Continuous Katherine Mortenhoe) is a complex novel of a woman whose cure from a terminal disease is televised as a part of a national series of such documentaries. Her life is secretly recorded by miniature cameras that are implanted in a companion. He, finally unable to withstand his voyeuristic function, blinds himself, as Katherine and he attempt to escape lives of overexposure and recognition.

(If you like the work of D. G. Compton, you might try that of Richard Cowper.)

MICHAEL G. CONEY. One way for a writer to approach science fiction is to place a person or society in a situation of their own or other's making and then study the reactions. Coney postulates strange futures under such strange conditions.

What if, for instance, a culture uses released convicts as bonded servants for those who can afford them, especially if bondservant means one who is to supply a leg, an arm, or another organ to their master if necessary? Coney sets up such a society and then has a free member of that society fall in love with a bondmaiden in *The Jaws That Bite, The Claws That Catch*. He develops the story along these lines and uses the outcome as a medium of speculation on human emotion. Character and emotional development are basic to this type of novel and Coney does a good job to it. Other possibilities of alien human environments are studied in *The Hero of Downways*, a post-holocaust novel depicting remnants of humanity living in vast complexes of underground tunnels, and in *Friends Come In Boxes,* where Coney weaves his tale through a society that has immortality; simple enough; just transfer your brain to the body of a six month old child. When you run out of bodies and have to keep your brain in a box, complications can arise. Careful attention to detail in building these cultures and societies make them come to sometimes horrifying life for the reader.

Rax is a departure for Coney, and a bit of one for science fiction. Whereas most novels depict human interaction, either with other humans or with aliens, *Rax* is a love story of aliens themsleves. The psychology and emotions of the maturation of Aliks-Drove, a young male at a time of planetary crisis, are well developed and the characterization of the various persons involved is detailed, as in Coney's other novels and his collection of short stories, *Monitor Found In Orbit*.

(If you like the work of Coney, try that of Gordon Eklund.)

EDMUND COOPER is an English novelist who writes as if he were American, and except for a propensity for overexplaining what-led-to-where-we-are-now, his novels are fast paced, adventurous, and often more than casually engrossing. In *A Far Sunset* only one Earthman survives when disaster strikes his ship after it touches down on Alatair Five, a planet with humanlike but alien inhabitants. Earth and Alatair Five meet on the couch, marry, reproduce, and the lady is killed by her peers. They don't approve of miscegenation. The Earthman becomes ruler of Alatair Five, his own eventual assassination a part of his accepted power. His equivocal position is further complicated when a rescue mission appears and he must decide between remaining as a doomed god or returning to the life he has known.

Cooper explores future anthropology, too, in the earlier novel *Seed of Light* in which survivors of an ultimate Earth disaster travel into space in quest of a new planet on which man may continue, and more recently in *The Overman Culture,* a melancholy novel about peculiar children in some ghastly London of the future. Throughout his work Cooper deals freely and graphically sometimes, with sex, giving it the due it so often doesn't get in the genre. As a stylist, Cooper isn't much, but he writes neat swift prose that serves his tales.

Writing under the name Richard Avery, Cooper emits a muscular adventures series called *The Expendables.*

(If you like Cooper, try Mack Reynolds.)

ARTHUR BYRON COVER is a writer represented by only a small body of work. A novel, *A Sound of Winter,* is set in a post-holocaust United States, and is about a highly political young man who is banished to the wild lands with his deaf-mute sister. Cover has a collection of short stories, entitled *The Platypus of Doom and other Stories.* Cover's style is somewhat uneven, but does have moments of humor.

RICHARD COWPER is an English novelist whose work follows no definable tradition. Cowper's thoughtful books are idiomatically contemporary and deal more with the nature of man than that of the universe. His sciences are the softer ones.

Breakthrough is a carefully and provocatively crafted tale of ESP. Its characters are literate and they behave, within the precepts of the story, rationally. *Kuldesak* postulates a subterranean remnant of mankind who believes that the surface is uninhabitable, taboo. Topside is, in fact, constantly harvested of its grain; tended by programmed robots, abandoned by man. An adolescent, Mel, finds his way to this abundant surface and brings others with him, leaving the repressive and superstition-filled society they have known. *The Twilight of Briarius* is a complex and very subtle novel dealing with the after-effects of a super nova on Earth. Most men are sterilized and the climate is chilling toward a new ice age. But there are saviors; those who are linked in mind, and some of them are fertile. *Clone* is a wry, parodistic story of a teleporting clone whose antics have odd repercussions.

Cowper's short fiction, the novelettes "Paradise Beach" and "The Custodians," and the acclaimed novella, "Piper at the Gates of Dawn," support his reputation as a superior teller of gentle tales.

(Cowper's fans might also try J. G. Ballard, Michael Bishop, and Edgar Pangborn.)

JOHN CROWLEY is a young author whose second published novel has received much favorable notice. *The Deep* concerns a strange feudal world whose warring aristocracy is divided into Red and Black factions, complicated by a quasireligious order of Grays and a revolutionary group who call themselves The Just. Into this world from somewhere else comes a stranger, sexless and memoryless, who is immediately involved in its struggles. *The Deep* is a strangely ambiguous work that can be considered science fiction, fantasy, or surrealism.

Beasts takes place in the next century, where the USA has been replaced by the USE (Union for Social Engineering), a pseudo-government desperately trying to make order out of the social chaos into which the country has fallen. Chief among the characters are animals with human intelligences (the dog Sweets) and beast men fashioned a la Dr. Moreau by genetic engineering (Reynard, half fox and half human, and Painter, outlaw leader of a pride of lion-humans). Crowley has made the interplay between these strange but believable creatures, and the humans of a crumbling American society, singularly fascinating.

The talent shown in these novels has raised the hope that John Crowley might be a major voice in science fiction in the years to come.

(If you like Crowley's work, you might try that of authors as divergent as Ballard and Vance.)

RAY CUMMINGS must have been just what the doctor ordered for Hugo Gernsback when he was looking around for science fiction authors to fill his pioneering new magazine, *Amazing Stories,* which was going to print nothing *but* science fiction! Not only had Cummings had an established hit novel in the magazine *All-Story Weekly* called *The Girl In the Golden Atom,* but he had worked as house organ editor for Thomas Alva Edison. It was just the mating of science and fiction that Gernsback wanted, and Cummings proved his staying power by a writing career that went well into the 1950s.

In those early days of the s-f magazines, it was indeed true that there was almost a set formula to their plots; on the other hand, most of the creativity went into the science fictional concepts. A vast majority of the stories *were* original on that basis, and Ray Cummings' were among the most original. *The Girl In the Golden Atom* is a case in point; casting about for an exotic locale and dismissing the future of another planet as old hat already, Cummings thought of infinite smallness. The girl is an inhabitant of a microworld in an atom of the wedding ring of the hero's mother; the hero catches sight of her in his microscope and invents a means of shrinking himself to join her.

Cummings set several stories on that sub-atomic world, and reversed the formula for *Beyond the Stars,* wherein the Earth is an atom of a larger universe.

He proved his originality in another direction too, with his Tama stories; a female protagonist was almost unheard of in science fiction at the time. (That these stories were set on Mercury gives them added panache; the littlest planet doesn't turn up often as a locale.)

Cummings also wrote a lot of good, solid space opera not quite so adventurous in concept, but still jolly good fun. The title of *The Insect Invasion* tells its own story, as does *Into the Fourth Dimension.* And he didn't neglect the possibliites and impossibilities of time travel with works such as *The Man Who Mastered Time* and *The Shadow Girl.*

Cummings is s-f at its exuberant, adventurous, youthful best, and what his work lacks now in sophistication, it more than makes up for in the delight of discovery.

(If you like Cummings, try the work of Burroughs, Kline, Hamilton, and Merritt.)

AVRAM DAVIDSON began writing s-f short stories in the mid-'50s, and won a Hugo award in 1958 for his "Or All The Seas With Oysters."

In 1962 Davidson became the editor of *The Magazine of Fantasy and Science Fiction,* but left in '64 to write full-time. Davidson's first novel was a joint effort with Ward Moore, called *Joyleg.* The novel is about a Tennessee hillbilly whose moonshine happens to be an elixir of immortality.

Davidson has a knack for setting his adventure in normal, almost mundane, surroundings. In *Clash of the Star-Kings* he invokes realistically all the boredom of a sleepy, impoverished Mexican village, then builds up tension very slowly as more and more bizarre events occur. The culminating battle between hostile alien races, as seen through human eyes, is made a strange and memorable exercise by simply showing the alien actions rather than explaining them to the reader.

Other books of the period include *Masters of the Maze, Mutiny in Space, Rork!, Rogue Dragon,* and *The Kar-Chee Reign.* All have the same feel of verismilitude, of making the strange seem even more abnormal by contrasting it with the familiar.

Since 1970 Davidson's work has been moving away from s-f and toward fantasy. In *The Island Under the Earth* he explores the land which is the source of all the legends of Earth. It is an unusual book, rather like the fantasies of George MacDonald.

(If you like the work of Avram Davidson, we suggest that of L. Sprague de Camp.)

L. SPRAGUE DE CAMP's first name is Lyon, which somehow seems appropriate for an author whose fiction can best be described as "swashbuckling." Be that as it may, de Camp's erudition in many areas, particularly history, is staggering, and while most of his stories are grand romps, their backgrounds can be vastly, if subliminally, educational.

Like many authors of that generation, discovered and nurtured by John W. Campbell for the magazines *Astounding Science Fiction* and *Unknown* in the late '30s and '40s, de Camp can (and does) write across a broad spectrum from the purest fantasy to scientifically accurate s-f. And among his most popular books are those written in collaboration with Fletcher Pratt.

Probably his most ambitious science fictional works are those concerning the *Viagens Interplanetarias,* in which a Brazilian-dominated, Portuguese-speaking Earth discovers and interacts with other worlds of the Galaxy. While their plots tend toward good old fashioned action-adventure, the social background of this universe is strongly and intelligently conceived. In *Rogue Queen,* de Camp hypothesizes about what happens when an expedition from Earth encounters an intelligent humanoid race whose social system is similar to bees, hive oriented and female dominated, and introduces the idea of democracy. *The Hand of Zei, The Search for Zei,* and *Hostage of Zir* are other *Viagens* novels, and there are numerous short stories in the loosely knit series.

Another de Camp classic is *Genus Homo* (written with P. Schuyler Miller), in which, anticipating a popular film and TV series by 30 years, a groups of humans survive a million years of suspended animation and awake to find a world dominated by evolved, intelligent apes of several species. *Lest Darkness Fall,* because of de Camp's broad knowledge of history, is one of the best time travel stories ever written, in which an American in ancient Rome attempts to prevent the Dark Ages.

De Camp has written an excellent biography of H. P. Lovecraft, a manual on the writing of science fiction, and a series of highly inventive historical novels which will appeal to the s-f reader.

(If you like the works of de Camp, we suggest the works of Fritz Leiber, Lester del Rey, and Avram Davidson.)

SAMUEL R. DELANY makes bright, sparkling images; his universe is peopled with many-faceted characters. Delany plays with words and ideas like a conjurer—he seems to toss them out at random, but with well practiced skill makes them tumble into wonderfully controlled patterns.

Delany's work falls into two distinct periods; the seeds of his future brilliance are to be found in his early books, but you have to look carefully and with judicious hindsight. He was something of a prodigy, seeing his first book, *The Jewels of Aptor,* in print at age twenty. *Jewels* is a quest novel, more fantasy than s-f perhaps, but remarkable for its invocation and control of dream symbols and concepts. The plot is of little importance—the images are all.

In fairly rapid succession came *The Fall of the Towers,* a massive three part work about the final collapse of a decadent culture; *Babel-17,* an exploration into the limits of language; *The Einstein Intersection,* which shows considerable skill with mathematics; *Nova,* a tale of obsession *a la Moby Dick;* and numerous shorts and novellas.

Nova was published in 1968, six short years after *Jewels.* Delany had a name for good, soft-science, "new wave" s-f. He had a nice way with words, and he is prolific. Then for the next seven years Delany published nothing save short stories. But what short stories! He refined his style, honed his talents, and focused his imagination. His stories gave the s-f world some of its most enduring images: the Singers from "Time Considered as a Helix of Semi-precious Stones"; the frelks, neutered space-farers from "Aye, and Gomorrah"; and the poignant joy of amphibious life in "Driftglass." These stories (collected in *Driftglass*) were harbingers of a new Delany.

Dhalgren was published in 1975 and is a massive (880 pages) exploration of a dying culture. The place is the city of Bellona, possibly on Earth and in the present, possibly on Mars and in the far future. The protagonist is the Kid (with a capital "K") who might be William Dhalgren and possibly has been in Bellona before, and *maybe* wrote the book the *next* time around. There is nothing simple and straightforward about this book, but its logic and structure are compelling enough to make the "real" world seem very strange and pale.

Triton, which anti-climaxed *Dhalgren*, is a return to more traditional s-f values. It has a clearly "future" setting and classic extrapolation. There is no question, though, that the author of Triton is a mature writer who has found his style and is exploring its limits.

Most authors have a character or concept that pervades all their work, and Delany is no exception. In his case it is "the Kid," a character that embodies the spirit of Delany's work. The Kid first appears in *Jewels*, and is present in every novel, sometimes human, sometimes mutant, always a peculiar blend of innocence and sophistication that invokes elfin childlikeness. This elusive quality is the flavor of Delany's style, and the heart of his appeal.

(If you like Delany, we suggest J. C. Ballard, Ian Watson, Joanna Russ, Michael Moorcock's s-f, Norman Spinrad, and, at the risk of alienating the s-f community, James Joyce.)

LESTER DEL REY is both a writer and an editor of distinction; one of those able to recognize and encourage good work from others, as well as produce it himself.

The majority of del Rey's novels are juveniles such as *Attack From Atlantis* and *Mission to the Moon,* written for the old "Adventures in SF" series. Though perhaps a trifle naive, any of them would be a good introduction to the field for the young reader.

Del Rey's adult novels are from a different mold; in these books he demonstrates great skill of characterization and plotting, and an ability to conjure up a veritable sensory assault. A del Rey novel is marked by its engulfing smells, tastes, sounds and sights.

Nerves, first published in 1948, is possibly the earliest book to tackle the problems of nuclear power plants. Told from the point of view of a doctor involved in containing radiation after an accident at the plant, it is a powerful, sometimes frightening novel. Del Rey foresaw modern public opposition to nuclear generators, and presented good arguments for both sides of the question. This book is technical s-f of the best sort.

He is also adept with more human themes. In *The Eleventh Commandment* the world is ruled by a transformed Catholic Church, whose message to humankind is to be fruitful and multiply. The reader sees, feels, and smells life on a planet populated by ten billion people. In the end, del Rey presents a logical argument for unlimited population growth in the most sordid of environments, and is terribly convincing.

Pstalemate is about ESP; the theory is that telepathy is a mutation which ultimately drives the possessor mad. This is a mature and sensitive book, and displays del Rey's understanding of humanity rather than relying on any technical device. Other novels include *The Sky is Falling, Police Your Planet, The Scheme of Things,* and *Badge of Infamy*.

(If you like del Rey, we suggest Hal Clement, James Gunn, or Fred Pohl.)

PHILIP K. DICK. Twenty years or so ago, Philip K. Dick had a memorable piece in *Galaxy*, "The Defenders," a story about humanity living in shelters while its robots fought overhead, making the surface uninhabitable. The kicker, of course (Dick is prone to kicker stories), was that as soon as man had withdrawn into the shelters, the sensible robots called off the destruction and proceeded to fabricate films and other deceptive proofs that the war would continue. Ho-hum, you say? Not quite. What made this particular story memorable was that it wasn't *about* nuclear destruction, or robot take-over, or any of the stale themes it might have dealt with; instead it studied the *ersatz* existence of the shelters and their fostering of new diseases and psychoses.

In his prolific career Dick has created a cluster of more or less related futures in which his gimcrack plots provide opportunities for wondering *what if.* What if the boys in the back room come up with convincing substitutes not just for war but for us? What if the good citizen's first morning duty is to dial up the right mood from a bedside console? What if love, perception, consciousness itself, can be taped, synthesized, and manipulated? This is the stuff of much of Dick's generally unsummariz-able narratives.

For newcomers to Dick's worlds, the collection of stories called *The Preserving Machine* is a reasonable introduction. The Hugo-winning novel *The Man in the High Castle* is Dick's most painstakingly con-structed and chilling novel. Outwardly it is about an alternate world in which FDR is assassinated and Germany and Japan eventually divide up the U.S. But the ostensible subject of the book is mere machinery to take us to the imaginative construction of quirky, thoroughly convincing cultures for both conquerors and conquered. In Dick's book a science fiction writer lives in central, neutral zone of the U.S. where he is writing an alternate history novel in which the Axis *loses* the war!

Dick likes, occasionally, to deal with the inversions of real problems. In *Do Androids Dream of Electric Sheep* for instance, a falling popula-tion is the problem presented. And he likes too, to consider future enlargements of contemporary malfeasance. In *Ubik,* industrial es-pionage is carried out through the use of controlled telepaths, a step be-yond the facilities of such corporate techniques of now. In many of Dick's futures, schizophrenia is a cultural norm, paranoia is a constant theme, and drugs and machines are employed to provide skewed perspectives. *Eye in the Sky* exemplifies Dick's use of such anomalies: eight people live out their psychoses after having been subjected to a ray, and each private reality incorporates all of the eight as it unfurls. And in *Dr. Bloodmoney* Dick suggests that although enormous changes—biological mutations, telepathy, contact with spirits, etc.—take place after the usual Armageddon, people carry on melodramatically, much as they always have. Petty concerns aren't ob-viated by major upheavals.

Dick is among the most prolific of s-f writers: his numerous novels and stories all deal with similar concepts. Tending toward the surreal and the unreasonable, his work delights many who find in his whimsi-cality a great sense of play despite serious themes.

(If you like the work of Dick you will enjoy some of the novels and stories of Roger Zelazny.)

GORDON R. DICKSON, (sometimes he doesn't use the ''R.'') has written everything from nutz-n-boltz hard science to the most fanciful of fantasy. He is nothing if not versatile, but the books known as the Childe Cycle are representative of his s-f and are perhaps his best work.

These books make up a "future history," with the theme of a human race spread throughout the galaxy and splintered by philosophical differences. The various cultures each embody a single quality of humanity (faith, courage, mental discipline, creativity, etc.) carried to extremes. The first in the cycle, *Necromancer* (or *No Room for Man*, an alternate title), tells of the events which lead to the break-up of mankind. *The Tactics of Mistake* recounts the first stumbling efforts to build a new culture and economy; *Dorsai* and *Soldier, Ask Not* both tell of pivotal men who realize that humanity has diverged too much and must be brought back together.

In the mid-'50s Dickson collaborated with Poul Anderson on a series of short stories that are possibly the funniest s-f ever written. They chronicle the adventures of the Hokas, inhabitants of the planet Toka, and are collected under the title *Earthman's Burden*. The Hokas made a comeback in *Star-Prince Charlie*, merely as supporting characters, it's true, but with full Hoka irrepressibility.

It is impossible to consider Gordon Dickson without at least mentioning his fantasy. As an example consider *The Dragon and the George*, wherein a 20th Century college teacher is trapped in a fiendish device and transported to another world. He materializes inside a large, and clumsy but intelligent, Dragon. Fused together, the two set off to rescue a George (otherwise known as a damsel in distress) from the clutches of an evil knight.

Dickson writes adventure with a flair for the details that bring a person or place to life. He has a knack for creating aliens that are really ALIEN—not "just folks" in funny suits. When Dickson deals with military concepts (which is often), he shows a profound grasp of tactics and the realities of warfare far removed from the romantics of most space opera.

(If you like Gordon Dickson, try Poul Anderson, Robert Heinlein, Larry Niven, Arthur C. Clarke, or Mack Reynolds.)

THOMAS M. DISCH's *334* is a monument of contemporary science fiction. But it defies categorization; it has no kin, but many kith. Uniquely, *334* displays no exotic technology, no quantum leaps into or out of the mind, no aliens but you and me, and no adventure, high or low. *And,* no distance in time or space. *334* is set in New York City (334 East 11th Street) in a tantalizingly near future, a future in which we immediately and nervously recognize ourselves and all we know, at just a slight remove. Disch's uncanny ability to conjure up a future so inevitably projected from our pedestrian present provides for chilling prerecognition. It is a cry for help from ourselves just ahead. *334* is made up of vignettes, at first seemingly unrelated, of life as it is lived. As the structure adds to itself the form of the novel emerges. In the struggle for survival—of which 334 is the epicenter—similarities rather than differences describe the whole. The book is richly and familiarly peopled and it is through these characters, their tenuous or tempestuous connections, that these mini-stories become a novel.

Disch's first novel, *The Genocides,* is relatively conventional: Earth is a kitchen garden for some herbivorous but unseen aliens, and man suffers accordingly. *Mankind Under the Leash (White Fang Goes Dingo)* tells of man as pet to alien, and his eventual revolt. In *Echo Round His Bones* matter transmission creates an elusive interspace. *Camp Concentration* is a terrifying tour de force about artificially increasing the intelligence of political prisoners, experimentally and dispassionately, leading to the convulsive death of each chemically engineered supermind.

In such short story collections as *One Hundred and Two H-Bombs* and *Getting Into Death* the remarkable diversity of Disch's abilities and interests are evident, and the range of his keen observation illuminates each story. His work seems outside of waves and movements; from each novel to the next he takes a giant step in an oblique direction.

(Admirers of Disch's work might also enjoy that of John Sladek and Gene Wolfe.)

(Sir) ARTHUR CONAN DOYLE is, of course, the creator of Sherlock Holmes, but also one of the ancestors of modern science fiction. His *The Lost World* is a classic of the beyond-the-horizon to the strange and wonderful, written when there were unexplored areas in the Earth's maps where the strange and wonderful still might exist. In this case, it is a plateau deep in the jungles of South America, which has everything from pterodactyls to Neanderthal types co-existing cheek to beak.

Into this arena stumbles an expedition of turn-of-the-century Englishmen. The chronicler, a gauche young journalist proving himself a man to a vapid young lady named Gladys, Professor Challenger, the leader and organizer, determined to demonstrate that the "lost world" exists, his fellow scientist Professor Summerlee, equally certain that it doesn't, and Lord Roxton, big game hunter in search of (what else?) big game. That which ensues is the best sort of adventure, and also is at times very funny, as in what happens when they manage to get a pterodactyl back to London.

Doyle's Professor Challenger is a creation to equal Mr. Holmes. There are several more Challenger stories, including the novel, *The Poison Belt*. Other of Doyle's short stories also qualify as s-f, including the oft-anthologized "The Great Keinplatz Experiment." Alas, a novel written later in the author's life, *The Maracot Deep*, about the finding of Atlantis at the bottom of the ocean, is rather pallid Verne with mushily metaphysical overtones.

(Admirers of Doyle might find the same period charm in the works of H. Rider Haggard and George Allan England.)

GEORGE ALEC EFFINGER is a young writer whose books tend to read like instant nostalgia. His ongoing fascination (or is it preoccupation) with the American mythic themes of WW II and sports, plus his evident marinading in comics color virtually all of Effinger's novels and stories.

What Entropy Means to Me is all at once a parody, an allegory, and a fantasy, as it traces the double quest of two brothers who have mislaid their father. One travels and the other writes, the writer embroidering the traveler's true voyage with further adventures as the real quest is farther removed from him. The true quest, the invented quest, the allegorical quest, the imagined quest. Do you see? In the end the writing brother, too, begins a physical quest, and it isn't clear who will chronicle (or invent) his. *Relatives* further explores the theme of multiple identity, parallel story. More like a tapestry than a narrative, it bears no plot outlining; it has to do with a sort of triplicate incarnation.

Effinger's often entrancing often clever often captious stories frequently appear in various of the year's best collections, and he's been known to have produced a mainstream novel as well.

(If you like Effinger, try Philip K. Dick.)

GORDON EKLUND came into prominence when he and Gregory Benford won a Nebula for their novelette "If the Stars Are Gods" which was later expanded into a full-length book. He had previously published a novel, *The Eclipse of Dawn*.

Eklund writes essentially traditional s-f, but as with some of his peers there is a kind of off-the-cuff (not to mention the wall), insouciant wit endemic in the prose. In *The Grayspace Beast* Eklund uses the literary conceit of having the tale told *as* a tale by a narrator who is clearly privy to the story itself, but whose identity is never guessed (until too late) by the wiseass children who comment like a newspeak Greek chorus in the entre-actes. The story of the beast is a fragmentary one, filled with duplicity and intrigue as a strange crew is gathered to man a ship to penetrate the grayspace den of the Grayspace Beast. Wryly adventurous, the novel chugs along like a shaggy dog story, leaving its stock ending for the pen-penultimate paragraph. That the Beast is an experience beyond man needs hardly be said.

All Times Possible is an alternate history novel, a what-if the United States had taken a different turn historically. A leftist revolution succeeds in the 20s and an early activist, Bloome, is content until he finds that this is only one of a number of alternate histories, each of which he participates in, one way or another. Other Eklund books are *The Inheritors of Earth*, with Poul Anderson; *Serving In Time*, about a totalitarianly manipulated false paradise; and *Dance of the Apocalypse*, in which two friends, one mighty, one visionary, hope to renew a devastated world.

(Admirers of Eklund's work might take a crack at that of Michael G. Coney.)

HARLAN ELLISON wears many authorial hats, but clearly all on the one head. This writer has produced a staggering amount of print which may be divided into three categories: journalism, allegory, and science fantasy. Those who admire Ellison's science fiction will doubtless want to read his various books of critical/journalistic essays, as well as what might be called the "punk" books, those collections of New York street stories which so clearly represent a period in recent social history. Actually, Ellison's only s-f novels so far are the slender effort *Doomsman* and the earlier *The Man With Nine Lives*.

Ellison's s-f reputation is based mainly on a sizeable number of facile short stories, many with stadium endings, such as that of "The Silver Corridor":

"At the instant they both realized it—the instant they considered the other's viewpoint—the illusion barriers shattered, of course, and the red-hot lava poured in on them, engulfing both men in a blistering inferno." Whew!

This, and other Ellison s-f type stories are gathered, in part, in: *Ellison Wonderland, Deathbird Stories, I Have No Mouth, and I Must*

Scream, Alone Against Tomorrow, The Beast That Shouted Love at the Heart of the World. For some of these he has won seven Hugo and two Nebula awards, and his scripts for several episodes of Star Trek have kept new readers coming to his books.

Among Ellison's best known and most collected stories are "I Have No Mouth, and I Must Scream" in which the supercomputer that creates and controls civilization—or its sole remnant, the "I" of the title—fails to provide a mouth for its final creation; In "'Repent, Harlequin,' Said the Ticktockman" Harlequin (anarchist, civil disobedient, hero) makes himself and others late in a society governed by punctuality and the Ticktockman (authority, order, repression), which he does by dropping tons of jelly beans from his flier onto a moving sidewalk full of regimented workers; "A Boy and His Dog," which has been filmed, is a reasonably straight s-f story concerning a post-atomsmash America and a boy who talks telepathically with his superior canine (a pooch), finds his way into an underground land (which is all apple-pie and mom), is used as a sperm source by the virility starved undergrounders, takes a girl back topside and serves her cooked, to his ever-faithful starving, wounded, heroic, and dolphin-intelligent dog.

Ellison's writing is trendy and glib, and he uses freely the conventions of the avant-garde in the structure of his stories. Though no polymath, Ellison makes his knowledge of Classic and Jewish myth support his visions of alienation and despair, sometimes giving certain tales oddly moral overtones. Sex, in Ellison's canon, is usually a negative and demeaning experience, as is life itself; and the tone, though often wry and parodistic, is gloomy.

(If you like Harlan Ellison's stories you might try reading Norman Spinrad or Spider Robinson.)

GEORGE ALLAN ENGLAND was a heavy contributor to the fiction magazines of the early part of this century, before they began to specialize. Besides the typical action and adventure one might expect from his work, there is also a Wellsian concern with social comment. In *The Air Trust,* science learns to control the amount of oxygen in the air and the population is forced to pay for what they breathe; *The Golden Blight* is a result of a machine that makes gold disintegrate and causes profound economic changes; in *The Flying Legion* aviators led by a power-hungry scientist attempt to rule the world.

His best known work is *Darkness and Dawn,* confusingly published as a single volume, a trilogy, and a five book series.* It is an epic of adventure in a deserted world, as experienced by an engineer and his secretary who have survived a thousand years of suspended animation. *D&D* is still a marvelously exciting example of the post-catastrophe sub-genre of s-f, and the most currently readable of England's works.

(England owes as much to Verne as to Wells, so his fans might try the works of both if they haven't already.)

*See *"Last and First Books"* section.

RALPH MILNE FARLEY was a physicist with three degrees from Harvard and so it's quite natural that his stories would have a technical slant. He's best known for a series about Myles Cabot, the Radio Man, that originally appeared in the 20's in *Argosy All-Story Weekly* and other pulp magazines. Cabot is accidentally shot into space by his own invention and finds himself stranded on a Venus populated by intelligent antlike beings, hugh bees, and other assorted denizens. It is through his immense knowledge of chemistry, electronics, and most especially of radio, that he manages to overthrow the bad guys and set up a new civilization, in the novel *The Radio Beasts*. A sequel, *Radio Planet,* finds Cabot once again in trouble, after a short sojourn on Earth. He misjudges his transmission back to Venus and ends up on that planet, but in an area just as uncivilized as that he has first discovered. He has to build a technological society from scratch, in order to return to his adopted home and loved ones, half way across the planet.

Farley's work must be read with an acceptance of the limitations of scientific knowledge available to a writer in the 1920s and with a sense of perspective regarding the style of the pulp magazines for which he wrote. Character was usually supplied by a catchy name and a job description, or by a rock-hard jaw and steel-blue eyes, and came second to the science, around which the plot usually revolved. The science material, for today's reader, is quite out of date. It is fun though, to look at radio when it was a big, new phenomenon. S-f is the best form of literature for this sense of history compression and it is partially for this reason that Farley and others of the pulp writers are still read.

(Farley fanciers might try Burroughs, Kline, or Cummings.)

PHILIP JOSE FARMER. In the pulp magazine period of s-f, there was a strange dichotomy between the magazine covers and the contents. The covers usually featured a lovely and diaphanously clad young woman in some distinctly sexual predicament. A large tentacled beastie was reaching for her, or an obviously depraved human male had her tied up, or . . . Inside? A chaste embrace between space suits and *maybe,* once the protagonists had agreed to marry, an actual kiss on the lips. The entire industry could have been sued for false advertising.

Phil Farmer brought real, honest sexual motives to s-f, and he did it in 1952. He explored the themes of sex and love between human and alien, alien and alien, and human and human, producing some remarkable stories—sensitive works on a formerly taboo subject. *The Lovers,* his first novel, *Dare, Flesh,* and *Strange Relations* are all fine books, though perhaps best suited to mature readers. Two others, which could be called s-f (for sexual fantasy) are *Image of the Beast* and *Blown.* The two are tenuously linked. A *Feast Unknown* is an obscene version of Farmer's own Tarzan pastiches.

Farmer has written several books about other people's characters, updating them or telling the "true" story. He has done both Tarzan and Doc Savage (in *The Lord of the Trees,* and *Doc Caliban,* and in his "biographies" of the two); he picked up from Verne in *The Other Log of Phileas Fogg,* a lighthearted spoof which proves that Fogg was an alien; *The Wind Whales of Ishmael* moves Herman Melville's character into the far far future.

Farmer has yet a third persona, and the novels produced by this one are probably the best. He has outdone himself and many others with the sheer inventiveness of his Riverworld series. The Riverworld is a huge planet with one great river between two mountain chains. The river winds its way around and around the planet, much like a red and white striped barber pole millions of miles long. Along the banks of this river, one fine morning, every human being who has ever lived, or who ever will live, wakes up in a twenty-five-year-old body. How? Why? Farmer has written four books which concern the answer to these questions. Also of interest in this connection is an early book of Farmer's called *Inside/Outside. I/O* is either a "first" book in the series, or a premature effort to handle the entire vision in a single book.

Finally there is the World of Tiers series, which is now at five books. This is about a small group of extraordinarily powerful and immortal beings who can create entire universes, parallel to each other, and who fight boredom by fighting each other. This series is highly adventurous, with the characters hopping worlds and escaping death by a narrow margin.

One of the most amusing things about Farmer's work is that he almost always creates a character that is himself, usually as an incidental sidekick. This character can be spotted by the initials of his name, PF or PJF.

(If you like Philip Farmer's work, we suggest Jack Chalker, David Lake, Roger Zelazny, and E. E. Smith.)

MICK FARREN, retired underground celebrity and rock and roller, has published one novel, *The Texts of Festival,* a cocaine-oriented downbeat adventure set in England's gloomy near future, and a trilogy of madcap adventure fictions which capitalize on s-f conventions. *The Quest of the DNA Cowboys, Synaptic Manhunt,* and *The Neural Atrocity* romp through a staggering variety of source material. Comics, Bruce Lee, 007, Michael Moorcock, science fiction pulp stories, trendy culture and chic individuals (Elvis Presley and Oscar Wilde appear in the final volume) contribute to the anything-goes mosaic of the trilogy. This is the stuff of mod dreams: a power-mad, sadistic lesbian queen, an ill-assorted group of contemporary drug types who hang out together, and thread through the books, a sanctimonious group called the Brotherhood who train super kung-fu artists and send them, laser armed, to do battle with evil. Farren's trilogy is pulp space-opera in contemporary dress, populated by familiar modern stereotypes.

(Those who like Farren's work certainly should look into Michael Moorcock's s-f.)

JONATHAN FAST is the son of author Howard Fast, and is therefore one of the few second generation s-f writers. Jonathan has contributed novels that are space opera in a mystic vein. *The Secrets of Synchronicity* features a rather Candide-ish hero who is caught up in a struggle against big corporations and wage slavery in the asteroid belt. His ultimate achievement is to bring cosmic consciousness to all humanity.

In *Mortal Gods,* Fast attempts a transcendental detective story, with a plot so twisted that it eventually doubles back on itself.

(If you like Jonathan Fast, we suggest A. E. van Vogt, or E. E. Smith.)

HOMER EON FLINT wrote for the magazine of the teens and '20s, and is now really only remembered for his collaboration with Austin Hall, q.v., on *The Blind Spot,* and as the author of the two short novels which were combined by Ace under the enchanting name of *The Devolutionist and the Emancipatrix* (remember that for charades). Unfortunately, the period prose is not as interesting as the title.

ALAN DEAN FOSTER is basically a builder of worlds, races, and societies. His concern for detail in his description of human and alien planets, cultures, and individuals, lends a sense of reality to the constructed situations.

Foster's probably best known for his series about the adventures of Phillip Lynx (Flinx), an orphaned slave freed by his owner, and Pip, his venomous pet minidragon. The sheer scope of this series tends to boggle one's mind a bit; here we have not just a galaxy-wide civilization of humans, but the Humanx Commonwealth, made up of humans and the insectoid Thranx. The four novels that form this saga tell the story of Flinx's search for his mother and father through Foster's well structured cosmos. These books are first class space opera.

Besides this series Foster has written several other novels, among them *Icerigger,* tale of human survivors of a crashlanding on the frozen planet Tran-ky-ky, and *Mid-world,* a particularly well-done novel of life in a ferocious jungle world. It's essentially a guide to this world and its denizens, somewhat reminiscent of Murray Leinster's *Forgotten Planet.* These two novels are both connected with the Humanx Commonwealth series in that they take place in the same universe at approximately the same time, though Flinx and Pip do not appear.

Although characterization is not Foster's strongest point you do get to know and like his people, and the background against which they are met is usually wonderful in concept and detailed in execution.

Foster is also author of the Star Trek "Log" series, a number of novels following the continuing adventures of the indomitable crew of the USS Enterprise.

(The works of Piers Anthony, Joseph Green, and Fred Saberhagen might appeal to you if you like Foster's.)

RAYMOND Z. GALLUN, in the late '20s, wrote good solid science fiction novels and stories, along with the other pioneers of that period. Gallun's "The Crystal Ray" deals with conventional period stereotypes, the heroic Americans, the inscrutable and probably evil Orientals, and victory via a light ray projected through volcanic glass. It was vintage material treated in vintage ways.

Thirty years after "The Crystal Ray" Gallun wrote *People Minus X*, a novel far removed from the thrills and adventure stuff of the depression era. Here Gallun speculated about human resurrection, and he considered the ethical and moral climes of the human condition.

The Eden Cycle, a novel coming some 45 years after that primordial "ray," gathers in sophistication and considers the possibility of man achieving perfection of a kind, and being unable to withstand it. Gallun imagines that ultimately, having everything is the same as having nothing, as his Eden people live hedonistically under a beneficent alien rule.

Gullun's career has been long and is notable for the way the writer has grown and changed with the times. A gathering of his work, *The Best of Raymond Z. Gallun*, spotlights an interesting and remarkably encompassing body of work over a period that embraces virtually all of s-f's modern history.

RANDALL GARRETT was one of the "regulars" of John W. Campbell's *Astounding/Analog* of the '50s and '60s. The quality of his work varies enormously: his short story "The Hunting Lodge" is generally acknowledged to be a modern classic, but *The Brain Twisters,* co-authored with Laurence Janifer, is simple space opera spliced onto a detective story.

Garrett also collaborated with Robert Silverberg and Lin Carter. *Unwise Child,* the story of a humanoid android with the power of independent judgement, is well plotted and enjoyable. Garrett's best work is found in the "Lord Darcy" stories, first published in *Analog,* and collected in part in *Too Many Magicians.* Darcy, Chief Inspector of the Crown, inhabits an alternate world where magic is possible (but only under properly controlled conditions), and world history has taken some surprising turns. The detective stories are ingenious, and the world Lord Darcy inhabits is rich and believable.

(If you enjoy Randall Garrett, read Fletcher Pratt and L. Sprague de Camp's collaborative efforts.)

JANE GASKELL is best known for her unique fantasy series, the five "Atlan" novels, but she also proved she could write equally pyrotechnic science fiction with *A Sweet, Sweet Summer,* an unnerving portrait of an anarchistic Britain that makes *A Clockwork Orange* look like *Winnie the Pooh.* With luck, Ms. Gaskell will turn to other science fictional subjects; writing talents such as hers do not come along every day.

(If you like Jane Gaskell, try the work of Angela Carter.)

JEAN MARK GAWRON (the name is Polish and the "w" is pronounced like a "v") published his first novel, *An Apology for Rain*, when he was nineteen. It has only appeared in hardcover to date and is somewhat difficut to come by. It chronicles the search by a tall silver-haired young woman named Bonnie for her vanished brother, Philip, across a post-holocaust landscape, where pointless wars, telepathy, and celestial portents have become the norm. Gawron's second novel, *Algorithm*, appeared as a paperback original in 1978. On a future Earth, now out of the center of interstellar affairs, we follow the adventures of a bunch of media-personalities called "proets" during a carnival where a mysterious assassin has been sent from the stars to kill. . .just who, no one is quite sure. Gawron's writing is witty and lush. Characters speak in long, poetic monologues, the pages become tapestries of color, with much linguistic and philosophical play. (Gawron, as of this writing, is a graduate student in linguistics in California.) This is "science fiction as rhapsody." And very lovely and lively rhapsody it is.

(If you like Gawron, try Brian Stableford—who frequently uses a somewhat similar rhapsodic approach to story-telling, especially in his *Grainger* series.)

HUGO GERNSBACK was less talented as a writer than as an editor. He is called "The Father of Science Fiction"; that title should in all fairness be qualified as *American* science fiction (though he was born in Luxembourg, of all places), and more particularly American *magazine* science fiction, since he founded several magazines which initiated the era in which the magazines *were* science fiction.

According to s-f historians, Gernsback fell into a two-day feverish delirium when he discovered his first science fictional concept at age nine (it was Lowell's *Mars as the Abode of Life*). One might note that this seems to be a contagious fever which most s-f fans seem to fall prey to, and from which some never do seem to recover. In any case, Gernsback's place in the history of science fiction is an important one, covered more thoroughly in "The Spawn of Frankenstein" chapter. But as a writer of interest to current readers, he leaves something to be desired. His best known work is *Ralph 124C41 +* (read that as "one to foresee for one plus"). The titular hero is an evolved superman of the year 2660, and given the melodramatic plot (complete with "saturnine" Martian villain, a confusion of gods at best), that is probably all you really want to know.

But the novel was an absolute gold mine of predicted inventions that eventually achieved reality (not the least of which was the juke box). One of the problems of the novel is the enormous amount of wordage telling the reader how these things work. Gernsback was of the Vernian view of s-f as prediction (with a little literary decoration). He lived until 1967, long enough to see his "child" become the many headed monster that it is today, to be honored by the science fiction community at conventions and to have an annual award in the field named the "Hugo," and to be created an "Officer of the Oaken Crown" by the Grand Duchess Charlotte of Luxembourg.

DAVID GERROLD is one of the up and coming of the younger generation of science fiction writers. Much of his fame rests on his association with *Star Trek* for which he wrote one of the most popular episodes, "The Trouble With Tribbles." But aside from that, he has written several original and stylish novels that bode well for his future as a major force in s-f.

When Harlie Was One is the trials and growing pains of a computer, with more perils to his existence than those of Pauline, and a near love affair with his programmer. *The Man Who Folded Himself* takes a Heinlein premise, that of a convolution in time where the main character keeps meeting himself, and carries it almost *ad infinitum* if not *ad absurdum;* sex plays a great part in this one and narcissism has never had a more active solution. It's vastly ingenious and amusing. Changing his key entirely, Gerrold, in *Moonstar Odyssey,* sets the stage for an ambigendrous society on an artificially habitable planet where the moonstars, with their artfully planned eclipses, and the inhabitants, with a choice of sexuality at puberty, make for a complex created world. The creation of the legends of this world (Satlik) are particularly lovely.

Gerrold's demonstrated skills make one hope that he will continue to cultivate the art of science fiction.

(Those who like Gerrold's work might also enjoy that of Sturgeon.)

MARK S. GESTON has produced very little; nearly a decade passed between his first and third novels. In *Siege of Wonder,* the enduring conflict between technology and magic still rages. Ancient sorceries and modern investigative sciences, often seeking the same ends, exist in the novel, not so much as polarities, but as interfaces. Arden, a spy and activist, observes and equivocates as the magic of the Holy City fails before the encroachments of technological assault, and he becomes a near victim of the enchantments of the enemy, even as it is perishing.

In *Lords of the Starship* an enormous group effort is made to construct a mighty ship. When the herculean task is done, evildoers explode the ship and open the now weakened country to invasion. *Out of the Mouth of the Dragon* is a novel of endless war and final war, and Geston uses mythic archetypes to enrich his narrative. Mark Geston's s-f novels are polished and literate representatives of the genre.

(If you like Mark Geston and haven't read Jack Vance, it would be well worth a try.)

H. L. GOLD stands tall in the s-f field as an editor and anthologist; he was *Galaxy* magazine's founding editor. He also created and edited the Galaxy Reader anthology series, which from 1953 to 1962 gave devotees an annual dose of good short fiction.

Gold had another side though, as an infrequent writer of good and imaginative short stories. Twelve of these stories were collected in *The Old Die Rich and Other Science Fiction*. The tales themselves are witty examples of the writer's craft, and the accompanying comments by Gold are full of useful information on how one writer goes about it. And while it is not widely known, Gold also wrote a novel, entitled *None But Lucifer*. It was revised by L. Sprague de Camp and was published in *Unknown* (a lost, lamented pulp) in 1939. This novel has not seen the light of day since then.

(In the unlikely event that you have found and liked the fiction of Gold and not discovered that of Fredric Brown, by all means try the latter's work.)

FELIX GOTSCHALK is a writer who, in Robert Silverberg's words, is "maddening to some, delightful to others." He has written some 35 short stories and one novel, *Growing Up in Tier 3000*. Most of Gotschalk's stories (and the novel) are set in a future where energy supplies have run low and population grown far too large. There is a deadly but civilized war being waged between parents and children; the prize is life itself—warmth, food, shelter and other amenities of an energy dependent technology. All these are just the bones of his world; the maddening or delightful part comes because Gotschalk has a certain way with words. He makes them up or changes their meaning, or applies them in ways you and I never thought of. Although some readers may find getting into Gotschalk's world a little difficult, the effort is worth-while.

(If you like Felix Gotschalk, we suggest Harlan Ellison or R. A. Lafferty.)

RON GOULART after graduating college in 1955, spent a few years in advertising, writing what was called "off-beat" copy. Taking the term off-beat literally, i.e. slightly out of synch, it could well apply to his science fiction also. The mad futures of Goulart are indeed a little out of synch, and a great many readers find them funny. His writing is laced with plays on words, and he also enjoys taking playful slaps at authority, be it personified in a government official or a telephone company's computer.

Goulart's protogonists are usually super secret agents, or super detectives, or, as in *The Hellhound Project,* even a super ex-advertising man. A good example is super secret agent John Wesley Sand, free lance spy and bon vivant. *Clockwork's Pirates* begins with Sand being thrown off a sailing ship by clanking steaming robot pirates, and accelerates across a world populated exclusively by engaging rogues and eccentric victims. The plot twists come fast and furious and the humor is abundant. *The Emperor of the Last Days* concerns a group of amateur detectives masterminded by a semi-sentient computer named Barney who get involved in a political conspiracy aimed at world domination. Hero Dan Farleigh's new-found love, a go-get-em female reporter, is on to this and so disappears. Dan enlists the aid of Barney and thereby such unlikely characters as Professor Supermind, hypnotist of machinery (robots included), Tin Lizzie, a bionic political satire complete with an ex-President who makes more money as a was then he did as an is, and a current President who video-tapes everything (and that means *everything*) for posterity.

Goulart is a prolific writer, and has added many books to the lighter side of science fiction.

(If Goulart amuses you, try Effinger, Sheckley, and Kurland.)

CHARLES GRANT is one of s-f's more recent producers; his stories have been appearing with increasing frequency in the genre magazines—and have won several awards along the way—and several novels have elbowed their way onto the shelves; he also has edited a number of anthologies, including *Shadows I* and *II,* two collections on the supernatural. Grant's novel *The Shadow of Alpha* teases with its subjects—a long awaited starship, a techie who collects data under the dubiously watchful eyes of an android civilizaton, a human civilization devastated by a plague, the less-than-amiable attitude of the increasingly effectual androids. And to compound the confusion, the ship Alpha never does return. In *The Hour of the Oxrun Dead*—not really an s-f novel; Grant is more comfortable with the supernatural—the conventions of mass-market terror fiction, occultism, nebulous omens, and a properly bewildered victim, brew and stew a plot characterized by missing books, ignored murders and ominous presences. Other fictions by this writer/editor include *Legion* and *Ascension*.

(If you like the work of Charles Grant, try that of George R. R. Martin.)

JOSEPH GREEN. Certainly one of the delightful devices unique to science fiction is the creation of alien races, whether as menace or friend. Green is particularly good at race making; in *Conscience Interplanetary* he has invented a device which serves to introduce quite a few. It is a series of short stories woven into a "novel" about the Practical Philosopher Corps that is in the business of identifying and saving from exploitation worlds inhabited by intelligences. Among the unusual and likeable sapient species encountered are the inhabitants of Crystal, where a tree is like a corruscating chandelier and the intelligence a glittering bush, and of the planet Beauty, where a clay idol leaves one in awe. The background of political skullduggery and infighting adds humor and suspense.

The Mind Behind the Eye introduces the Hilt-Sil, a three-hundred-foot-humanoid race who are inexplicably trying to exterminate Homo sapiens.

Green's experience as a technical writer for NASA may be the basis for this talent for creating extraterrestrials; on the other hand, one wonders if that might have been more of an obstacle than an aid.

(If you are intrigued by Green's other-worldly "people," you might enjoy Alan Dean Foster's.)

JAMES GUNN is an educator and scholar well known for his critical analyses of s-f, who also writes fiction. While his scientific backgrounds are firm, his stories dwell on mankind's reaction to the technological world. Gunn has a sober view of our ability to adjust to the future.

In *The Joy Makers*, a company goes into the business of making everyone happy by helping remove all negative influences from life. There is no sickness, no pressure, no hunger, no unfulfilled dreams, no conflict for anyone who takes out a contract with them. This eventually evolves into a new world culture, the Hedonic society, which rules mankind. The breakdown occurs when the Hedonists can no longer make themselves happy, and turn over governing to a complex computer. It is a moving and compelling argument against the attainment of one's heart's desire.

The Listeners are huge radio telescopes which one day receive the entire history of an alien culture; Gunn describes the effect that this knowledge has on mankind. The theme is continued in *The Burning,* where people rise up in revolt against the technologists, because they are unable to cope with a machine society.

In all of Gunn's books there is a plea for moderation, a warning that if we become too entranced by or dependent on machines and progress we may lose touch with humanity.

In a slightly different vein is *The Immortals*, about a group of mutant humans who are truly immortal. This immortality can be passed to non-mutants by a transfusion of blood, and when this is discovered they are hunted by those who would like to live forever. The story is a frightening reminder of how easily common humanity can be brushed aside in the face of overwhelming desire.

(If you enjoy Gunn's work, we suggest Frank Herbert, or Lester del Rey.)

H. RIDER HAGGARD is another one of those ancestors of science fiction who is still thoroughly readable today (given, of course, the usual proviso of a little historical perspective on the part of the reader.)

Those who have already read Haggard's marvelous melanges of adventure, mysticism, and lost races, might well ask just how he fits into the genealogy chart of s-f. Well, when Haggard was writing—the end of the 19th century and into the 20th—there were still vast empty areas on the maps where wonders could be placed; no need to go into space or the future to wonder as you wander. And in the 19th century, the mystical or "occult" sciences were still considered almost as valid as the physical sciences (a viewpoint, I might add, that seems to be reviving today). And as well as speculation in that direction, Haggard speculated in anthropology and practically created the sub-genre of the classic "lost race" story.

She, one of Haggard's most famous novels, is a good example of all this going at once. Two Englishmen discover a formidable lady living among the decadent remains of an ancient unknown African civilization. She is immortal (through bathing in a mystical fountain of fire that, it is implied, is extraterrestrial in origin) and has been waiting around for several thousand years for the reincarnation of a lover that she had killed in a careless moment. Guess who one of the Englishmen turns out to be?

It's easy to make fun of Haggard's extraordinary plots; but it's also fun to read them. There are in all, four books about She (Her?): one, *Ayesha, the Return of She,* takes place, as implied in the title, after the events of *She,* in Tibet, of all the unlikely places; *She and Allan* brings together the formidable lady and Haggard's equally formidable great white hunter, Allan Quatermain, and the result—the mystic East meets the rational West—is curiously humorous; *Wisdom's Daughter* is about She's early life.

Both Edgar Rice Burroughs and A. Merrit, in very different ways, owe much to Haggard, and science fiction as a whole would have been much the less robust without him.

(If you like Haggard, give Merritt and Burroughs a try.)

JOE HALDEMAN. A (fairly) rare event in the science fiction world is for a first novel to win an award. Even more rare is its winning of both the Hugo and Nebula Awards. Haldeman managed this with *The Forever War,* a novelization of four stories that appeared in *Analog* magazine. An anti-war novel, often contrasted to Heinlein's *Starship Troopers,* it is the story of Private William Mandella, a draftee in the United Nations Exploratory Force. He doesn't want to go to war, and finds that war is a figurative if not a literal hell; he's fighting a species made enemy by mistake and the relativity problem brought about by faster-than-light travel enforces this hell. The characterization is good, the plotting is reasonable, and it has as happy an ending as one can expect considering the beginning and the middle.

Mindbridge is an experiment in style, and like most experiments, succeeds or not depending on the observer. The story is a good one, with matter transmission, telepathy, and even contact with an alien race thrown in.

His third novel, *All My Sins Remembered,* details three episodes in the career of Otto McGavin, Prime Operator for TB II, undercover guardian of the rights of aliens and humans under the Confederacion. Like *The*

Forever War, it is a violent novel revealing anti-violent attitudes.

Haldenman is a good writer, and although at times tending towards polemic, enjoyable, especially if you agree with his viewpoint.

(Try Gordon Dickson's work if you like that of Haldeman.)

AUSTIN HALL wrote fiction and some scientific romances for the general fiction magazines of the first quarter of this century. The only work he's remembered for is *The Blind Spot* (in collaboration with Homer Eon Flint) which has been in print on and off since then. Many modern readers may find its period charm less than charming, plus the fact that it has sometimes been called the worst science fiction novel ever published. This is unfair; the first part is a scientific mystery story, in which the mysterious phenomenon of "the blind spot" is tracked down in an old house in San Francisco; the second part takes place in the other-dimensional world that the spot is in reality a gateway to, and has some of the splendidly romantic vision of A. Merritt. The fact that all the major characters in the book disappear without a trace at the end just might be off-putting, however. But it's great fun with the usual invocation of historical perspective.

(If you like *The Blind Spot,* by all means try A. Merritt and John Taine.)

EDMOND HAMILTON. Zap! Bam! Baroom! Crashing suns! Star trail to glory! Battle for the stars! The sun smasher! Those are Edmond Hamilton titles, and from that you may well guess that Edmond Hamilton writes space opera. Right. Even more, he may well be the epitomal writer of space opera.

One of the simpler definitions of space opera is science fiction for the fun of it, and nobody has had as much fun over so much time as Hamilton. His has been one of the longest careers in the field (first story published in 1926), and a word count might show him to be the most prolific. His career seems almost a blueprint for every classic s-f writer; he began it in *Weird Tales* before the dichotomy between science fiction and tales of the supernatural had developed; he perfected the speed and facility necessary to make a living from the low-paying pulp magazines; he wrote across the lines of science fiction and fantasy, and he married another s-f writer, the wonderful Leigh Brackett of the sensuous prose. (Luckily for the librarian and bibliographer, they did not allow their work to become entwined as did Moore and Kuttner.)

Perhaps the greatest challenge of his career, as he might say about one of his heros, came when he took on the job of turning out a "novel" (pulp novels were closer in length to novelettes) once every three months for *Captain Future,* a pulp quarterly devoted to the adventures of science fiction's first true super hero. He accomplished this for four years with only a couple of lapses. Despite the inhibitions of such a format and schedule Hamilton's *Captain Future* series was consistently good, and over its length, Hamilton created a background milieu of some depth for "space opera." It was a Solar System of nine inhabited worlds, each with its own indigenous races as well as colonies or scientific settlements from Earth. Captain Future himself was Curt Newton, raised in an isolated spot on the Moon by his dead father's inventions, Grag the robot, and Otho the android; and with the help of Simon Wright, his father's partner, who was now an immortal brain in a maneuverable box (OK, it sound silly, but half the charm was Hamilton's ability to bring these things off).

Captain Future was, of course, a scientific wiz as well as super-endowed physically. He had arranged for the President of Earth to set off a flare at the North Pole whenever the System was menaced ("There's only one thing left to do," the President said purposefully. "I'm going to call Captain Future.").

The Captain Future stories were so good of their kind that they literally typed Hamilton. While science fiction was enlarging its horizons in Sturgeonesque, van Vogtian and Heinleinian directions, Hamilton kept the flame of action-adventure s-f going, but like the pro that he was, he didn't stay in one place. He presented a Captain Future type of a bit more maturity in his *Starwolf* series; Morgan Chane, the "Starwolf," comes close to being an anti-hero. His novels were still bursting with action, but the concepts became more subtle and integrated with the narrative. In *The Star Kings,* a contemporary man is thrown into an exceedingly complex future; in *City at the World's End,* an entire present day community is blown into the future by a super bomb.

And his short stories, which had always tended more than the novels to be atypical mood pieces or even fantasies, became more polished and thoughtful, as in "Requiem," where the last man on the Earth before it falls into the Sun regards with disgust the sentimental drivel about the event being broadcast to humanity, now inhabiting many other worlds. "World Wrecker" Hamilton was here destroying a world for effect, and not for the action implicit in the situation.

Hamilton had been affectionately dubbed both "World Wrecker" and "World Saver" by readers, but his long lasting talent has outgrown those easy labels.

(If you like Hamilton's work, try E. E. Smith, Jack Williamson, Bill Starr, and Harry Harrison.)

CHARLES HARNESS' slim output ranges from *The Paradox Men* (published over twenty years ago), with its bewilderingly complicated plot about the efforts of one man to end a global social injustice in a martial, totalitarian U.S. of the future, to *The Rose*, a baroquely decorated novel, romantically treated, about two beautiful people in love, two people whose beauteous deformity appears to be the pre-natal state of the next stage in man's evolution.

Ring of Ritornel is a pseudo-scientific novel of galaxy-wide meanders and circumferential time; its fabulous beasts and Harness' conception of anti-matter weave a plot more fantastic than science-fictional. The author's more recent *Wolfhead* is a novel of post-holocaust familiarity, mixing interesting brews of telekenetics, telepathy, surgical amalgams of the brain matter of wolf and man, and an archetypal underworld quest. Its pseudo-scientific doubletalk seems acceptable because of the literary frame. Harness makes highly literate pulp fiction.

(Those who like Harness' variety might find the same in the work of John Brunner.)

HARRY HARRISON was a machine-gun instructor during World War II and he may have given some instructions to his typewriter. Whatever the cause, most of his stories are fast moving adventures full of action and excitement. He is best known for two series: "Deathworld" (succinctly individually titled *Deathworld 1, 2 & 3)* and "The Stainless Steel Rat" (which includes also *The SSR's Revenge* and *The SSR Saves the World*).

Deathworld 1 is Pyrrus, one of the most vicious planets in the literature. Jason dinAlt, interplanetary gambler, tries to discover the reason for the apparently studied effort of an entire world's ecology to wipe out man. In *Deathworld 2* and *Deathworld 3* dinAlt and his Pyrran companions tackle other worlds, each in its own way as dangerous as Pyrrus. The Stainless Steel Rat novels follow the adventures of interstellar criminal and crook catcher James Bolivar diGriz, "Slippery Jim," who is a delightful character, prone to wisecracks, amorality, and cleverly designed and executed escapades.

Other novels in Harrison's lighter vein include: *Bill, the Galactic Hero,* a satire on the regimentation and brutality of the military; *Star Smashers of the Galaxy Rangers,* which (as you might guess from the title) sets out to out-space-opera space opera; and *The Technicolor Time Machine,* which chronicles the adventures of a crew of bumbling filmmakers shooting a historical epic not only on location, but in the past with the help of a time machine.

In a more serious vein, *Make Room, Make Room* (filmed as *Soylent Green*) is a detective story set in a future when man has finally depleted his living and food-production space, while *Captive Universe* is an intriguing variation on the spaceship as ark theme, with many civilizations preserved in a giant interstellar vessel, unaware of their true circumstances.

(If you like Harrison, try Gordon Dickson, Edmond Hamilton, and Heinlein.)

M. JOHN HARRISON. After a few sit-up-and-take-notice short stories in British magazines, Harrison published his first novel, *The Committed Men,* an appalling vision of man degenerated, psychotic and clawing, in an ecologically deranged future; it is a book much affected by the early novels of Ballard. *The Pastel City,* a narrative of desperate quest and vicious combat in a landscape of demolished and forgotten technology, might seem a sword and sorcery tale, but its wondrous prose and deeply etched dramatis personae raise it above that subgenre. *The Centauri Device,* expanded from a seminal short story, is the space opera-like saga of John Truck, a hobo flyer of *My Ella Speed,* a tin lizzy ship. Space-spanning fights, intrigues, brawls, and political huggermugger surround Truck's equivocal center position in the search for the enigmatic centauri device. A novel of blood and guts, often graphically described and impeccably depicted in Harrison's inventive prose, *The Centauri Device* has the kind of antic madness that saves the British from contemporary dismay. It is as speedily pell-mell and adventure filled as *Star Wars,* and its visions of intergalactic spaceports and drugged flyers are both funny and fearsome. *The Machine in Shaft Ten* is a collection of Harrison's shorter fiction, each piece of which is as tense and wryly turgid as the other.

(Fellow Britishers Ballard and Aldiss might appeal to those who like M. John Harrison's work.)

ROBERT A HEINLEIN. One is tempted to stop right here. What can be said in this brief space about the writer who is, to many science fiction readers (and non-readers, for that matter), *Mister* Science Fiction? And who, despite the endless controversies engendered by his work, probably deserves that appellation more than any other?

His style is straightforward to the point of non-existence. His novels are often shapeless and (particularly in the later ones) shamelessly, self-indulgently preachy. His philosophies have enraged people into going so far as to call him "militaristic" and "fascistic." Many readers consider the best part of his work a series of juvenile or "young adult" novels he wrote between 1947 and 1962.

Despite, and partially because of all this, Heinlein is the most influential writer to emerge from the golden age of magazine science fiction, with the possible exceptions of Asimov and Clarke. He was exactly what John W. Campbell was looking for in his attempt to make s-f something more than pulp adventure; Heinlein's first story was published by Campbell in 1939. It was called "Lifeline" and dealt, in a negative way, with what would be one of the major themes of Heinlein's works, mortality and immortality.

His best-known novel, *Stranger in a Strange Land,* became a campus cult novel of the '60s (giving the word *grok* to our vocabulary), though it is considered by many to be far from his best work.

Much of Heinlein's special quality comes from the fact that he views the speculative matters of science fiction as much from an engineering viewpoint as a strictly scientific one; one might say he's as concerned with *how* things work as *why* they work, whether it be a time machine or a future society. And that leads to extrapolation about the most minor details; no one has ever made a more real portrait of what day-to-day living on a spaceship will be like, for instance.

Heinlein does have several main themes running through his many novels and short stories. Probably his most famous character, Lazarus Long, is by some genetic chance longlived to the point of immortality (he first appears in the early *Methuselah's Children,* leading the revolt and escape of a genetically engineered long-lived segment of humanity; he reappears in the far future as the protagonist of *Time Enough for Love,* the enormous later novel which is in part his memoirs).

Another major theme is that of the circle in time, which he uses in several different ingenious variations. One of the first was the short story that has become a classic in the field, "By His Bootstraps," in which every character is the same character at various points of a circular time trip. *The Door into Summer* takes the theme into a novel: the hero submits to artificially induced suspended animation to reap the profits of accumulated interests; everything goes wrong that can go wrong and by a conveniently invented time machine he returns to Go to correct matters, which includes getting the right girl. The time circle also enters into *Time Enough for Love,* enabling Lazarus Long to return at the right time to have an affair with his mother.

A third important theme for Heinlein is that of revolution, always of course, justified and usually that of a colony that claims the right to run its own affairs. The best example of this one is *The Moon is a Harsh Mistress,* the revolt of Earth's colonies on Luna (initially begun as penal colonies, as were those of Australia).

The juvenile novels that Heinlein wrote in the '40s and '50s were responsible for an enormous part of that generation being introduced to science fiction. And most of them still make fine reading for adults. *Citizen of the Galaxy,* for instance, is one of the best s-f novels written for any age. It is the ultimate Horatio Alger story, taking the boy Thorby from slavery to becoming one of the most powerful men in the inhabited galaxy, and on the way from the slave planet of Jubbul to Earth itself we were introduced to a score of cultures, human and alien, that are brilliantly realized.

It is only when you are about nine-tenths of the way through *Glory Road* that you realize you are not reading a rousing sword and sorcery novel with dragons, beautiful princesses, and the other usual accountrements; it is really science fiction, with valid rationales for these phenomena, and succeeds in gently satirizing all those thud and blunder novels while being a damn good one at the same time.

And mention must be made of *Starship Troopers*, a *tour-de-force* extrapolation of what the military of the future will be like.

It is perfectly possible that Heinlein might not be to your taste. On the other hand, there are those who claim that if you haven't read Heinlein, you haven't read science fiction.

(Heinlein's influence is practically pervasive in s-f, but works by Piper, Panshin, and Busby are particularly suggested.)

ZENNA HENDERSON is a marvelous lady, an ex-school teacher who has the uncanny ability to home in on childhood fantasies. Henderson has created a group of alien human beings who have fled the destruction of their home planet; they are living among us now. These aliens have telepathic and telekinetic abilities—the gifts and persuasions as Henderson calls them—and they are very very nice people. In fact, they call themselves The People, to distinguish from the native Earth variety.

The People stories can be found in two books, *Pilgramage: The Book of the People* and *The People: No Different Flesh.* These constitute a history of their flight to Earth and their adventures once here, spanning about 100 years. Henderson uses the goodness of the People as a yardstick for measuring humanity, our attitudes toward difference, and for exploring the childlike wonder of our world.

Henderson has written a number of other, unrelated, short stories; these have been collected in two volumes, *Holding Wonder,* and *The Anything Box.* She is particularly good at catching the feel of children, and her love for them glows throughout the stories.

(If you like Zenna Henderson, we suggest Clifford Simak, Anne McCaffrey, or Naomi Mitchison.)

FRANK HERBERT has written what is often called psychological s-f since his first novel, *The Dragon In the Sea* (since re-titled *Under Pressure*), an interpersonal thriller set aboard a submarine. Although Herbert wrote s-f regularly for a decade after that, he published only short stories; these further explored mankind's probable reactions in a multitude of settings and situations.

In 1966 Herbert published a novel which was a considerable departure from the style and content of his previous work. The book was *Dune*—it had a considerable impact within the s-f community and an incredible impact outside of it. People who had never had a good word for s-f read it and were impressed.

Dune is a massive novel which details the lives of the inhabitants of the planet Dune and the political machinations of an interstellar empire. The plot is based loosely on the life of Mohammed (which may account for the huge popularity of *Dune* in the mid-East). The story of Paul Atrides is compelling, but the real hero of the novel is the planet itself. Herbert has carefully and exhaustively described Dune's ecology, culture, religion, and technology; Dune has been called the genre's most effectively evoked world.

There are two sequels to *Dune, Dune Messiah* and *Children of Dune*, which continue the saga of the Atrides family. Herbert has announced a fourth volume, untitled at this writing.

Following the publication of *Dune*, Herbert continued the interplay of humanity and environment. His books are all complex and inventive investigations of what makes people tick and how they will adapt to the future.

Hellstrom's Hive and *The Green Brain* are both novels of ecological disaster which make a case for the necessity of insects to life on Earth, and also for the desirability of hivelike social organization. In *The Green Brain*, mankind has undertaken to wipe out all insect "pests" on the planet; this brings on famine, and finally Mother Nature fights back by creating a symbiosis between men and bugs. *Hellstrom's Hive* was the inspiration for a rather silly and melodramatic film called *The Hellstrom Chronicle*. The book is a well done effort at establishing a society based on the organization of a beehive. The film was simply an exercise in close-up photography and creepy-crawly horror.

The Santaroga Barrier is another closed community novel; this time a small valley community which avoids all prolonged contact with outsiders. The novel is framed as a detective story, and the young investigator is slowly but relentlessly pulled beyond the mental and physical barrier.

Herbert wrote a dystopia in *The Eyes of Heisenberg;* here human beings are as carefully planned and molded as their society, with the goal of eliminating all chance and uncertainty. The novel is an early and sobering warning of the dangers of genetic manipulation and social engineering.

(If you like Frank Herbert, we suggest John Brunner, James Gunn, Gordon Dickson, or Ursula Le Guin.)

WILLIAM HOPE HODGSON was English, the son of an Anglican priest, a seafarer, a disciple of the great bodybuilder Eugen Sandow, a lecturer, a winner of the Royal Humane Society medal for heroism, a crusader for seamen's rights, and one of the most talented of early photographers. He was killed by a shell burst near Ypres, in 1918.

This extraordinary man wrote one extraordinary novel which assures him a special place in science fiction. His other fiction was primarily horror tales of the sea, and quite hair-raising they are, too. But *The Night Land*, equally hair-raising in parts, is a vision of the future, and a stranger one has never been conceived.

The land is dark. The sun is dead. What remains of humanity lives in an eight-mile-high pyramid, the Last Redoubt, protected by radioactivity from the strange creatures and stranger things that prowl the land. But a telepathic call comes across the land. Another remnant of humanity had established a lesser Redoubt whose defenses have been breached and which is now open to the evil forces of the Night Land. One man sets out to rescue whom he can. The entire novel, *of 200,000 words*, is a minute-by-minute, blow-by-blow account of that journey.

For reasons known to himself, Hodgson tells this tale as a sort of future "memory" revealed to a man of the 17th century, and the entire story is cast in a curious, semi-period language which many readers find difficult going. After getting into it however, this conceit adds its own peculiar color to the narrative and some patience is more than rewarded by one of the oddest and most original epics in the history of science fiction.

FRED HOYLE is a s-f writer who writes *science*-fiction. It has been said that Hoyle has never written an implausible word, and some of his speculations are so accurately worked out that the novels are used as teaching texts in astronomy classes. (Hoyle is himself a noted astronomer and has been knighted for his scientific contributions.)

Sir Fred is particularly intrigued by the question of extra-terrestrial intelligence; how it would be organized, how it would communicate, and whether it would recognize the intelligence of humankind.

In *The Black Cloud,* a huge mass (by the standard of interstellar vacuum) of gaseous material approaches the solar system and envelops the sun. The early part of the novel is a realistic and amusing sketch of the life of a working astonomer and a critique of governmental meddling into science. The mathematics are accurate, and the extrapolation is of a quality to deserve publication in a scholarly journal. Needless to say, the cloud turns out to be an electrically based intelligence, and somewhat of a philosopher.

Hoyle continues his quest for the nature of communication in *A for Andromeda* and its sequel, *Andromeda Breakthrough* (both written in collaboration with John Elliot).

In *October the First is Too Late* Hoyle departs from rigorous scientific realism a bit, and enters fully into the realm of philosophy. All the time periods of Earth are scrambled, leaving England in the present, Europe in 1917, Greece in the time of Pericles, and Mexico in the far future. The resulting confusion offers an opportunity to explore changing human values, and to contrast ways of life and technologies.

Fred Hoyle is that all too rare creature, the scientist who can write clearly and with some style; he brings wit and drama to what are often dry and dusty themes.

(If you enjoy Fred Hoyle, you will like Arthur C. Clarke, Hal Clement, and James Gunn.)

L. RON HUBBARD is best known for writing *Dianetics, The Modern Science of Mental Health* and for founding the cult of Scientology. But before this Hubbard wrote science fiction.

In *The Final Blackout* (first published in 1940) Hubbard expounds the theory that military-style discipline is the only way to mobilize and revitalize a nation in the aftermath of war. It is an incredibly persuasive piece of propaganda, and Hubbard's best-written work. In *Fear,* he experiments with horror in the vein of Lovecraft and Machen. *Fear* is a puzzling and scarey novel, and the final pages will send you leafing back to check for the clues. (It is bad form to reveal the punch line, especially in a mystery. Read it if you want to know.)

Typewriter in the Sky is an intentionally funny nudge-and-wink about the writing "game." The hero of the novel becomes trapped in the world created by a bad writer, and is cast in the role of chief villain.

Hubbard stopped writing s-f before he found a style that suited him, and before he had a chance to rise above the derivative.

(If you like Hubbard, we suggest C. M. Kornbluth or Mack Reynolds.)

ZACH HUGHES. This writer certainly has something to offer space-opera buffs, if you don't mind the cliches.

For Texas and Zed is an amusing exercise in translating a book from one genre (the horse-opera) to another (the space-opera). Hughes has done a remarkable job of coining new names for old things; witness *airors,* a contraction of "air horse," which is a one-man unit of transportation on the planet Texas. Also, the *Darlene Space Rifle,* which shoots a lead pellet and is the weapon of choice on Texas. The plot? Well this young fellow from Texas named Lex, gets himself seduced by the Emperor's cousin, and in a fit of wild oats he kidnaps her. His papa gets real mad at him, since the girl knows the location of the maverick planet. After a few adventures, and an epic battle or two, Lex and a few friends defeat the Galactic army and Lex becomes Emperor.

In another book by Hughes, *The Stork Factor,* the future military and fundamentalist movements have joined forces to rule the world. After making contact with an alien civilization, a young dissident develops his latent ESP powers, returns to Earth, and cleans the place up. *The Stork Factor* presents a bleak future for mankind, yet allows for the effect of one brave man on the course of history.

(If you like Hughes, we suggest John Rankine or John Norman.)

JOHN JAKES seems to have written more books than Andre Norton and Michael Moorcock added up. But only a few of this multiproclivitied writer's forays have been into what is thought of as science fiction. Jakes is now well-known to the mass-market public as the author of the American Bicentennial Series.

Along with the fantasy-hero series *Brak the Barbarian* and the Conanesque fantasy *Mention My Name In Atlantis*, Jakes has published *Black In Time*, unique in its Black protagonist and its speculation about alternate Black history; *Six Gun Planet*, which somehow explains itself in the title—yes, the Old West on the planet Missouri; and *On Wheels*, an interestingly thought out whimsy about a fully rounded society living, literally, on highways—it is not allowed to travel at less than 40 mph. And in *Time Gate* Jakes continues his familiar pell-mell adventure style as the closely guarded time gate of the title is taken over by a proverbial madman who not only alters the course of history but threatens the extinction of man altogether. A heroic team tears through capsule histories in pursuit, and time grows short.

(If you like Jakes' s-f, you might like the equally pell-mell stories of Mack Reynolds.)

LAURENCE JANIFER is billed as having written a large number of books, most of which are not s-f, and most of which are published under untraceable pseudonyms. (He did collaborate with Randall Garrett as "Mark Phillips," not to be confused with Princess Anne's husband.)

In two works of s-f published under the name of Janifer the theme is violence and the survival of humanity in the face of violence. *Bloodworld* is a convoluted and extremely graphic account of a world where people are sundered into the Lords and the Bound—slaves upon whose bodies and minds the lords exercise all of their violent urges.

Survivor is a lighter, and much more fun adventure yarn. Gerald Knave, a sort of future Simon Templar or James Bond, has the knack of living through the most horrendous happenings (fires, gun battles, poisonings, alien invasions, etc.) and ultimately defeating the originators of dastardly deeds. In the process he generally saves "civilization as we know it.''

(If you like Janifer's work, try the books of John Norman. If the appeal is Knave's adventures, you will find Poul Anderson's Flandry and Keith Laumer's Retief exciting.)

D. F. JONES. There is probably an ancient Chinese proverb about the abacus that turned on its creators and tried to rule the world. If not, the theme of man being challenged by his creations has certainly been common in science fiction ever since Mary Shelley put pen to paper and constructed Frankenstein's monster.

Jones takes this theme of a computer that is sentient, and in *Colossus* makes of it a well-done suspense novel (which was made into a good s-f film) with two sequels, *The Fall Of Colossus* and *Colossus and The Crab*. Charles Forbin is the chief computer scientist on the Colossus project and the trilogy revolves around him and the megalomaniacal computer he's created. The three novels follow the relationship between the two as it evolves from man/machine through a sort of benevolent parasitism to a quasisymbiosis.

Jones' other works, among them *The Floating Zombie* and *Denver Is Missing,* successfuly combine the elements of suspense and science fiction, in tense gripping novels of intellectual adventure.

(If you like the work of D. F. Jones, try that of Zach Hughes and Dean R. Koontz.)

NEIL R. JONES is a good example of the toilers of the pulps, those all but forgotten writers who filled the pages of the magazines of the '20s, '30s, and '40s with hastily written stories, many of whom nevertheless added their bits to the growing conceptual traditions of the field. Jones' major claim to fame is his Professor Jameson series, which has the distinction of being the longest running series of any in a field loaded with series; they were published from 1931 to 1951 in three different magazines, and also chalked up as the most series wordage, according to those who keep count of such things.

Professor Jameson, of Earth, find himself in three things: suspended animation, an early artificial satellite, and in orbit around the Earth. More correctly, he *is* found, long after all life disappears from our planet, by the Zoromes, star-hopping entities who have built themselves super robot bodies. They provide the good professor with one such, and we're off on a sort of endless travelog of the wonders and dangers of the

Galaxy. These were the only works of Jones' to see book form; sixteen of the stories were published in five books.

Unfortunately, Jones' literary style is such as to cause most contemporary readers acute discomfort. However, there's a certain period pulp charm to such lines as "...he saw that which caused him to nearly drop over, so astounded was he" or "...even the double suns are not numerous, but among the trillions of suns in space they are not hard to find" or "If I possessed bones, it would have chilled them." Given a large dose of historial perspective and an ear for camp prose, Jones is still fun to read.

(As are the rather better writers of the same period, Ray Cummings and E. E. Smith.)

RAYMOND F. JONES is one of a number of pulp writers who shaped the pages of *Astounding* magazine when it was under the aegis of John W. Campbell.

This Island Earth was filmed—very different from Jones' original novel, but serviceable as a film in which Earth is visited by aliens who need help in warring with another planet. In *The Secret People* Jones strayed from the formulas of pulp s-f to deal with mutants in a post holocaust world, and Prime Press, one of the pioneers in the field, published his *Renaissance,* an interesting novel of our world and a parallel one.

Still writing, Jones has produced Doc Smith-like space adventures in formula pulp style, neither challenging nor taxing.

(Also try Edmond Hamilton if you like Raymond Jones.)

COLIN KAPP, while working as a technician in an electronics research lab, has turned out several enjoyable and innovative novels.

Manalone is a mystery suspense novel set in a future where the past is hidden by government decree and a too-inquisitive archeologist could end up in a concentration camp. Manalone is a computer systems analyst who fights the machinery of this police state to find the answer, and a chilling one it is. The society in this story is well described; crowded humanity, computer control, et al. The details of Manalone's discoveries build to a nicely constructed and surprisingly plausible conclusion.

In *The Chaos Weapon* Kapp comes up with a far flung space opera built around an intriguing concept of chance: time, and entropy used in a weapon designed to help in the invasion of our universe by beings from an alternate one. The major protagonist of the story is Space Marshall Jym Wildheit, and Kapp gives the tale a twist by having the Marshalls in this society accompanied by multi-dimensional gods in a semi-symbiotic relationship. The plot-line is complex, with inclusions of extrasensory perception, relativity, and cosmological theory, but Kapp weaves in all the threads and brings the story to a conclusion in which everybody in the universe lives happily ever after.

Kapp's experience in electronics and in research discipline helps with the plausibility of his scientific concepts, and his attention to detail in description and character development is more careful than most writers in the field.

(If you like the work of Colin Kapp, try that of Jack Williamson and Brian Stableford.)

DANIEL KEYES has written very little s-f, although he was an editor in the field in the early '50s. He is best known for one short story which he expanded into a novel; he won the Hugo award for the story and a Nebula for the novel.

The story and book are *Flowers for Algernon,* which was adapted into the film, *Charly,* which also won several awards.

Flowers for Algernon is about Charlie Gordon, a mentally retarded experimental subject. Charlie is given a drug which enhances his intelligence—first into the normal range and then into a blaze of genius. The book is Charlie's diary; the reader grows to see the world as Charlie does.

This book is a profoundly moving exploration of humanity, of intelligence, and our society. It is capped by an agonizing description of Charlie's regression to idiot status as the drug wears off.

(If you like Keyes, we suggest you try Robert Silverberg.)

OTIS ADELBERT KLINE is generally considered an inferior imitator of Edgar Rice Burroughs, what with his pure hearted heroes galumphing around unlikely civilizations on Mars and Venus, committing mayhem with their swords against villains and beasties all intent on doing in the pure hearted heroines. You will like them if they are the sort of thing you like.

There are two Kline Mars books, three Venus novels, and one set on the Moon. They are not as continuously connected as are Burroughs' series; Kline's heros have a confusing habit of moving from planet to planet by exchanging their consciousnesses with a local inhabitant, so the Martian Borgen Takkor exchanges bodies with Harry Thorne, who has lots of adventures of Mars, but Borgen gets bored sitting around on dull old Earth, so *he* exchanges identities with the Venusian prince Zinlo...you *are* following all this, aren't you?

Kline is also very big on assorted monsters, who can be counted on to turn up when the action begins to flag. ("A great ordzook approaches from the north!" is a typical prelude to one more attack from a some-thingie crawling, flying, or swimming.)

Mr. Kline also wrote popular songs and screenplays, one of which, taken from his book *The Call of the Savage,* was filmed with Dorothy Lamour and sarong.

DAMON KNIGHT has been described as a "writer's writer," which all too often means that the person so honored is inaccessible and abstruse to the average person. Not so Damon Knight. His short stories are witty extrapolations, often based on misunderstandings, or the mis-interpretation of a turn of phrase. Often reprinted, highly praised, and frequently copied, his stories include: "To Serve Man," in which altruistic aliens arrive on Earth and make it a paradise (the only catch is that their handbook, *To Serve Man,* is a cookbook); another enduring image created by Knight is from "Not with a Bang," where the last woman on Earth allows the last man on Earth to die, because she won't go into a men's room.

Knight's novels include *Hell's Pavement,* where the human race is controlled by artifically induced neuroses, while given the illusion of perfect freedom; *The People Maker,* where a sort of Xerox for human beings is invented; and *The Rithian Terror,* a novel of espionage set in the 26th Century, with occasional side-trips into social satire.

Knight's novels and short stories are good, no question; it is, how-ever, as an editor and anthologist that he takes his place among the great. Knight is responsible for some of the finest anthologies in exis-tence. The *Orbit* series, the *Nebula Award* series, *Tomorrow X 4, The Dark Side,* and *Cities of Wonder* are all his work. If a book says "Edited by Damon Knight," you can be sure of quality contents.

(The stories of H. L. Gold might appeal if you like those of Knight.)

DEAN KOONTZ. Although his recent work has been commercially mainstream oriented, Dean Koontz has written a number of s-f novels and stories, one of which, *Demon Seed,* became a film. Using techniques unusual to the genre (interior monologue, whole paragraphs in upper case, dreamlike wandering sentences), his style is, for the most part, standard s-f adventure prose; lots of Hemingway-like sentences; lots of dialogue.

In *Beastchild* a galactic society decides that Earth's mankind is not fit for the Universe and a process of extermination begins. Along the way a boy is befriended by an alien official whose determination to eliminate Earthmen wavers and softens. The relationship between boy and alien is delicate and thoughtful. Another kind of boy figures in *A Darkness in My Soul,* a "child" in appearance, but a monster withall; an intelligence and creation with universal implications. Simeon Kelly, a genetically engineered man, is ordered to probe the brain of Child, using his artificial esp. Once inside Child, a universe of horror, intellect, and creative fecundity is opened to him; but it is a vicious, destructive, insane mind, one that takes all of Kelly's all, and more, to withstand.

In *Nightmare Journey* Koontz projects a very far future feudal society in which the masses are fabulously mutated through eons of voluntary genetic engineering and are suppressed by the Pures, unmutated masters. Koontz's interest, not to say preoccupation, with xenophobia is evident here, as it was earlier in *Dark of the Woods* and *Soft Come the Dragons.*

(Some of Koontz's themes are also explored by Gerrold, Geston, and Russell.)

C(YRIL) M. KORNBLUTH had a brilliant but tragically brief career as an s-f writer; he died in 1958 at the age of 34. Although there are not a few readers who are convinced that Kornbluth's first name was "Pohl-and," due to his collaborative efforts with Fred Pohl (such as the ever popular *Space Merchants*), Kornbluth working solo produced some memorable books and stories.

He began writing at age 17, under the name of Cecil Corwin; these first stories were mostly fantasies. Later in his career the Corwin name was appended to stories that Kornbluth considered minor works.

Kornbluth's novels include *The Syndic,* a story set in a future America where the Mob and the Syndicate have gained full control of the government. Their rule is surprisingly benevolent, and the novel is a good argument for "family" style rule.

With *Not this August,* published in 1955, Kornbluth drew the attention of the mainstream of s-f. *Not This August* is a cold-war polemic which warns of the communist threat, but even within these confines he manages to say something about the dangers of playing at war.

Kornbluth's other novels elaborate on his concerns about big-government interference and the danger this poses to individualism. Kornbluth was very much a part of the John Campbell rationalist school and his stories have a feel for the style of the period.

(If you like Kornbluth's work, we suggest you read Mack Reynolds, L. Ron Hubbard, and, of course, Frederick Pohl.)

MICHAEL KURLAND wanders along a tight-rope between story and style. His plots are imaginative and his relating of same is damnably clever. There are double and triple entendres and inside jokes about science fiction and its writers. This approach is particularly evident in *Unicorn Girl,* in which he develops a very plausible theory of parallel universes within an exciting adventure while playing games with words, sentences, and what are essentially writing exercises.

The Whenabouts Of Burr, a tongue-in-cheek novel in which alternate universes result in the disappearance of the U.S. Constitution and its replacement with one signed Aaron Burr instead of Alexander Hamilton, and *Tomorrow Knight,* where aliens separate Earth into historical periods and use it as a sort of intergalactic Disneyland, are much the same type of science fiction, clever in content as well as in titles.

(If you like the work of Kurland you might try Robert Sheckley, Fredric Brown, or Ron Goulart.)

HENRY KUTTNER. One is tempted to say, "You name it. Henry Kuttner wrote it." He is perhaps the prime example of the pulp writer who began turning out stories by formula and went on to become a competent stylist and a more-than-competent creator of those wonderful ideas on which science fiction is dependent. His output was enormous and incredibly varied: tales of the supernatural (his first published story was in *Weird Tales;* it has the none-too-original title of "The Graveyard Rats" and is a bit Lovecraftian around the edges); sword and sorcery fantasy (a series with the engagingly names hero, Elak of Atlantis); humor (or at least what passed for humor in the early days of science fiction). The two short s-f novels published together in book form, *Tomorrow and Tomorrow & The Fairy Chessmen,* were intricately confusing in the style of van Vogt. *The Dark World* and *Mask of Circe* are second only to A. Merritt's scientific romances for their poetically purple prose and art deco visions.

Fury, with its immortals and undersea cities, somehow smacks of Heinlein, and there is a series of robot stories only less better known than Asimov's. And we won't even mention the detective stories.

To compound confusion, many of these were written under a variety of *noms-de-plume.* And after he married the equally gifted writer C. L. Moore in 1940, they more often than not collaborated on stories that might appear under either of their names or under yet more pseudonyms. (The above mentioned *Fury* is one of these.)

Things got to such a point that when Jack Vance began writing, there arose a persistent rumor that this was yet another Kuttner alias; so persistent that it still emerges now and then.

Yet Kuttner is not just imitation Lovecraft, or van Vogt, or Merritt, or whatever. True, one cannot sort out any work and say, "Well, this is typical Kuttner." But there is a distinctive freshness in his stories no matter whose path he was following.

If one has to choose particular Kuttner works to talk about, it should probably be the Gallegher stories and the "novels" he wrote for *Startling Stories.*

The Gallegher stories (there were five of them) revolve around an inventor who only functions when drunk and his foremost creation, a robot named Joe who is insufferably uppity and superior. An anthology of authentically humorous s-f stories might well be the shortest book in the field; until recently most of it was the "booze and broads" variety, with more emphasis on the former. Modern readers might find the Gallegher stories a little broad (in the other sense of the word), but they are period pieces with a certain naive charm.

Kuttner's scientific romances are another matter. Spinning off from the great A. Merritt, they usually take a modern hero and translate him into another "time-stream" or continuum, with invariably exotic cultures and strange super- (or pseudo-) scientific phenomena that smack of more magic than science. These worlds are obviously not futuristic; that of *The Dark World* (which became a sort of touchstone of excellence) was vaguely medieval, with a flavor of Norse mythology about it. In *The Mask of Circe,* our hapless hero, a descendant of Jason, is thrown into a classical mythological world where the gods are real, but are simply wielders of enormous powers that are rational, not supernatural. He is caught up in the battle between Apollo and Hecate, with the twist being that Apollo and his minions are the villains. These works are often thought of as fantasies, but they are given just enough of a scientific rationale to qualify as s-f.

Since his work was so varied and appealed to so many different science fiction readers, Kuttner's death in 1958 was a severe loss felt across the entire spectrum of the field.

(As you may gather from the above remarks, if you like Kuttner's works, there are many directions you can take. Just for a start, let us suggest Brackett, Moore, Merritt, Asimov, and van Vogt.)

R. A. LAFFERTY is possessed—a madman, a wild talent. He has created a grammar and syntax all his own, virtually a language all his own, despite the fact that taken one by one all the words he uses are English. One simply *cannot* begin a Lafferty story and mistake it for anyone else's.

To detail the speculative elements or plots of his major novels would be meaningless, since plot, while undisputably present, has little or nothing to do with Lafferty's charm and appeal. The speculations are toss-offs, believable in context but not real extrapolation. His novels are: *Fourth Mansions, Past Master, The Reefs of Earth, The Devil is Dead, Space Chantey, Arrive at Easterwine, The Flame is Green, Strange Doings, Not to Mention Camels,* and *Apocalypses.* They vary considerably, but the basic theme of Lafferty's work is power: mental, physical, or political. The end result of his style is the complete annihilation of the fabric of reality.

In Lafferty's world there are strange forces at work. Aliens studying Earth life who know that the planet will kill them. A corporation that leases miracle-makers and god-effects. People who are identified only by the color of their auras. Mindweaves that cause earthquakes. Killing machines that are activated by treasonous thoughts or actions, as defined by the machine. Land masses that appear and disappear at whim. Umbrella men who can change reality.

Lafferty's world is not always comfortable, since he takes particular delight in subtly twisting the meanings of words. His world is usually delightfully absurdist, and often bristling with pins to prick the soap-bubbles of whatever you hold sacred. Lafferty is fun, sophisticated, and utterly insane.

(There is no one who writes like R. A. Lafferty, so if you like one of his books, find some more.)

DAVID J. LAKE is a relative new-comer to s-f; his books are adventure science fiction, with some wildly inventive speculative biology.

Walkers on the Sky is set on a delightful, though possibly impractical, planet which has been colonized and terra-formed by human beings. The planetary engineering is such that there are three concentric force shields around the planet, rather like an onion. This creates, in effect, three separate planets one inside the other. Though invisible, the force shields will bear considerable weight; the inhabitants can literally walk on the sky. The lead character, a barbarous young man, manages to break through the skies and visit all the levels.

Two other books, *The Right Hand of Dextra* and *The Wildings of Westron,* take place on the planet Dextra, and are somewhat connected. The premise is that Dextra is an Earth-type planet, a veritable garden of Eden, but with one problem. All of the living molecules on the planet are the mirror images of the ones on Earth. This makes it impossible for humans to obtain nourishment from the local produce.

Both *Right Hand* and *Wildings* ar good light reading; the biology is not too heavy, and there are amusing characters and classical references to move the plots along.

(If you like Lake, we suggest Roger Zelazny or Philip Farmer.)

SIMON LANG, although certainly a science fiction author, has a style reminiscent of mainstream or fantasy, with careful development of character and a poetic use of words and sentence structure to evoke emotion.

Another aspect of her (Simon or not, she's a woman) work is the complexity of her plots and the manner of development. *All The Gods of Eisernon* begins with a short prologue, an excerpt from "The Book Of Han," which reads as if it were translated from a rich, embroidered tapestry, and then sends the reader through a sometimes confusing, but always interesting, mixture of characters and cultures to a heroic and poignant ending.

Although one gets to know the characters in a round-about way, a chapter here and a paragraph there, they do emerge as real people, warm, loved, and loving. In the same style Lang develops the Einai (People of Eisernon), Earthlikli (Human) and Han (hunted, hated telepathic descendants of both) as knowable, admirable cultures, with imaginative detail such as the "shun-daki," a ritualized duel in the dark.

The Elluvon Gift is a sequel to *All The Gods...* in that Dao Marik, who is a Han and one of the prime protagonists of the first book, is also a focal point in the second.

Lang is a good writer, capable of nice imagery, full characterization, and poetic prose; her work requires full concentration, but she makes it well worth the reader's time.

(Those who like Ms. Lang's brand of science fiction would do well to try Ursula Le Guin and Marta Randall.)

STERLING LANIER. A particularly well-known (mostly through films) species of science fiction is the post-holocaust rebuilding story. Here there usually has been a world- or nation-wide war or other form of destruction; what's left tries to get its act together in one way or another. Lanier takes this and does some very good things with a time-honored formula in *Hiero's Journey*.

The glossary at the end of the novel is in itself a delight to read: *Batwah, Leemute, Groken,* and the *Glith* are some of the intriguing terms Lanier has invented, not to mention the wonderful *Morse*, the mutated horse-moose who is man's (or at least Hiero's) best friend in the troubled times of a totally destroyed civilization. And there are the Eleveners, those of the brotherhood of the Eleventh Commandment ("Thou shalt not destroy the Earth or the life thereon").

These are some of the elements in this quest-across-a-post-holocaust-world. Per Hiero Desteen, priest of what is left of the Catholic Church, is sent to the lost cities of the South in the hope that some forgotten knowledge will be found to help the Church combat the Dark Brotherhood, Masters of the Unclean. We follow Hiero's journey as he and his morse travel south from what was Canada into what was upstate New York through unhealthily mutated swamps and agents of the Unclean villains. Along the way they are joined and helped by Gorm, a telephatic bear, and Luchare, a runaway princess and potential human sacrifice from and for some primitive new societies that have appeared. The imagination Lanier has shown in decorating an old and tired theme has made the fact that his output is spare to the point of minimal (there are a few short stories) a source of aggravtion to science fiction readers.

(But you might make do with Marion Zimmer Bradley's equally skillful blends of fantasy and s-f.)

KEITH LAUMER. The Mobius strip of time is the playground of Keith Laumer. He and the reader run in and around this multi-one dimensional realm and usually come back to find themselves watching. *Dinosaur Beach*, a time travel classic, stacks paradox upon paradox and then pulls the clock out from under you. *Worlds of the Imperium* and *The Other Side of Time* (really a two part novel) go from a *now* to another *then* and back again. All of Laumer's postulates and theories of time are consistent and believable.

In many of Laumer's works, there is a sense of humor present. In *The Monitors*, an invasion of benificent aliens wreaks goodhumored havoc on Earth by forbidding violence. The Retief stories (collected in *Envoy to New Worlds* and *Retief: Emissary to the Stars)* are the adventures of an intergalactic diplomat who specializes in conniving to cut through red tape. (Presumably Laumer picked up some basically absurd material through experience in the U.S. Foreign Service.) Humor amid multiple dimensions is the basis for the Lafayette O'Leary series, which includes the novels *Time Bender, Shape Changer,* and *World Shuffler.*

Laumer also has a penchant for future warfare; *Bolo* is a series of connected short stories concerning futuristic war machines, and *A Plague of Demons* has humanity acting as mercenaries in alien hostilities.

Earthblood, written in collaboration with Rosel George Brown, has a human searching for the legendary planet Earth in the far future, and has the unusual background of an interstellar circus.

Laumer's work is not of the earthshaking or epic style; it is, however, many-faceted and consistently imaginative.

(Barrington Bayley, Laurence Janifer, and Christopher Stasheff might appeal to Laumer's admirers.)

TANITH LEE's rise to science fiction stardom was rapid, and justified. Discovered by Donald Wollheim, she made an auspicious debut with an epic novel called *The Birthgrave*. It could be argued that this was a fantasy, an epic quest across a strange and phantasmagorical landscape with, for a change, a female protagonist. But its hardedged reality and relentless logic appealed to science fiction fans also.

She immediately changed her pace with *Don't Bite the Sun*, a piece of true s-f set in a city—a "utopic" city—of the far future akin to Clarke's Diaspar of *The City and the Stars*, but rather like that splendid town gone completely and dippily amok. What Ms. Lee revealed here was that rarity of all rarities, a science fiction writer with a sense of humor. The adventures of her adolescent heroine in Four BEE (the city), in a society whose young people spend their time killing themselves, being rejuvenated, changing sex, and shoplifting, are very funny indeed, particularly the running misdeeds of the pet that she shoplifted in a moment of carelessness, a flopsy object with too many legs. The pet creates an unexpected serious finale that presages the second part of the whole, *Drinking Sapphire Wine*; the two are one novel chronicling the maturing in most unusual circumstances of a most unusual heroine (sometimes hero).

Ms. Lee, a prolific writer, has veered between the two extremes of *The Birthgrave* and *Don't Bite the Sun* in her later novels; between the fantastical and the science fictional, the epic and the personal, the touching and the humorous. A protean talent indeed.

(If you like Tanith Lee, you might try Ursula K. Le Guin, in one direction, or C. J. Cherryh in another.)

URSULA K. Le GUIN has a beautiful prose style that is both evocative and unobtrusive; that she has chosen to grace s-f with her talent is both fortunate and a compliment to a genre bottom-heavy with purple prose. Her stories are rich in human detail, her science is perfectly plausible; the tales she finds to tell seem inevitable once told. The s-f community has recognized her skill by awarding each of her major works with both Hugo and Nebula awards.

Le Guin's early novels are typical s-f, exciting and good fun. They show the signs of her later development although they are not themselves important works in the field.

Rocannon's World was Le Guin's first book; it is the story of a Galactic League scientist stranded on a primitive planet, and under attack by aliens hostile to the League. This novel is important to understanding Le Guin's work, since in it she outlined her working theory of the future. Here also she describes the governmental structure, her space drive, and the *ansible*, a hyper-light-speed communications device, which constantly reappear in her books.

There followed two more short novels, *Planet of Exile* and *City of Illusions,* both about human/alien conflict. Atypically, the aliens are not presented in a terribly flattering light.

Two years later, in 1969, Le Guin's masterpiece was published. Used here, the word masterpiece is intended in its original meaning, that of a work of art which proves beyond any doubt that the artist has mastered his craft and developed his own unique style. The book was *The Left Hand of Darkness,* one of the most widely acclaimed, highly recommended, and pivotal works of s-f produced in many a year.

The Left Hand of Darkness is about the culture of the planet Winter, as seen by Genry Ai, an emissary from the Galactic League. On Winter (which, as the name implies, is an extremely cold planet), human beings have developed or mutated into ambisexuality; each person is capable of becoming either male or female during estrus, and is nongendered at all other times. The implications of this reverberate throughout the culture. Genry's own unchanging maleness creates a psychological barrier to his understanding of Winter, and creates resistance on Winter to the Galactic League—the natives see Genry as a pervert. *Left Hand* won a Nebula Award in 1969 and a Hugo in 1970; it is an outstanding example of the quality and subtlety of which s-f is capable.

The Lathe of Heaven is about George Orr, who has "effective" dreams—dreams which change reality. He goes to a psychiatrist who at first doesn't believe this is possible. When he sees that it is, the psychiatrist uses George's ability to give himself absolute power over the world.

In 1973 Le Guin won a Hugo award for a short novel called *The Word for World is Forest*. *Word for World* is about a planet which is being commercially exploited by a development company without regard for the indigenous intelligent life forms. The story is about power, machismo, and culturally induced blindness to reality. As a prediction of what will happen when human beings finally arrive on another planet it is probably too accurate; if you don't believe it, remember what Europeans did to the American Indian.

The Dispossessed won her another set of awards, Hugo, Nebula, Jupiter, and John Campbell Memorial, when it was published in 1974. It is subtitled *An Ambiguous Utopia,* and because of its structure the reader must decide for himself what is meant by that. *The Dispossessed* is set in a planetary system where two large worlds revolve around each other; the mother world, Urras, is much like Earth, and has a planet-wide system of monopolistic capitalism. The sister planet is Anarres, which was settled by a group of dissident anarcho-syndicalists exiled from Urras. The protagonist is a scientist who was born on Anarres and goes to Urras in search of recognition.

This novel is an exercise in contrasting values, a cogent and non-didactic debate on social theory. Its well developed characters and settings, combined with Le Guin's skill and uniquely effective style, make *The Dispossessed* a superior novel in any field.

Recently Le Guin has turned to the short story, and in collections titled

The Wind's Twelve Quarters and *Orsinian Tales* she is pushing harder and harder at the boundary between fantasy and reality.

Although not s-f, three other books by Le Guin are worth more than a passing glance. She has written a trilogy for children about magic and a magical world. It is known as the Earthsea Trilogy, and concerns the rise of Ged, a magician, from obscurity to great knowledge and fame. The Earthsea books rival Lewis' Narnia series in magic and delight; they are not just for children.

(If you enjoy Le Guin, we also suggest Marta Randall, Frank Herbert, James Tiptree Jr., and James Gunn.)

FRITZ LEIBER is another of those authors who have written many works in so many veins that there is no way in the world of conveying the full breadth of his skill. Like other writers of his ilk, he is a graduate of the great era of the magazines, which must have been wonderful practice grounds for the arts of being prolific and many-faceted. Otherwise all that was needed was talent, which Leiber has in plenty. The usual criticism of writers of that period was that they had marvelous ideas but little writing skill; this was never heard said of Leiber.

His stories of the supernatural are suitably chilling. His heroic fantasies have made him one of the top names in *that* field; it should also be noted that he managed the rare feat of satirizing a field before it even existed. His Gray Mouser stories are wonderfully light-hearted send-ups of the sword and sorcery school; the amoral Mouser and his friend Fafhrd appeared first in the magazine *Unknown* in 1939, long before there were enough like stories to constitute a sub-genre.

His science fiction is unique, not quite like anyone else's, and as one-time editor of *Science Digest,* his concepts are as convincingly valid as Clarke's or Asimov's. But as the son of a great character actor (the Fritz Leiber one so often sees in the cast lists of '30s and '40s films was his father) and as a former actor himself, perhaps the greatest aspect of Leiber's fiction is the drama, seldom melodrama, usually controlled theater at its best.

A superb example of this is his Hugo-award winning novel *The Big Time.* It observes the classic dramatic "unities" of a single location in space, a continuous action in time. But what a space! And what a time! Leiber speculates a great war, fought across the cosmos of infinity and eternity, between the snakes and the spiders—aliens of unthinkable power and unknowable realities. All beings are enlisted in this war, humans among them, and the war is engaged in time as well as space. History itself is changed in favor of one side or another, and to those involved, all other beings are "zombies," since their historical reality and they themselves can be wiped out in the second of a reality change.

The action of the novel takes place in a rest and recuperation area outside the possibilities of time change. There, "hostesses" and warriors from various eras of Earth mingle with aliens in a small drama that reflects the macrocosm of the time war, which is never made clear to the reader, much less the participants. It is an extraordinary tour de force with no equal in the literature of science fiction.

Leiber has also written other stories about the snakes' and spiders' change war; they again never tell you of the whole thing, but only recount small episodes, therefore making the concept even larger and more terrifying. Most are to be found in the collection, *The Mind Spider.*

Then there is *The Wanderer,* the first part of which is the ultimate disaster novel, following various characters as they cope with natural upheavals after the arrival of a planet which settles close enough to the Earth to cause immense disturbances. However, this action is topped by the revelation of who and what is guiding the planet; *The Wanderer* has been called the ultimate motorcycle epic.

The classic *Conjure Wife* (filmed twice, the second time confusingly under an A. Merritt title, *Burn, Witch!*) is a bloodcurdlingly convincing story of modern day witchcraft, taking place on what was, at the time of its writing, one of the most placid of all contemporary environments, the American college campus. Here the faculty wives manipulate, torture, and even kill by magic, to gain status for their husbands. But this is not just a fantasy of magic in a modern setting. Leiber hypothesizes that magic is as logical a method of cause and effect as any of the sciences, if you know the rules. And by creating what is in effect another science, to be used logically, he has made as valid a work of science fiction as if he were giving us semantic gobbledy-gook about hyperspace, as other s-f writers have done.

There are two things certain about Fritz Leiber's work; any story that you see with his name on it is not going to be incompetent, and it is not going to be dull. What it *is* going to be is entirely up to the prolific Leiber talent.

(Leiber's many facets have some counterparts in the work of Isaac Asimov, Alfred Bester, and Jack Vance.)

MURRAY LEINSTER was the pen name of Will F. Jenkins, and while the title of science fiction writer with the longest career is subject to a lot of debatable variables, Leinster is certainly one of the three or four front runners, with an initial story ("The Runaway Skyscraper," about a New York City office building that shifts in time) published in 1919 in *Argosy*. He was still actively writing when he died in 1975.

Because of the longevity of his career, he was known as the "dean of science fiction." This general designation might also imply his lack of specialization; he was never identified with any particular type of science fiction in the way that Edmond Hamilton, for instance, was "Mr. Space Opera."

Not that Leinster didn't write space-opera. Many of his works were tales of the Wild West or the high seas translated to outer space. There was *Miners in the Sky,* where the 1849 Gold Rush is taken to the Asteroid Belt, and *The Pirates of Zan,* with jolly Roger in a space suit.

He wrote series, of course. The "Joe Kenmore" novels are the adventures of a young man involved in the early days of space travel, complete with spies and romance. And he was one of the first to build a series around a career, as in the Med Service stories, about Calhoun of the Interstellar Med Service and his assistant, an alien named Murgatroyd. The two save worlds from medical disaster, mental illness, and malevolent exploiters.

Forgotten Planet is one of Leinster's works that can certainly lay claim to classic status. The titular world is one being readied for human habitation; found sterile, it is "seeded" with micro-organisms, plants, fish, and insects. Before animals and man can be added to the recipe, the planet's file card is mislaid and it is forgotten. Then a ship crash lands there and the survivors eventually revert to savagery. The story is actually that of Burl, descendant of the survivors, and his struggle toward civilization. Botanically and entomologically accurate, this tale of struggle against the by-now mutated and gigantic flora and fauna is prime adventure.

Leinster did not neglect the short story as a form either. The Hugo-award-winning "Exploration Team" is about just what the title says; the team, however, consists of a man, four bears, and an eagle. And another classic, "First Contact," deals brilliantly with the dilemma of a human ship and an alien vessel meeting in space and, wanting peace, still not daring to give away their home planets' location by returning. What do they do? Read it; it's one of the most anthologized stories in the field.

Perhaps Leinster's career of solid science fiction writing can best be summed up by pointing out that *The Forgotten Planet* was, like so many s-f "novels," originally published as several shorter pieces, in this case, three. The first saw print originally in 1920; the third in 1953. In a field that has changed so rapidly over its brief history, this kind of continuity is a notable achievement.

(If you like Leinster's work, you might move to that of John W. Campbell and Alan Nourse.)

STANISLAW LEM is Polish and is certainly the most renowned s-f writer *not writing in English* since Jules Verne. His books have been translated into more languages than you can shake a stick at, and his fame in Europe considerably preceded his introduction to the U.S. Clearly a polymath, Lem draws as much on mythological and folktale sources as he does on science; his work is often purely allegorical—in the sense that the writing of Borges, Bruno Schultz, or Italo Calvino often is—and both satire and philosophical speculations play major roles.

The Star Diaries is typical of the antic Lem: twelve minitales about one Tichy, a kind of globe-trotting diplomat whose adventures, mostly inadvertent, involve menacing potatoes, sexually deranged robots, and other madnesses. The Diaries make for speedy and bumptuous reading. And in *The Cyberiad* Lem gives us the two wonderfully insane robot inventors, Trurl and Klapaucius, and their fantastic machines (for example: a device which can, on command, create anything beginning with the letter n). In this loose-knit collection of tales, anecdotes and fables— many of which have a didactic quality—Lem treats science as if it were legerdemain, and time like a toy, while he presents confrontations between men and their machine creations. Which is finally which, is tantalizingly unclear.

Earlier adventures of Tichy (at the Costa Rica Hilton this time) are in *The Futurological Congress,* a novel of aimless violence, Costa Rican terrorism, and hallucinogenic drugs used as weapons.

Because of the Soviet film made from it, *Solaris* is undoubtedly Lem's most read novel. Considerably different in tone and intention from the aforementioned books, *Solaris* is a serious, not to say ponderous, novel about efforts to communicate with a presumed alien intelligence inhabiting the planet-wide sea of Solaris. Scientists study the ever changing, ever same ocean in an attempt to plumb its depths—as it were—and glimpse its essential *alienness,* but they are limited by their ultimate inability to transcend their own frames of reference. It is a puzzle, and makes for a puzzling novel. In *The Invincible* a giant title-role spaceship travels to an away planet to ascertain what happened to a sister ship and its crew. They are met and confounded by a hostile society of evolved-by-natural-selection machines, and man's pride is in question.

Often maddening and fascinating by turn, Lem's wide-ranging work encompasses a galaxy of styles, influences and intentions from the grandiose and quasi-profound to the ludicrous, with intriguing way-stations of insight and invention.

C. S. LEWIS was a remarkably versatile writer and thinker, able to encompass theology, fantasy, and science fiction. Many philosophers have used fantasy as a vehicle for their views, but most have made use of the sub-genre of allegorical fantasy. Lewis, at heart more a writer than a teacher, abandoned the heavy-handed approach in favor of beguiling his readers.

Lewis' contribution to s-f takes the form of three connected novels and a handful of short stories. The three novels (often called the Space Trilogy) chronicle the adventures of a philologist named Ransom, a character based on his close friend J.R.R. Tolkien. In the first book, *Out of the Silent Planet,* Ransom is kidnapped by a megalomaniacal scientist named Weston. He is packed into a spaceship and taken to Mars, under the illusion that the Martians require a human sacrifice before they will permit Weston to mine their planet. On Mars, Ransom meets three species of *Hnau,* or rational beings with souls, and is finally brought to the Oyarsa, a sort of sub-deity in charge of Mars. Oyarsa sends Ransom back to Earth, but remains in contact with him.

In the second book, *Perelandra,* Ransom is sent to Venus, where a re-enactment of the fall of Adam and Eve is taking place. Lewis' vision of Venus is an unusually lovely one: the planet is a water world with floating islands, and the cloud cover creates a diffuse golden light over everything.

In the final book, *That Hideous Strength,* Ransom is faced with evil on Earth, and must use the strength and knowledge gained in space to combat it. The battle ground is small, a college town in fact, and the ultimate evil is the abandonment of personal integrity to a faceless bureaucracy. It sounds somewhat banal, but when Lewis has finished bringing in Merlin, the Pendragon, an artificially maintained talking head, Gestapo tactics, and the final descent of the gods to Earth, it is anything but.

After Lewis' death in 1963, an incomplete manuscript was found among his papers which seems to be the beginning of a fourth Ransom novel, entitled *The Dark Tower.* Here a friend of Ransom's invents a device which acts as a window on a parallel universe. This world is a truly horrible one; it appears that having tackled bureaucracy Lewis was about to take on dogma, propaganda, and blind loyalty to any cause.

It is tempting to hope that at least a plot synopsis for *The Dark Tower* will be uncovered by Lewis' executors—and frightening to think that someday, someone will decide that the work should be farmed out for a posthumous collaboration.

FRANK BELKNAP LONG began publishing stories when the related fields of science fiction and the supernatural were much closer than they are now. (His first published story was in 1924.) A ghostly visitor from Beyond or an alien visitor from a spaceship were all one to the readers of that period—frightening. Long has carried on that tradition by being equally prolific in both genres, as well as in the hybrid horror tale a la Lovecraft; perhaps his most famous short story, "The Hounds of Tindalos," is about ravening beasts from the curious angles beyond our spatial and temporal geometries. (Long, incidentally, was the first writer permitted by Lovecraft to use aspects of his Cthulhu mythos in his own work.)

Long's work, as opposed to that of Lovecraft, shows a humanism and sometimes a sly humor. In "Census Taker," there is a brief and horrifyingly funny warp in time that involves a perfectly ordinary man and his fiancee with a census taker from a future whose tax laws are decidely something else.

A different sort of hero was invented by Long for a series of short stories: John Carstairs, botanist-detective of the future, "the curator of the finest Botanical Exhibit in the Solar System," who gallivants about the planets collecting specimens that are often ambulatory and usually dangerous.

Other science-fictional themes explored by Long are aliens on Earth (*Journey into Darkness, Lest Earth By Conquered, Mission to a Star*); robots (*It Was the Day of the Robot*); and futuristic intrigue and power struggles (*Mars is My Destination, This Strange Tomorrow*).

(If you like Long, you might look into Lovecraft, or in another direction, Manly Wade Wellman and Murray Leinster.)

HOWARD PHILLIPS LOVECRAFT is the dean of 20th-century horror story writers, the "successor to Poe," the chronicler of supernatural terror in New England. Why, then, are we including him in a round-up of science fiction writers? Because he wrote a lot of science fiction, that's why.

A full exploration of the uneasy boundaries of s-f lies elsewhere in this book, but to reiterate, the simplest test of logical inclusion here is, if a writer of fantastic or speculative fiction gives a scientific or pseudo-scientific rationale for his fantastic or speculative elements, he's writing science fiction.

And this Lovecraft did, probably more often than not. His multi-tentacled, horrid thingies were true aliens, from other places, "spaces," time, or dimensions. By their inherent powers they could cross the gulfs between them and us, always with malefic intent. Lovecraft was the prime xenophobe: in his period (the '20s and '30s), extraterrestrials, particularly non-humanoid ones, were almost never friendly anyhow; they were usually portrayed as carrying off the scientist's daughter, for purposes certainly that had nothing to do with sex, considering their comparative anatomies. But Lovecraft carried this to an extreme; his slimy horrors were the true heroes of his stories, out to get any hapless human that lets them "through." Anything that comes from *out there* is just trying to get a foothold to conquer, or reconquer, the Earth.

This is essentially the basis of Lovecraft's famed "Cthulhu mythos" (Cthulhu is one of the major villains, and the majority of his works were infinite variations on the theme of the unwitting investigator (often of his own ancestors) who goes too far in his investigations and is enthralled one way or another.

Much of HPL's fiction is laid in New England, particularly the two fictional towns of Arkham and Innsmouth, and having to do with Arkham's Miskatonic University, named for the river that runs through the town. A little noticed aspect of his talent is the gloomily unpleasant atmosphere he gives to his fictional backwoods New England, with its inbred and bestial inhabitants, as frightening as his cosmic terrors, if not more so.

To cite specific stories, his two most science fictional "novels," *At the Mountains of Madness* and *The Shadow Out of Time,* were published initially in *Astounding Science Fiction,* (to further make the point). The former concerns an Antarctic expedition (from Miskatonic U., of course), that uncovers some freeze-dried aliens who immediately thaw, and all hell breaks loose. The latter is about a scholarly gentleman who "dreams" that he is living in a prehuman civilization, and finds more and more clues that he is not dreaming.

Probably Lovecraft's most successful stories were the shorter ones (though even his "novels," in his magazine-oriented period, were hardly lengthy). Many consider "The Colour Out of Space" his best work, a chilling and relatively underwritten (for Lovecraft) tale of a rural Massachusetts family and a malevolent object they think to be a meteorite which lands on their farm. Another favorite of Lovecraftians is "The Dunwich Horror," in which the hills around Arkham are laid waste by a terrifying invisible thing, revealed at the end to be a result of cross breeding between a particularly decadent family and something from "out there." (Perhaps the only HPL story with a true surprise ending—usually the reader can spot the awful final revelation pages ahead.)

It's easy to have fun with Lovecraft's florid prose and cosmic conceptions. Many contemporary readers find his prose unreadable because of its verbosity and reliance on adjectives like "unspeakable," "unnameable," etc. Nevertheless, given a chance, it can get to you. No one has yet bettered him in the creation of nightmarish paranoia set in a stylized but still believable reality, and his concepts reflect one of the truly original minds ever to write science fiction.

It might be noted, as a saddening postscript, that Lovecraft, who died in 1937, made a meager living through editing and ghost writing, and the tiny sums he obtained for his stories from magazines. He saw only one of his works between book covers before he died and that was a small private printing. And yet, in his way, he has probably influenced more writers in the field than anyone except John W. Campbell.

(Among the many influencees, Frank Long and Clark Ashton Smith certainly have their own voices, but are *de rigeur* reading for HPL fans.)

SAM J. LUNDWALL, who is known for his introductory *Science Fiction: What It's All About,* is also a dj, a singer and recording artist and TV producer. In his spare time he writes novels, and their eclectic nature reflects Lundwall's considerable knowledge of the s-f genre.

2018 A.D., or The King Kong Blues suggests by its title the kind of picaresque, hip book it is. A minor corporation executive is sent out to quest for a Miss Armpit for a deodorant commercial. Lampooning his way along, Lundwall introduces such familiar devices as an international computer bank of information on private citizens, the modern energy crisis, Arab power, and TV preposterousness. Mostly, *2018* is a caveat masquerading as a satire, and Lundwall uses the novel to warn us about all of the awfuls to come. That he does it with wit, madcap situations, and occasionally considered extrapolation takes a bit of the curse from the we've-read-it-all-before.

(Lundwall fanciers might like the equally madcap Michael Moorcock.)

RICHARD A. LUPOFF is a fan turned professional, one of the new generation of s-f writers. He began by publishing a fan-magazine called *Xero,* which won considerable recognition for its quality. Lupoff then wrote a biography of Edgar Rice Burroughs, along with several critiques of his work, which established him as a scholar of s-f adventure. Lupoff has since written five novels, three of which, while not world-shaking, are quite respectable s-f.

Into the Aether is a parody of early Verne and Wells. It is a very funny story of a young Victorian man who is entangled by his respected professor into making a space voyage in a coal-burning spaceship. Combine ''Doc'' Smith with H. G. Wells, and you get the idea.

In *The Triune Man,* Lupoff postulates a crazy comic book writer who is incarcerated in a mental hospital after developing a multiple personality. The trouble is, he really *does* have a multiple personality, and they aren't all in the same body.

The Crack in the Sky is about the inevitable ecological disaster which is waiting for us around the corner. In it, Lupoff pits political expediency against physical need, and ties up the package with needless tragedy.

(If you like Lupoff, we suggest you try Roger Zelazny and Philip Farmer.)

BARRY N. MALZBERG's fiction, not to mention his persona, has engendered controversy ever since his first works began to appear. Although a life-long fan and expert in the s-f genre, Malzberg has never chosen the easy way; he has never chosen to work within the framework of traditional s-f materials or style. His versatility and remarkably large output, plus his terse, dense and self-examining prose, have long given critics (and fans, the self-appointed critics) much fodder for their polemics.

Among Malzberg's earlier works are *The Falling Astronauts,* a psycho-fantasy whose protagonist's psychic make-up governs the skin of plot and motivation, and *Beyond Apollo* which explores similar material, both always focusing on the writer's lonely, existentially alienated characters, their oblique dialogues and outlandish human environments. In the latter novel, after a disastrous mission to Venus an only survivor returns to proclaim the insanity of the program, giving various ostensibly conflicting versions of what went wrong. Typically in Malzberg, surfaces are merely present and never explored; it is the intangible which interests him, the ineffable that entices him. Malzberg readers must work!

Concern with real contemporary events and their implications become metaphors in such novels as *The Destruction of the Temple,* in which an urban center, long since abandoned by "civilized" people, is used as the set for a *verismo* film about the assassination of John F. Kennedy, and others, and *Herovit's World,* about a science fiction writer, uncertain as to the value of his work and often bewildered by the elusive other self of his nom-de-plume to whom he can never measure up, is disturbingly involved in the mini-cosmos of an s-f convention.

Sex, or more accurately, the disappointments of sex, figure as a leitmotif in Malzberg's work; sexual protagonists experience failures, embarrassments, vacuous successes and often dismal emptyness. In Malzberg, man is both pivotal and small—as in *The Gamesman,* which begins with a failed human coupling, itself the first episode of some absolutely incoherent but rigged "game," which is the skeleton of the novel. Unsatisfactory sexual encounters and relationships, alienating but desperately necessary experiences, weave through Malzberg's involuted, but fascinating plots. *Scop* again focuses on the murders of the Kennedys, and the effort of Scop to time-travel and prevent the killings. Scop sees total moral breakdown and human decline as inevitable sequences to the assassinations, yet his tampering only makes the inevitable killings easier.

The Last Transaction is a remarkable and often chilling excursion into the political near-future of the United States. Its president tries to deal with the ever-mounting insanity of civilization, the madness rampant in his government, and the painful disarray of his personal life. William Eric Springer, in first person memories, speculations, intensely intimate monologues and ruminations, slowly and tentatively constructs the novel. Malzberg's on-the-mark references to recent and memorable political horrors, *real* ones, give the whole novel a kind of preternatural realism—even though we know that *The Last Transaction* is fiction and guesswork fiction at that.

Among Malzberg's many other books (and he has published outside of the s-f genre extensively as well), are the critically aclaimed *Guernica Night;* a moving and challenging young adult novel, *Conversations;* and under the name of K. M. O'Donnell are found *Universe Day, The Final War,* and *Dwellers of the Deep.* Much of Malzberg's short fiction is gathered in two collections: *The Best of Barry N. Malzberg,* and *The Many Worlds of Barry Malzberg.*

GEORGE R. R. MARTIN, a fast up and comer, has produced two impressive collections of stories, *A Song for Lya* and *Songs of Stars and Shadows,* and a large and somewhat unclassifiable novel, *Dying of the Light.*

Martin's Hugo Award winning title story, "A Song for Lya," is a fascinating vision of a human who is willingly, to the horror of her mate, consumed, as it were, by an alien brain/consciousness polypart oneness. *Dying of the Light* tells of an Earthman who, on a virtually abandoned planet, finds his long lost, but she belongs in some unimaginable way to a remnant ruler of the planet. The alien culture is thoroughly and imaginatively worked out, as is the solution to the protagonist's predicament; and along the way those mythic virtues, decency and chivalry in battle and love, get their due.

RICHARD MATHESON's writing has been more for the screen (he has written many Hollywood movies, and his name appears on the tube frequently) than it has for the book, but several collections of his horror stories have had a vogue and two novels, *The Shrinking Man* and *I Am Legend* (each having received screen treatment), stand as minor classics. Matheson's work is arguably not science fiction, but in *Shrinking* and *Legend* sufficient rationales are provided to supply the necessary cachet.

I Am Legend is something of a tour de force—a one character, self-told story of a man who is, ostensibly, the only *normal* survivor of a bacterial disease which has caused vampirism in all others, some of whom are *dead,* and some of whom live diseased. Barricaded in the house he once shared with his wife and daughter, Neville lives a kind of mad, determined, alcoholic, hopeful but resigned existence. He systematically kills such vampires as he can during the day and he tries, too, to solve the cause of the disease through research. It is all, of course, futile, but Neville has become a legend to the living vampires, and having found a way to begin a new society they must eventually come to grips with him.

In *The Shrinking Man,* Matheson details the diminishing life of a man who, having been exposed to some vague vapor, finally fights a titanic struggle with a basement spider now exactly twice his size, *after* having escaped being eaten by his house cat who can now look upon master as mouse. Only the writer's attention to fascinating detail and his careful writing lift this novel above the conventional modern horror story.

ANNE McCAFFREY has brought a strong element of humanity into s-f, exploring as she does the human angle of any situation. For the most part McCaffrey leaves technical explanations for others to work out.

The Ship Who Sang is a collection of related short stories, about a spaceship which is directed by the cybernetically installed brain of a little girl. Unlike many stories of this nature, Helva is not a victim, nor is the tale one of frustration and pathos. Helva is happy, human and delighted to be free of her deformed and useless body.

In *Restoree,* which McCaffrey herself calls a "spoof," a human woman finds herself on an alien planet. This is a gothic romance cast in s-f mold and set free. If you read it seriously it loses a lot of charm. *Decision at Doona* is a case of interstellar misunderstanding; two highly intelligent and technological civilizations (one of them ours) survey the same planet, and, since it has no indigenous intelligent life forms, decide to colonize. When the two colonies meet, each thinks the other is an overlooked native species. The book has some excellent speculation on first contact.

A series, planned as a trilogy, is set on a world called Ireta. This planet is surprisingly Earthlike, to the surprise of a survey team from the Federated Sentient Planets. Intellectual puzzles are quickly thrust aside, though, when the crew realizes that their rescue vessel isn't coming back, and they are stranded in a primitive world. The first book is called *Dinosaur Planet.*

Finally, one cannot overlook McCaffrey's most popular books, her Dragon series. The planet Pern, colonized hundreds of years past by humans, suffers from periodic invasions of spores from a neighboring planet. To combat this threat to life, a cadre of men and telepathic "dragons" is maintained, even through the 200-year intervals between "threadfall." The dragons and their riders live a communal existence in great caverns, called *wyers,* and are governed by the rider of the queen dragon. The series opens, in *Dragonflight,* with the search for a new queen and the subsequent ascent of Lessa to that high but sometimes dangerous office. It continues with *Dragonquest* and *The White Dragon.*

As counterpoint to the tale of Lessa, McCaffrey has written a second series set on Pern. This tells of the same events from the point of view of a young girl, Menolly, as she seeks recognition as a harpist. This series is comprised of *Dragonsong, Dragonsinger,* and *Dragondrums.*

(If you enjoy McCaffrey, we suggest Marta Randall or Marion Bradley.)

J. T. McINTOSH is Scots, and his forte is storytelling, an often lauded virtue in the realm of s-f. When readers used to talk of "a good read," or worse, "yarn," McIntosh was the kind of writer they were referring to.

Mostly standard ideas provided the armatures for his well-told stories. In *The Million Cities* the notion is that of Earth entirely covered by one sprawling city, and *Flight From Rebirth* investigates scientifically conceived and controlled reincarnation. Artificial enhancement of animal intellect is explored with its appalling results in *The Fittest,* and in another study of the survival of the fittest, *One in Three Hundred,* Earth is doomed by the Sun's nova, and only a chosen and determined few can migrate to Mars; of those allowed only some make it, and once on Mars (presumably unaffected by the nova!) stringent conditions mitigate against survival, but some do and therein lies the tale.

McIntosh has written a goodly amount of novels, each with reasonably ingenious science, but often bland in characterization and written with a kind of pedestrianism that dulls the essential sense of wonder. His people and their thoughts are one-dimensional, but they act in complex and often interesting frames of reference.

(McIntosh's themes have been also explored by Asimov, Clarke, and Cowper.)

VONDA N. McINTYRE won a Nebula Award for her vigorous and poetic novelette "Of Mist, Grass and Sand," which evolved into the novel *Dreamsnake,* which also won a Nebula, and intrigued readers had to wait three years for her first novel *The Exile Waiting,* its title, not surprisingly, a line from a poem by Ursula Le Guin. McIntyre's affinities are humanistic and societal, and her point of view, her vantage point, is vitally female.

The Exile Waiting is a sinuous and complex tale set in a demolished and hopeless Earth, rampant with thievery, duplicity and murder. Mischa partakes of all of these, but feels that she might, with help and a change of venue, turn her talents to good. Her drug demented brother is dying of despair; her wretched uncle holds her sister literally, and Mischa telepathically. How Mischa comes to escape Earth for a better (artificial) planet, and how various interesting aliens and genetic constructs are involved in her adventures and her departure, makes for engrossing storytelling, and it is well done. But *Exile* has much more to say than its mere narrative indicates. . .

Though few and far between, McIntyre's thoughtful short fiction is eagerly sought as it appears in magazines.

(As you might gather, a McIntyre fan might well enjoy the work of Le Guin, and also that of Marta Randall.)

RICHARD C. MEREDITH is a devotee of the Time War theme, an s-f tradition where an elite corps of time travelers shuttle back and forth fighting a momentous war throughout all history. As a basic plot, it is intriguing, as it allows the writer to extrapolate from the past into the present. You know, like "What if Lincoln weren't assassinated?" or "What if Hitler had won the war?"

In *At the Narrow Passage* the war is between two alien races who are fighting for control of all the continua of Earth, using human pawns. One soldier in this war discovers the true situation and sets out to discover a way to defeat the aliens.

Run, Come See Jerusalem is begun in a theocratic future, where a despotic new Church Militant has discovered time travel. One of the "chrononauts" is party to a plot to overthrow the government by going back in time to assassinate the mother of the man who founded the church. It is all rather confusing, since Meredith postulates alternate time lines rather than a single changeable line.

As a writer of war stories, Meredith excels. His battles are on a grand scale, and his flair for intrigue makes him an exciting spy story/adventure writer.

(If you enjoy Meredith, we suggest Gordon Dickson or Poul Anderson.)

JUDITH MERRIL began writing s-f in 1948, when the field was dominated by men and men's concerns; her stories presaged the feminist movement. She wrote about the way things were and the way they might be; her heroines are strong and resourceful without denying compassion and gentility.

Some of her stories are collected in *The Best of Judith Merril*, which includes the incredible "Daughters of Earth," about six generations of pioneer women. Merril collaborated with C. M. Kornbluth on *Gunner*

Cade and *Outpost Mars,* and on her own, wrote several novels. Among them are *The Tomorrow People,* which contrasts the first Mars expeditions with a global power struggle and her finest novel, *Shadow on the Hearth.*

Shadow on the Hearth chronicles the life and death of a suburban housewife and her children after New York is destroyed by an atomic bomb. Written in 1950, this novel, with its understated tone and horrible normalcy is a chilling statement about an all-too-possible future.

Merril, also a fine anthologist, is actively engaged in bringing good writing and mature plotting to s-f.

(If you like Merril, we suggest Tiptree, Pohl, or Wilhelm.)

A. MERRITT. Abraham Merritt's works seem to leave no one neutral. The lush, art-noveau prose and classic adventure plots of his epitomal "scientific romances" are hard to take for certain modern readers, especially those of the nuts and bolts school of science fiction, but the rise of the romantic strain in s-f in the past decade has won him a whole new host of admirers. His influence cannot be ignored; like his contemporary, Edgar Rice Burroughs, he is one of the granddaddies of American science fiction.

His output was comparatively slight in the light of some of his more prolific peers: eight novels (plus two unfinished at his death) and a score of short stories. Of the novels, three can be loosely described as occult (though dealing with matters that were in the '20s and '30s legitimate areas of scientific interest), one is the purest fantasy, *(The Ship of Ishtar,* and a classic it is), and four are given the pseudo-scientific rationales that qualify them as science fiction.

In all of these, Merritt spins off the classic "lost race" form of H. Rider Haggard: somewhere on (or in) the globe there was still room for undiscovered cultures of various exotic varieties. These are not, however, mere leftovers from the cultural mainstream. In *Moon Pool,* they are the decadent remnants of the Lemurians, living in the great cavern under the Pacific formed when the Moon was ripped from the Earth. In *Dwellers in the Mirage,* it is a strange hybrid Norse-Mongolian-Indian civilization, worshipping a Lovecraftian god from other dimensions. In *The Metal Monster,* it is an extraterrestrial hive mentality of metal entities, flourishing in the remote Himalayas.

Naive or unrealistic as these may seem to us now, there was nothing unsophisticated about Merritt's handling of these themes. Particularly strong is the element of tragedy untypical for its time. The three god-like aliens who guard the caverns of the Moon Pool must fight against their own creation, a creature of pure energy, "The Shining One." The Snake Mother of *The Face in the Abyss* is the last of her unhuman race, immortal and tired of immortality; perhaps Merritt's strongest character. Several of the novels (and we won't say which, for obvious reasons) have tragic endings; the hero (inevitably from our "world") and the heroine (always a lovely creature from the exotic culture) *don't* live happily ever after.

Merritt's style—"lush" to his admirers, "purple" to his detractors—is unique in one quality: its poetic evocation of scientific phenomena. Where, for instance, another science fiction writer might describe a matter transmitter or projector, usually trying to make its appearance in a story as realistic as possible by giving, obviously or subtly, a technical description of how and/or why it works, Merritt does it thusly:

"...within the roseate oval, two flame-tipped shadows appeared... and still it was as though their bodies passed back through distances; as though, to try to express the wellnigh inexpressible, the two shapes we were looking upon were the end of an infinite number stretching in fine linked chain far away, of which the eyes saw only the nearest, while in the brain some faculty higher than sight recognized and registered the unseen others."

You may not end up knowing how it works, but you've sure got some beautiful pictures instilled in your mind. (This is probably the place to add that one of those rare creative combinations of talent occurred in s-f when the noted fantasy artist Virgil Finlay began to illustrate Merritt's work. Somehow he caught visually the extraordinary effects that Merritt gives in words.)

No, no one seems neutral about Merritt. Brian Aldiss has snidely remarked about him: "His world ends not with a bang, but a simper." But no one else had ever succeeded in creating the visions that Merritt has dreamed and communicated to us. And that may be the secret of his unending popularity.

(The only writer that came close was Henry Kuttner in his more romantic fantasies. You might try them if you like Merritt.)

SAM MERWIN, JR. is best known as an editor of some distinction. In 1945 he assumed that pose for *Thrilling Wonder Stories* and *Startling Stories,* and remained at the helm until 1951. It was Merwin, in those magazines, who introduced the concept of a thoughtful, intelligent and most of all, responsive letters column. We have grown so accustomed to information and ideas in today's s-f letters columns that few people realize that such things didn't always exist. It is perhaps this interplay between readers and writers of s-f that gives the genre both its great strength and its insularity.

Merwin also writes s-f; he has produced a number of short stories and several novels. *The House of Many Worlds,* and its sequel, *Three Faces of Time,* are adventure novels liberally laced with politics and assorted skull-duggery in parallel worlds. In 1953 Merwin somewhat anticipated the backlash to Feminism with a book called *The Sex War.* In it he portrayed a maniacal women's underground whose sole aim was to kill all men (not a very practical goal). Later he returned to the theme with *Chauvinistro;* in it the world is governed by women, but there is a secret political party composed of those who have realized that only men are capable of running a government. Merwin's writing style is somewhat primitive, but energetic and not without imagination.

(If you like the work of Sam Merwin, try that of Mack Reynolds.)

WALTER MILLER. The case of Walter Miller is, though not unique, a special one. Several decades ago his stories began appearing in the genre magazines, and they appeared with considerable frequency. Then he published three novellas which became the basis for his tripartite ("Fiat Homo," "Fiat Lux," "Fiat Voluntas Tua") novel *A Canticle for Leibowitz.* Published in its final form in 1959 it has stayed well at the top of the s-f heap, and is now commonly assigned in various literature courses.

Canticle can be read and understood on many levels. It is a novel of ideas rather than action; speculation more than narrative; provocation more than surface engagement. In the U.S. southwest desert, a post-holocaust time, a bleak and empty time, Francis, a novice priest, finds the "relics" of one Leibowitz, a nuclear technician involved in the final war. From the neo-medieval world in which they ply their Catholic trade the priests and brothers fearfully and tentatively deal with such remnants of technology as they find. Francis involves himself in a futile pilgrimage. Bewildering, symbolic characters thread through the book: the two-headed tomato lady; Benjamin, the wandering Jew. The monastery develops electricity in, appropriately, "Fiat Lux," and that symbol of the rebirth of technology points to the novel's inevitable deduction: history repeats. As yet another final atomic horror begins, various clergy and laity escape to elsewhere in the newly reinvented spaceship. A genuine classic, *Canticle* is a novel of monstrous power and vision.

In all, Walter Miller wrote some forty short stories and one novel. Some of his stories are collected in *The View from the Stars* and *Conditionally Human*. Recently the reclusive author has vanished into what Norman Spinrad has called "public obscurity."

(If Miller's work appeals, try that of Edgar Pangborn and Robert Silverberg.)

NAOMI MITCHISON is that rarest of rare birds, an author from outside the genre who managed to write a good science fiction novel (two, to be exact). Too little known in the U.S., but noted in Britain for her historical novels, she may have accomplished this feat because she is sister and daughter to the noted scientists Haldane; she herself has achieved a reputation as a biologist.

Her first science fiction novel, published when she was 65, was *Memoirs of a Space Woman,* an episodic account of the life of a human empath, bred and educated to achieve the maximum communication possible with alien races. In addition to constructing a fascinating future human society and some equally intriguing alien ones, it had a good deal to say about the place of the female in *our* society quite some time before the subject was chic. Her second s-f novel was *Solution 3*, a post-holocaust story in which humanity is attempting to rebuild itself on a social basis of homosexuality and cloning.

Would that every mainstream writer who attempted science fiction were so successful.

(Mitchinson's social and anthropological base is shared by Le Guin, Bishop, and Cherryh.)

MICHAEL MOORCOCK is unquestionably the most varied and prolific of s-f authors. Still young by writer's standards, he has published some fifty books and if his annual output were in barrels of oil England's energy crisis would be much relieved.

Moorcock's work can be roughly divided into three types of imaginative fiction: the "straight" s-f novels, sword and sorcery, and science fantasies. On the straight novels, three were written under the name of Edward Bradbury: *City of the Beast, Masters of the Pit,* and *Lord of the Spiders* are "Martian" novels in a fairly standard mold; high on adventure and blood-and-thunder conflict. In *The Black Corridor* the passengers of a spaceship travel in suspended animation while their captain, Ryan, fantasizes and frolics with terrible imaginings about the ship and its destiny. *Breakfast in the Ruins* and *Behold the Man* (award winning novella expanded to a novel) are related books, and are indicative of Moorcock's ability to deal with a staggeringly wide variety of subjects. Unconventional writing techniques mark these novels: *Breakfast* is told in a series of news clips, dialogues and vignettes from past, present and future history, in which Karl Glogauer (an everyman neurotic) is both perpetrator and victim. In *Behold the Man,* Glogauer travels through time to impersonate Jesus when he finds that the worthy child is, in fact, moronic.

Warlord of the Air and *The Land Leviathan* are outrageous and often highly amusing scientific romances, rather in the style of Wells; they feature secret manuscripts, time travel and expert boy's adventure, albeit with much ribaldry and satiric overtone.

Moorcock's sword and sorcery is a far cry from the definition: in Moorcock heroes and heroics are always mitigated by human foible, though this curiosity enhances rather than diminishes the magic and adventures. By the very nature of its construction and its endlessly intertwining character and story, it tends to confuse and frustrate its devotees. There is the Elric series, the Corums, the Count Brass series and the Runestaff. The author has been revising some of these, particularly the Elric books, to give them a greater consistency and cohesion. (Whether he has lessened or compounded the confusion remains to be seen.) Moorcock's fantasies are heroic fantasy with bathos, and Elric *et al.* are multi-dimensional characters, not simple-minded mugs such as Robert Howard's Conan. It is here that Moorcock's debt to Edgar Rice Burroughs is paid, and the account closed.

Two major non-fantasy but not quite s-f series are those featuring Jerry Cornelius (now a cult figure of considerable albeit wrinkled, proportion) and Jherek Carnelian (those into nomenclature have great games with Moorcock's character names). In these books women finally find a strong place in Moorcock's work; Katherine Cornelius and Una Persson, among others, are far from stereotypes, and they, no doubt, pave the way for his new titular heroine, *Gloriana*. In the Cornelius novels and stories the urbane, studish, wiley and eternal (death and resurrection are equally common) Jerry, who is a kind of James Bond parody, careers about the globe on improbable if not intelligible missions for—one hopes—mythic agencies. Conquest and defeat, potency and impotency, manner and matter are stewed in an outlandish but palatable way, and for all the maverick preposterousness there is often an underlying seriousness here. The Cornelius books are *The Final Programme, A Cure for Cancer, The English Assassin,* and *The Condition of Muzak,* and there are also various ancillary Cornelius stories, collected and uncollected.

The Jherek Carnelian trilogy (*Dancers at the End of Time*) consists of *An Alien Heat, The Hollow Lands,* and *The End of All Songs,* plus a book or two of satellite stories. Here, in Earth's remote future, the small remaining population is outlandish, wealthy, decadent and more than a little jaded. Sex and technology are both seriously atrophied, and life is lived best by sybarites. Jherek time-trips into the past, partly to alleviate his boredom and partly to romance a Victorian lady. He gains and loses her over the millennia (and through all three books), and finally secures her in his own time and place. Jherek's mother, the Iron Orchid (orchid is Greek for testes), is one of Moorcock's more memorable characters, representing a kind of focal point for both fears and securities.

Throughout all of his work Moorcock's writing is speedy (sometimes too speedy) and agile. Event and character come and go with insouciance; plots twist in apparently arbitrary ways; reason is defied, and eclectic is the way to go. Some early Moorcock s-f novels, unrelated (it says here) to any of the series, are: *Fireclown, The Sundered Worlds, The Wrecks of Time,* and *The Twilight Man.*

(Moorcock's madness can in some ways be matched by Alfred Bester, Mick Farren, R. A. Lafferty, Sam Lundwall, and Christopher Priest.)

C. L. MOORE is really Catherine Lucille Moore; the initials were adopted to disguise her sex in the mainly masculine world of science fiction in the '30s. Despite (or perhaps because of) her gender, her rise in popularity was rapid due to such stories as the Northwest Smith series, where her rough and ready spaceman hero meets alien horrors on Mars ("Shambleau"), Venus ("Black Thirst"), and various other exotic locales. These were that combination of horror and science fiction, dubbed "science-fantasy," which *Wierd Tales* was specializing in at the time, and that Lovecraft and Clark Ashton Smith were creating at the highest level it was to achieve.

Knowledge that C. L. Moore was female seeped slowing through the science fictional grapevine. She probably blew her cover by unveiling a female "hero"—Jirel of Joiry; almost unheard of in those days. However, science fiction readers, adjusted to coping with all varieties of extraterrestrial species, took the female writer in their stride. As her stories leaned more toward science fiction and away from fantasy, she began to write for *Astounding Stories*.

The vision of H. P. Lovecraft as a matchmaker is an unlikely one, but knowing that a young author named Henry Kuttner had been greatly impressed by C. L. Moore's fiction, he arranged a correspondence between the two which eventually culminated in their marriage.

As noted in the article on Kuttner the marriage was professional as well as personal; few stories by either of them after the event were by one of them alone. Dual efforts would appear under either name, not to mention any one of nineteen (!) pseudonyms.

Of the works that Moore concedes to be her own, two exceptional novels are noteworthy, *Judgement Night* and *Doomsday Morning* (despite the complementary titles, there is no link between the two). *Night* is of a far future and a decaying Galactic Empire, with a pleasure planet that set the style for all following pleasure planets; *Morning* is the near future of an America run by an omniscient political "machine" called Comus (Communications U.S.). A far cry from Northwest Smith's brawling adventures, but just as skillfully done.

There's a special excitement inherent in Moore's short stories from the '40s; the excitement that went into making that period at least one "golden age" of s-f. It was the time of playing with ideas; every story was an adventure in concept and while sometimes the idea didn't work, the adventurousness was still there. Moore's stories vibrate with this, and something further to boot. She had a skill, rare for the field at that time, of extracting the human drama from a science fictional idea. In "No Woman Born," for instance, a great dancer finds herself, after an accident, in a rebuilt, "robot" body of great beauty and abilities—but unhuman beauty and abilities. Moore presents the personal drama here as well as the technical speculation.

And in "Vintage Season," which is more than a few people's favorite science fiction short story, three strange people take rooms in a modest house in a contemporary city. The owner realizes that they are time travellers from the future—but *why* are they here? Not for the world would we tell you here...

C. L. Moore has been inactive in science fiction for many years, devoting her talent to a successful career of writing scripts for television. We can only hope that some day she will return.

(If you're impressed by C. L. Moore, try Leigh Brackett or Clark Ashton Smith for something similar in a different key.)

JOHN MORRESSEY has published a few essentially traditional—in both manner and matter—contemporary space operas, filled with the customary assortment of goings-on.

Stardrift features Jolon Gallamor, a peripatetic space orphan who is tagged for a hit by the murderers of his father. Changing identity with every planetfall with the ease given him by his natural wit and native abilities as a man of daring, gamesmanship and good aim, he spins through worlds of gangsters, petty dictators and assorted nasties, searching, searching, searching.

The Extraterritorial recounts the plight of a man who works in an ambiguous matrix of intergalactic skullduggery; even he is more than unclear as to just what the organization does. Through what appear to be dreams, he comes to realize the atrocities he has perpetrated through the manipulations of the organization, and his own horror leads him to plan for revenge.

(If you like the work of John Morressey, try that of Mack Reynolds and Keith Laumer.)

LARRY NIVEN is generally recognized as one of the most scientifically oriented writers in the field. He uses his extensive knowledge of the sciences to build a completely consistent milieu in which to ensconce his concepts and characters.

The majority of Niven's work is part of a vast "future history," one of the most detailed in the field, the Known Space series. This series covers a thousand years of time, with corroborating data from over a billion years in the past. The preponderance of the stories (short stories and novels) take place in Human Space, the area of space colonized by man (a sphere approximately sixty light-years in diameter by the end of the series), or in Known Space, the much larger area explored by humans but controlled by other species.

The future history begins around 2000 A.D. with slight variations from our own timeline, such as advanced organ transplant technique, civil rights for all *three* intelligences on the Earth (humans, whales, and dolphins) and manned exploration of the Solar System, and proceeds through over a thousand years of scientific and technological progress, cultural and sociological evolution and revolution, and contacts with several intelligent alien species.

This is an extremely complex interlocking series with the advantage that any part can be read separately and understood as an entity within itself. *A Gift From Earth* is a novel speculating on the extended use of organ transplant technology on a colony planet, and the effects on its class structure by a revolutionary advance in that technology. Other novels in the series include *World of Ptavvs,* about a human/alien mental link and *Protector,* in which a similar mode details the conversion of a man to an alien philosophy and technology by an advance scout for an expanding race near Galactic center. And there's *Ringworld,* probably the best known component of the series, an awe-inspiring technological tour-de-force which sends two humans, a mad member of the cowardly Puppeteer race, and a Kzinti, an individual of a viciously warlike species, to investigate an enormous hoop-shaped object completely encircling a star. This is world-building in the truest sense, with the science sound in theory and the extrapolation breathtaking in practice. Throughout these novels and the collections of short stories which compose the series, although science is basic, characterization is by no means left to fend for itself; Niven creates races and individuals and imbues them with a breath of life through the detail and warmth of his writing.

Even leaving Known Space aside, Niven is a fairly prolific writer; *The Flight Of The Horse* is a collection of eight very intelligent, slightly tongue-in-cheek short stories of time travel, our hero, generally operating at the whim of a mad emperor of the future, sent to capture denizens of the past such as unicorns and leviathans. Other collections, of unrelated short stories and articles of speculative science, include *The Shape Of Space, All The Myriad Ways,* and *A Hole In Space.*

With Jerry Pournelle he has co-authored *The Mote In God's Eye,* a far-flung space opera, *Inferno,* a science fiction writer's trip to Hell, and *Lucifer's Hammer,* a present day disaster-suspense novel. Another collaboration, this time with David Gerrold, resulted in *The Flying Sorcerers,* a humorous science fiction adaptation of *A Connecticut Yankee In King Arthur's Court.*

Niven, although his scientific knowledge is among the best in the field (other authors have him check their manuscripts for accuracy), uses it only as a base; his characterization is well developed, his extrapolation mind-boggling, and he's just plain enjoyable to read.

(If you find Niven's work to your taste, sample the output of Hal Clement, Poul Anderson, Robert Heinlein, and Arthur C. Clarke.)

JOHN NORMAN. One of the oldest themes in science fiction is the Earthman transported to another planet one way or another (just so it's quick and we don't have to waste time and details on the voyage). He's strong, handsome, and a general macho type. Burroughs did it epitomally with John Carter and Mars. Norman has a slightly more modern counterpart in Tarl Cabot.

In *Tarnsman of Gor,* the first of the long Gor series, Cabot (ostensibly of Earth) receives a message from a long-lost father, boards a spaceship and is transported to Gor, "counter-Earth." There he trains with sword and lance, learns to ride the huge, fierce, roc-like birds called tarns, and sets off to capture a princess (what else?), steal a sacred Home Stone, and is finally sent floating down a river to die. He doesn't (otherwise no series, of course), and in the two following novels—*Outlaw of Gor* and *Priest-Kings of Gor,* Cabot searches for the mysterious rulers of the planet, the cruel and implacable Priest-Kings. Norman has created a well developed culture, or actually a variety of cultures, in these novels, and there is action and adventure enough to suit the most pulp-hungry tastes. The style is solid, earthy, and (unlike its genre predecessors) there is more than just a suggestion of sex.

Gor became so popular with readers after the first three books that Norman has continued the series with *Nomads, Captive, Raiders,* etc. of Gor. There is usually an evil man, a women subjugated, the woman freed in such an heroic manner that she chooses voluntary enslavement to her rescuer, and they all live happily ever after (or at least till the next novel).

Time Slave does not take place on Gor. In this novel, the slave is a time-travelling woman of the 20th century and the enslaver is a Cro-Magnon man.

Imaginative Sex is the first science fiction sex manual. It is a book of 53 scenarios designed to give lovers a chance to tie each other up.

(Aside from their particular flavor, Norman's books are in the long tradition of the interplanetary adventure series of Burroughs and Kline; other contemporary practitioners are Lin Carter, E. C. Tubb, and Alan Burt Akers.)

ANDRE NORTON is a prolific writer of science fiction; although most of her output is considered "juvenile" this is primarily due to the age of the majority of her protagonists. They are generally young persons, male and female, aged anywhere from twelve to twenty-five and are set in and against an adult world that doesn't always give them credit for the sense they usually have, until at a crisis point they come through with flying colors.

One of the talents prevalent in Norton's heroes and heroines is telepathy, although it is usually restricted to communication with animals. *Beast Master* and *Lord of Thunder* are sequential novels following the emotional rather than physical maturation of Hosteen Storm, ex-commando of the Galactic Federation forces, rank: Beast Master. The term should probably be Beast Partner, as Norton's love and respect for members of the animal kingdom is quite apparent in these books, as in many others. Storm is teamed with an African Black Eagle, two Meerkats, and a dune cat, and keeps them with him after he leaves the service. His relationship with animals is developed with a simple but telling skill by Norton. And the team's interaction with society, as Storm, a Navaho Indian seeks atonement for a tribal dishonor, is equally well described. (The respect Norton holds for the American Indian evident in these two novels is also inherent in *The Sioux Spaceman,* where Indian heritage and values save a world for mankind.) Although communication between Hosteen Storm and his team is primarily verbal on Storm's part and emotional on the animal's, Norton carries this theme a bit further in *Catseye,* a novel in which Troy Horan becomes a fully communicating equal to a kinkajou, two foxes, and two cats, while in *Storm Over Warlock* and *Ordeal In Otherwhere* the animals are a pair of wolverines.

Youth tested is the basic theme for a lot of Norton's work, including the series of novels detailing the adventures of Dan Thorson and the trade ship *Solar Queen*. The galactic background against which the four stories are set are consistent, the character of their characters well detailed, and they're very good low key space opera. *Daybreak 2250 A.D.* (originally published as *Star Man's Son 2250 A.D.)* is another tale of a young man facing responsibility and challenges, this time on a post-holocaust Earth.

Adults are also the protagonists of some of her books; Ross Murdock is hero of four novels of space/time travel and cold war one-upmanship, *Star Rangers* has characters who are at least physically mature, while Blake Walker is prominent in *The Crossroads of Time* and *Quest Crosstime*. In these, as in most of her work, the theme of man fighting successfully against the greed and viciousness of his nature is basic, and in all but a few of her later novels, optimism is like a light at the end of a tunnel.

Although by no means all of Ms. Norton's work has been detailed above, most of it is similar; her characterization is simple but completely adequate, her imagination is wide-ranging, and a story usually ends on an up note. Fascinating people and places, animals and aliens abound, and unless as a reader one is fond of stylistic writing, search along the Norton shelf; you'll probably find something you like.

(Norton's special appeal is hard to duplicate; what come closest are probably Heinlein's "juveniles" and the works of James Schmitz.)

ALAN E. NOURSE writes what is generally referred to as juvenile fiction. This categorization is caused by the fact that his protagonists are usually young people, and by no means indicates that adults can't enjoy his work. He specializes in tightly-plotted, fast action stories, usually with a medical slant, which isn't surprising, considering that Nourse is a doctor. *The Mercy Men* is one of his best, a novel of twists and surprises. In a future time there is the Medical Center, last resort of people hard up for cash; volunteer for an experiment, the higher the risk, the higher the pay. Jeff Meyer, seeking the man he believes murdered his father, must become one of these mercy men. The climax is unexpected and Nourse's speculations on the future practice of medicine are stimulating. Futuristic medicine is the background for *Star Surgeon*, too; Earth is attempting to enter the Galactic Federation and jealously defends its ace in the hole, medical knowledge. Dal is a young man from the planet Garvia, and the first off-Earth person to be accepted as a medical student. There are several exciting adventures in which Dal and his mysterious pet play an important part, and, by showing its ability to teach, Earth is admitted to the Federation to learn. The relationship between Dal and his fellow interns/shipmates is developed with humanity and compassion.

Nourse strays from the medical in *Trouble On Titan*, a free-wheeling adventure set on Saturn's moon. It's the old story of the descendants of convict colonists mining a desolate lump of rock, but with a few interesting fillips, including, as Nourse says in his intro, an interstellar drive that exists right now. It also considers the extent to which a person will go to be free.

In a more "adult" vein, *Psi High And Others* is the story of Earth's reaction to three crises being observed by the Watchers from the Galactic Federation. It is the job of the Watchers to decide on a future of freedom or quarantine for humanity based on three criteria: whether it uses its knowledge of physiology and biochemistry for good or ill; how it deals with arising extrasensory powers within its own members, and reaction to first contact with alien intelligence. The three episodes are intelligently and provocatively developed, and the Watchers' decision hangs like the proverbial sword over the situation.

Nourse is also notable for his short stories, nine of which are found in *Tiger By The Tail.*

(If you like Nourse, you should try Murray Leinster's Med Service series, and the writing of James White.)

PHILIP NOWLAN, by his creation of Anthony Rogers, became the father of all that was epitomal of science fiction to the general public for several decades. The creation of who? You may ask. Would it help to point out that Anthony Rogers' nickname was Buck? That he had a girlfriend named Wilma Deering? That he fell into suspended animation in the 20th century and awoke in the 25th? Yes, Philip Nowlan was responsible for the phrase, "That Buck Rogers stuff" as applied (infuriatingly to s-f readers) to science fiction.

The fury was justified if by that phrase was meant simple-minded comic strip s-f, but unjustified if the original novel is examined. *Armageddon 2419 A.D. (not* one of those titles that stays easily in the mind), published in *Amazing Stories* in two parts in 1928 and 1929, is a creditable example of the s-f of its day. Buck awakes to find America ruled by naughty Mongols (those were the days of the "yellow peril," remember) and joins a guerilla group. Between the super science of the Mongols and the surprisingly prescient portrait of modern guerilla warfare, it's quite a lively story and perfectly readable today.

Once Buck became established in the comics, Nowlan wrote no more fiction. He died in 1940.

ANDREW J. OFFUTT came of literary age during the foment and "revolution" of the '60s in the U.S., and his work reflects a definite if not vicious anti-establishment attitude.

Though most of Offutt's work is of the sword and sorcery genre, he has written a few true science fiction novels: *Evil Is Live Spelled Backwards* tells of a future of religious tyranny and oppression rebelled against by a Satanist underground, while *Castle Keep* is a graphic depiction of civilization tearing itself apart. The "meaningful" themes and the skill with which Offutt develops his characters and cultures were typical of his early work and earned him inclusion in the iconoclastic anthology *Again Dangerous Visions* with the short story "For Value Received."

A lighter work from a not-so-rebellious period is *The Galactic Rejects,* the story of three of Earth's front-line fighters, being sent home as worn-out casualties of the Earth-Azuli war, stranded on a backward planet. They settle into the society, using their extrasensory powers in a circus, until the Azuli land. Then they instigate guerilla warfare against the enemy. It's a fast action adventure with intriguing use of the powers of telekinesis, telepathy, and teleportation.

Offutt's quite a good writer, fleshing out his innovative concepts with solid characterization and a facile skill at building cultures and societies.

(If you like Offutt you might try Piers Anthony.)

CHAD OLIVER is another example of the s-f fan become professional. His intelligent letters were a mainstay of the magazine letters columns of the late '40s; in the '50s he published fiction strongly influenced by his vocation as an anthrolopogist.

Almost all his stories are variations on the theme of humanity's contact with alien races. In *Shadows in the Sun,* a human discovers a small town in Texas to be a colony of extraterrestrails, "scouting" Earth as a potential member of a Galactic union. In *The Winds of Time,* aliens stranded on Earth go into suspended animation until our race reaches a stage of being able to help them. *The Shores of Another Sea* contrasts man's sometimes academically cruel study of anthropoids with another race's study of man. The several collections of short stories also explore the infinite possiblities inherent in the "first contact" sub-genre.

Though he published a novel as recently as 1971, Oliver's output has been minimal in the past couple of decades. One hopes that he will bring his anthropological expertise to science fiction again in the future.

(If you like Oliver's anthropological slant in s-f, try Michael Bishop's intelligent works on the same theme.)

EDGAR PANGBORN. "I'm Davy, who was king for a time. King of the Fools, and that calls for wisdom." So begins the warm, wonderful adventures of a youth traveling to adulthood through the northeastern United States of a post-holocaust world. *Davy* is a special book, not just for its story, but for the way in which it is told. Pangborn's characters are people you want to meet and talk with, his places are real and you feel you've been there with him.

Strangely enough, even though *Davy* and two other of his works, *The Judgement of Eve* and *Company of Glory,* are set in worlds destroyed by man, there is an optimism and a love for humanity in his novels which can't be denied. This optimism is also evident in *A Mirror For Observers,* in which after thousands of years of Martian nurturing of Earth's civilization and culture, one Martian exerts an evil influence on the potential initiator of an age of ethics for mankind. The conflict arises when another Martian opposes him.

Basically, Edgar Pangborn was a marvelous writer who happened to pick science fiction to write. Science fiction readers profit by this choice.

(If you like Pangborn, try Theodore Sturgeon, James Schmitz, and Walter Miller, Jr.)

ALEXEI PANSHIN made a name for himself as a more-than-promising author, but of late has concentrated on, with his wife Corey, the criticism and historiography of science fiction (which, one might note, s-f badly needs).

His Nebula-award winning *Rite of Passage* has been called "the best Heinlein novel not written by Heinlein" which is probably unfair even to bring up. Though it employs a Heinleinian female adolescent first person narrator, and an equally Heinleinian attention to the minute details of life aboard a spaceship, it also is strikingly original in its story of a young girl's life aboard a ship fleeing from a post-catastrophe Earth, and her survival test on a distant planet.

In an entirely different vein, his three Anthony Villiers novels are probably the closest that science fiction has come to the Victorian comedy of manners. Recounting the adventures of an unusually likeable rogue and his intelligent giant frog of a companion in a dizzily far-fetched future, they are authentically funny, something that can be said for few of s-f's excursions into "humor." Helping the hilarity are the author's asides to the reader, a device that could be cute, but in Panshin's hands really works.

While the Panshins' critical and historical work is of great value, we hope it does not preclude more of the authentic wit Alexei has shown in the Villiers novels, a quality equally needed in the field.

(The sort of humor displayed by Panshin can also be found in the work of Keith Laumer and Tanith Lee's science fiction.)

H. BEAM PIPER was a late beginner; his work began appearing in the magazines when he was already in his 40s. But his comparatively brief career (he died in the mid-'60s) resulted in several novels that continue to be popular, and for good reason. There are strong similarities to Heinlein, particularly that singularly satisfying plot-form that could be described as Horatio Algeresque of the underdog, outsider, or seeming born loser triumphing against adversity *and* wicked opponents whose wickedness is absolutely wicked; no moral shilly-shallying here.

The prime example is *Little Fuzzy*. On one side, a self-sufficient prospector on the planet Zarathustra, who discovers a race of tiny beings who have the koala beat to hell in sheer adorableness, and are probably sapient to boot. On the other, the corporation who owns the rights to the planet's natural resources *if* there are no intelligent indigenes. By pluck, luck, and dogged determination, prospector, friends, and fuzzies take on corporation and win, with a lot of intrigue and adventure on the way. Jolly good fun, as is *Fuzzy Sapiens* (initially titled *The Other Human Race)* which continues the Fuzzy chronicles. There's some interesting intellectual and philosophical points made on the way, too.

Lord Kalvan of Otherwhen is really a Pennsylvania state cop thrown into an alternate time stream where the Aryans have arrived in America the other way around from the west, resulting in a feudal and rather backward culture. Luckily, he lands in with the right crowd immediately, those in favor of social progress and against the naughty theocracy that has a monopoly on gunpowder. Keeping an eye on all this is the Paratime Police, who guard the crosstime dimensions and were responsible for the accident that got "Kalvan" there in the first place.

The Cosmic Computer (originally and more accurately called *Junkyard Planet)* gives us the inhabitants of a jerkwater planet living off the detritus of an interstellar war and their search for an omniscient computer supposedly also left on their world. *Space Viking* tells the tale of another interstellar backwoodsman in the fading days of a Galactic Empire that, like the Norseman-Normans taking over the shreds of the Holy Roman Empire, goes a-Viking and ends up inheriting the whole kit and caboodle. Rousing is a barely adequate word for this one.

As is evident, Piper was adept at adapting historical precedents into valid and exciting future situations. His work is probably epitomal of the sociologically-inclined, post-space opera, action adventure science fiction.

(If you like Piper, by all means try Heinlein and probably Asimov.)

DORIS PISERCHIA first appeared with a short and somewhat florid novel called *Mr. Justice,* all about a vigilante with a time machine. Mr. Justice, as he called himself, could literally return to the scene of the crime and obtain evidence against the criminal. Piserchia weaves a good plot by contrasting public outrage and private satisfaction at Mr. Justice's activities.

Star Rider is a story about a girl and her horse: only in this case the horse is a weird telepathic and teleporting beastie. The book has a lingering effect; the reader, sometimes years later, will wonder where that strange image came from.

In *Earthchild* and *A Billion Days of Earth* both, Piserchia seems to be finding her own voice. The style is faintly Lafferty-esque, with his characteristic half-mad play with words and concepts. Piserchia also reveals a whacky sense of humor in her situations and characters. *Earthchild* is about the last human child born on Earth, and raised by friendly aliens. *A Billion Days of Earth* is set in a bizarre future where Mankind has become godlike, and a new race of intelligent beings has evolved from rats.

(If you enjoy Piserchia, we recommend R. A. Lafferty, or Joanna Russ.)

FREDERIK POHL has been around a long time, although you wouldn't know it to look at his stories. He has been writing s-f since 1937, when he was first published in *Amazing Stories,* the magazine that Hugo Gernsback founded. In forty-plus years of writing s-f, Pohl has produced a massive body of work (although not so large as to vie for the title of most prolific), each piece of which is remarkably well suited to its time. Pohl has changed, matured, and always been willing to try something new in his fiction; in fact, Pohl has been something of a daring writer all his professional life.

Pohl is at his best in the short story, where he can explore a single aspect of a culture or technology, and display his skill at the rapid sketching of character and milieu. His stories have been anthologized time and again, and there are several fine collections available.

In his novels, Pohl delves into the effect of technology on the human condition, epitomally in the Nebula-award winning novel, *Man Plus.* In the not-too-distant future, the problem of colonizing Mars is attacked, not by changing the environment of Mars, as so many have speculated, but by changing the nature of man. Through surgical and cybernetic techniques, a man is adapted to Martian conditions and thus cut off from all humanity. Pohl's detailing of the effect of this transformation of Roger Torroway and the people around him make this an unusually compelling novel; furthermore, the science is sound.

A much earlier work, *Drunkard's Walk*, tells about an elite group of telepathic immortals who rule the world (a not uncommon plot) and all of the "normals." The only safeguard against mental control is to be mildly inebriated. These two are but a taste of Fred Pohl's work.

One of s-f's most productive and delightful collaborative relationships existed between Pohl and Cyril M. Kornbluth. It began in 1952 and continued until Kornbluth's death; the Pohl/Kornbluth team is funny, sophisticated and the master of the *ad adsurdum* argument.

The first book they wrote was *The Space Merchants* which was based on the premise that Madison Avenue advertising techniques effectively rule the world. The book grew from Pohl's experiences as a copy writer for an advertising firm. As satire and social criticism in 1953 it was delightful. It is less funny today, possibly because we have come a long way farther on the road to the world they described. *Gladiator-At-Law* is set in the same sort of world, where corporate "wars" are fought in the arena.

Other works by the two include *Search The Sky* and *Wolfbane*, and numerous short stories.

Pohl also collaborated successfully with Jack Williamson.

(If you like Pohl's work, we suggest you try Williamson, Jack Vance, and Arthur C. Clarke.)

JERRY POURNELLE appeals to that in the human animal which enjoys a good fight. Not violence, really, but fast efficient action by competent people who know their jobs, and his knowledge of combat tactics and strategy contributes to believable and exciting reading. *A Spaceship For The King* sends an ex-military man to an alien planet to find the means for achieving a spaceflight, thereby enabling his planet to join a Galactic Empire on an equal footing with the other members. The bulk of the novel is taken up with well described and detailed training and battles using, primarily, Roman Legion tactics. *The Mercenary,* as well as showing a knowledgeable use of tactics and strategy, also concerns political machinations and begins to set up a "future history" of galactic progress. In this history, shortly before the year 2000 a series of treaties between the U.S. and the Soviet Union create the CoDominium and establish world government. Space begins to be settled by voluntary and involuntary colonists, and the colony planets are patrolled by the CoDominium Navy and Marines. At the start of the novel the date is 2085 and nationalism has reared its ugly head on Earth, threatening the CD. Due to having irritated a politician, Colonel John Christian Falkenburg of the CoDominium Marines is "allowed to resign" and the story concerns his continuing efforts to keep the CoDominium from falling apart. This novel sets the scene for what is probably Pournelle's best known work, *The Mote In God's Eye*, a collaboration with Larry Niven. *Mote* is a long novel, a grand space opera about a human expedition sent to the Coalsack Nebula to search for suspected alien intelligence. The protagonists of the book are really a species rather than individuals and the depiction of the alien Moties is intriguing. As both authors are technically oriented, the science is also plausible and innovative.

Other collaborative efforts with Niven have produced *The Inferno*, a retelling of Dante's classic, and *Lucifer's Hammer*. *The Inferno* is about a science fiction writer who goes to Hell, and the tongue-in-cheek treatment, with modern villains and jibes at science fiction writers and fans is fun reading. *Lucifer's Hammer*, more suspense than science fiction, is about the discovery of a meteor on a collision course with Earth, and the aftermath of that collision.

(For those who enjoy Pournelle, try Gordon Dickson or Christopher Anvil.)

FLETCHER PRATT is probably better known in science fiction than he should be—and that is not as unkind a remark as it sounds. His activities in s-f were in great part peripheral, as translator, and as collaborator with Laurence Manning and later, with great success, L. Sprague de Camp. The latter pairing resulted in a series of highly popular fantasies in the 1930s and '40s for the magazine *Unknown*, and they were certainly on that odd borderline between genres. Harold Shea, for instance, in the series which bears his name (*The Incomplete Enchanter*, etc.), is thrown into some wacky fantasy worlds based on Norse myth, Spenser's *Faerie Queene* and such, but the device by which he is thrown is as rational as any used for time travel, space travel, or any of those good old s-f conveyances.

Pratt's line of expertise was American and European military history, in which he had an extremely good reputation. His best solo writings were two fantasy novels of created worlds in which magic works, *The*

Blue Star and *The Well of the Unicorn,* and they are as convincingly presented as any science fictional planet of Clement's or Anderson's. But he has been called "a dilettante author in science fiction" which might well be true. His comparatively few science fiction works saw magazine publication; even fewer made it to book form (one that didn't, for instance, was *The Wanderer's Return,* a short novel attempting to put Homer's *Odyssey* into futuristic terms).

CHRISTOPHER PRIEST, a recent British arrival, has some interesting and remarkably divergent novels to his credit. *Indoctrinaire* postulates a strange encampment deep in the Amazon wastes; a two-century future place into which our protagonist stumbles. Is it physically, or only metaphorically real? In *Fugue for a Darkening Island* Britain of the near future is, like Gaul, divided into three parts by a civil war. *The Inverted World* deals with a very elusive geophysical notion, and Priest's imparting of that concept is not entirely satisfying. The City of Earth must be laboriously moved on a mighty track; it must be moved because the earth, on which Earth moves, is slipping away (rather like the edges of a fish-eye photograph) under stress of ever increasing G forces. Or is it?

Although Priest's work is stylistically traditional and narrative, *The Space Machine* represents a different departure for the writer. Here we are given a Wellsian pastiche, if not parody (and if so, heavy handed), dealing with both a time machine and an alien invasion, a *Martian* invasion. In the sense of the standard yarn, *The Space Machine* passes muster.

Priest's short stories have been collected under the title *Real-Time World.*

(If you like Christopher Priest's books, certainly give those of Michael Moorcock a try.)

MARTA RANDALL is one of the young women writers who are making an impact on contemporary s-f. She has an elegant yet controlled style, and a fine sense of character.

Islands, published in 1976, concerns a mortal woman in a human society that has become immortal. Tia Hamley is, as far as she knows, the only person on earth who is immune to the immortality treatments. She alone of millions has aged, and will die; *Islands* is about her conflict.

Randall builds on Tia's isolation to show the powers of the human mind. Ultimately Tia transcends the physical immortality denied her and achieves that state of free mentality so often heralded as mankind's final evolution, by writers from Stapledon to E. E. Smith to Arthur C. Clarke.

In *Journey* Randall painstakingly chronicles the life of a family, the Kennerins, who have homesteaded the planet Aerie (in this universe, people can own worlds). Aerie has its own sentient species, and with their help Josh, Mish, and their three children are able to live quietly and alone. The novel opens with the arrival of a large group of human refugees, rescued by Josh from their own war-torn planet. Values and customs clash, and the Kennerins are all affected, positively and negatively, by this invasion of their home. *Journey* is a moving, sometimes funny (as the eldest son lives out his space-opera fantasies), blending of s-f and mainstream traditions, drawing on the best of both.

(If you like Marta Randall, we suggest Ursula Le Guin, Joanna Russ, or J. G. Ballard.)

JOHN RANKINE is the pseudonym of Douglas R. Mason, the headmaster of a rural British school. Perhaps in reaction to this, he writes almost classic space opera. Under the Rankine name he has produced a series of books about Dag Fletcher, a brooding, hard driving, and occasionally berserker interplanetary "trouble shooter," reminiscent of James Bond. These include the *Blockage of Sinitron, Interstellar Two-Five,* and *One is One.*

Among his other works is *Binary Z,* where a British headmaster and an English teacher meet and conquer an alien menace. *Binary Z* is primarily remembered for its portrayal of intelligent and sensitive people caught up in red-tape. Rankine also writes the *Space: 1999* series of novelizations.

Under his real name, Rankine has written a number of good short stories, published in U.S. magazines but rarely anthologized.

(If you like Rankine, we suggest E. E. Smith, Zach Hughes, or Eric Frank Russell.)

MACK REYNOLDS displays special knowledge of politics, economics, ancient civilizations and warfare, the stuff of which most of his works are made.

A good many of Reynolds novels are set in a future that is presented from a socio-economic viewpoint and are usually fast action spy or detec-

tive tales evolved within this framework. Don't worry about not understanding the basics of this society. At some point in the novel you will
encounter someone who says something along the lines of, "Say, how
did all this come about, anyway?" And out will pour the history of
Negative Income Tax, trancs, and the Universal Credit Card. The lec-
tures on politico-economic theory and systems are pervasive but don't
really get in the way of the plots concerning underground organizations,
government agents, revolutionaries, and would-be revolutionaries. One
of the stories set in this future is "Time Gladiator," in which a professor
of Etruscan history and ancient warfare enters the national gladiatorial
combats. The nation uses the winners of these competitions as
representatives in any international squabble that may come up, and
after our hero wins there is a flareup that could mean world war. With
plenty of action, and knowledgeable detail of gladiatorial weaponry and
hand-to-hand combat, it's typical of Reynolds' work.

Politics and desert warfare are the elements in the sequential novels
Black Man's Burden, Border, Breed, Nor Birth, and *The Best Ye Breed*
while economics and future warfare are encountered in *Mercenary From
Tomorrow.*

Reynolds slips his tongue into his cheek writing of Section G of
United Planets. In this series humanity has colonized some 3,000
worlds, most of them settled by homogeneous groups representing practically every crackpot idea in the human spectrum. The main job of
United Planets, the organization to which they belong, is to leave them
alone and let them go where they want in their own way. Then evidence
of a war-like alien race is found, and advances in science and technology
are necessary if man is to meet the aliens on an equal footing. Some of
the planetary political and economic systems are not compatible with
progress and so must be overthrown, and Section G comes into being,
staffed by super secret agent/revolutionaries. The worlds visited by these
agents are well constructed, and in this series Reynolds' familiarity with
political structure and revolutionary technique provides the basis for
adventurous escapades.

(If you enjoy Reynolds' work, you might equally enjoy that of Hubbard, Heinlein, and Kornbluth.)

KEITH ROBERTS is another of those articulate, thoughtful, *intelligent* and often poetic contemporary English s-f writers. Nurtured by
several avant-garde British magazines and their venturesome editors,

Roberts soon made his mark in a big way with *Pavane*, a widely read and praised alternate history speculation.

A true tour de force, *Pavane* postulates the assassination of Elizabeth One of England in 1588 and the subsequent victory of the Spanish Armada. (For an English writer this is a painful postulation!) Repressive and absolute church rule slow England's pace, technology is woefully limited, such major progressive thrusts as the Renaissance and the Industrial Revolution don't appear until now—the late 20th century, and by the time of the inquisition and revolution, England is still essentially a primitive country. The revolution's inevitable success leads to a modern age, but the venerable Fairies, ancient spectators, tell of the values gained during the extended feudal period; man has, perhaps, come into his own at a point much farther along the maturity scale, and the pain may have been worth it. *Pavane,* like Roberts' more recent novel *The Chalk Giants,* is actually a kind of mosaic, composed as it is of fragments and short stories which cling together and accumulate, into a whole.

The Chalk Giants is so manufactured of self-intact parts that although the sections are often powerful and memorable, the whole of the novel is difficult to discern. In a post-armageddon civilization, presumably in Britain, Roberts creates various fragmented visions of the future: "The Beautiful One" focuses on feudal anomaly; in "Monkey and Pru and Sal," (previously an effective short story) fascinating and contemporary mutants wander the devastated landscape, and Potts, a kind of modern everyman, weaves through the complex story giving ostensible texture to it. Like many English writers, Roberts is capable of finding and articulating some very *verismo* imaginings for his tales of fear, endurance, beauty, and horror in a world of future madness.

Earlier Roberts' novels are the psi-oriented *The Inner Wheel* (see Theodore Sturgeon's *More Than Human* and Stapledon's *Odd John)* and *The Furies.* Roberts' nuclear short stories are found in *Men and Machines* and *The Passing of the Dragon.*

(Those taken by Keith Roberts' work might try that of M. John Harrison, Christopher Priest, and Ian Watson.)

SPIDER ROBINSON is one of that rare breed—a critic who ventures into his area of criticism. In other words, he was an s-f reviewer who started writing s-f.

Callahan's Crosstime Saloon takes the old and honored device of the many stories emanating from a bar, which has been used even in science fiction several times. (Clarke's White Hart and de Camp and Pratt's Gavagan's are the two most honored bistros in the field.) Robinson's humor, as befits its environment, is on the punny side, and the references are very hip.

Telempath is a post-holocaust novel on an oddly personal level; the hero is out to get the guy who unleashed all the destruction. On the way are speculations on alpha feedback and meditation, and eventually the world gets saved, if not restored.

(Spider Robinson fans might enjoy the works of Harlan Ellison and Norman Spinrad.)

WILLIAM ROTSLER, frequent contributor to and correspondent in various genre fan magazines, has published two novels, the first of which, *Patron of the Arts,* is the considerable expansion of a much talked-of short story. In it the author puts his own interest in the plastic/electronic arts to use, and the *sensatron*-woman he commissions from a famous electronic artist is a fascinating concept. *Patron's* protagonist, a super-wealthy man named Throne, achieves his artifact—or is it a woman in fact?—only to have both artist and art vanish. Thorne chases, finds himself the target of killers on Mars. Hugger-mugger and tumult decorate the escapade. In his second novel, *To the Land of the Electric Angel,* a world famous architect is hired to design a tomb for an unimaginably rich eccentric, Voss. Voss and his lover, Rio, enter the hidden tomb, intent on travelling to the future where their temporal problems will be obviated. Unwanted by Voss, the architect sneaks along for the time/travel ride and they all debouch into a future of civil and religious strife. Naturally, they become involved, with Voss on the bad guy side and architect/hero and pulchritudinous Rio on the other.

Rotsler writes with a kind of chic and trendy literateness, and his books are chock-full of nifty moments and witty conceits, even when they suffer near-collapse from unthoughtout structure.

(If you like William Rotsler you might try Harlan Ellison, Alfred Bester, and Ed Bryant.)

JOANNA RUSS is a speculator in human nature, who peers unflinchingly into the depths of the human soul, then makes you laugh when she rubs your psyche with sand paper. People are her concern: how they behave, why they do what they do, and how they got that way. She twists time honored plots and devices to her own use, and pokes not-so-gentle fun at much of establishment s-f.

The first of Russ' Alyx stories appeared in 1967; bored by the typical muscle-bound sword and sorcery heros (see Robert E. Howard's Conan) she gave us a heroine. Alyx is covered with scars, fast on her feet, good with a sword—a thief, a mercenary, a murderess...in short, all that a great hero should be. Her adventures are good reading, and not nearly as simplistic as those of her brothers at arms.

The short stories were followed by a novel, *Picnic on Paradise*, which features Alyx as lead character. *Picnic* is pure s-f, despite Alyx's genesis in sword and sorcery. A group of tourists vacationing on a planet called Paradise are caught up in a corporate war, and someone has to lead them overland to an evacuation point. Alyx is pulled in by the Trans Temporal Corporation (a sort of free-lance time patrol) to do the job. Out of this plot Russ succeeds in developing a biting narrative about civilized people confronting the realities of a primitive culture they profess to admire.

In *And Chaos Died* Russ examines psi powers, and their probable effect on a human being who suddenly acquired them. This book was followed by *The Female Man*, a time spanning, dimension-hopping exploration of the female condition. The heroines, Janet, Jeannine, Joanna, and Alice explore the attitudes of their various worlds and times, sometimes together and sometimes separately. The book is a challenge to many accepted s-f conventions, and has inspired both acclaim and revulsion. These reactions to *The Female Man* are typical of public response to Joanna Russ' work. It is perhaps a tribute to her skill in making the unthinkable real, the impossible all too immediate. Readers either love her or hate her, but are never, never bored.

(If you like Joanna Russ, we suggest Samuel R. Delany, Vonda K. McIntyre, or James Tiptree, Jr.)

ERIC FRANK RUSSELL has created some of the most endearing of aliens in science fiction. The influence of Stanley Weinbaum is evident in many of his short stories, especially "The Prr-r-eet," about a being named for the sound it makes. (As a note of interest, the Prr-r-eet's parting gift to Earth was a color/sound musical instrument. The idea for this instrument was supplied by one Arthur C. Clarke and the 10% commission was the first money Clarke earned from science fiction.) Russell enables the reader to empathize with his aliens to such an extent that you generally want to take them home for a glass of milk and some cookies. "Dear Devil" is one of his most lovable creatures, a Martian poet who is voluntarily stranded on a post-holocaust Earth, who helps the shattered remnants of humanity on the return road to civilization and to the stars. Another is Maeth, "The Witness" on trial for illegal entry to Earth. The prosecutor paints a picture of an evil spy in advance of an enemy horde. Things look bad for Maeth until the defense attorney brings out the fact that this monstrosity is actually a frightened little girl heroically escaping a totalitarian society. There is also an intriguing example of an alien/human symbiotic relationship.

Strangely enough, Russell, though having created some very nice people "out there," is perhaps best known for his novel *Sinister Barrier*, which advances Charles Fort's idea that "We are property." The masters in this case are the Vitons, floating globes that feed on the nervous energy of their human cattle. The frightening thing about the story is that Russell uses common inexplicable occurences as evidence of the Viton infestation, and one again begins to wonder if we are alone on our planet.

Another facet of Russell's work is evident in at least one short story and two novels: Terran chauvinism and clever maneuvering abound in "Diabologic," in which an Earth scout confounds aliens with questions such as "If a planet has a southern hemisphere of water, and a northern of land, is the water a lake? or is the land an island?"; *Space Willies* has as its hero a human POW who confounds his alien captors with an invisible, omnipotent doppelganger, contacted through a block of wood and a twist of wire; *Wasp* ponders the question, "If a little wasp can cause a huge human to lose control and wreck a car, what might one human do to a huge enemy culture?" This is a fast paced action story with secret agent James Mowry reducing an entire planet to utter confusion.

Russell wrote from the '30s through the 60s'; the style may be a bit dated, but there's a warmth and humanity in his writing that's worth experiencing.

(Try the works of John Rankine and Stanley Weinbaum if you enjoy those of Eric Frank Russell.)

FRED SABERHAGEN is best known to s-f readers for his bizarre Berserker stories, and the novels which grew from them: *Brother Berserker* and *Berserker's Planet*. Berserk, from the old Norse, means bear-skin, a concept remote from Saberhagen's enormous, solid-state, robotic, one-track-minded monstrosities, productions of a nuts-and-bolts culture and dedicated to the extermination of all sentient, organic being in the universe, and beyond. And somewhere there are still some omniscient and pacific, not to mention elusive people who don't care for the situation. Filled with E. E. Smith-like tempestuousness *and* periodic enlightening reflections on the nature of conflict, Saberhagen's Berserker books offer more than merely diverting space opera.

In other novels and stories Saberhagen tends toward indulgences in the quasi-occult and wooly, though his extrapolations of incredibly far future times in *The Changeling Earth,* with science obviated and magic everyday, are fascinatingly thought out.

(Saberhagen admirers might equally enjoy Alan Dean Foster.)

MARGARET ST. CLAIR has been writing s-f since the '40s; in fact she has had two careers as an s-f writer. The first was under her own name, beginning in Thrilling Wonder Stories and continuing to the present. The second was as Idris Seabright, a regular contributor to *The Magazine of Fantasy and Science Fiction* after its birth in 1949. As Idris Seabright she wrote some of the most interesting non-technical science adventures of the period. Idris faded away, leaving Margaret to her technical stories and periodic novels.

Sign of the Labrys tells of a group of super-normal people who are able to survive a massive plague which destroys most of humanity. This book has an underground setting which is postively Dantesque and which rivals the Kuttner/Moore offerings of the same sort. *The Dancers of Noyo* is extrapolated for the communal movement so prevalent in America of the '60s, with the added seasoning of cloned androids who are very near to seizing control of the Earth.

In *The Dolphins of Altair* she presents a cogent argument for the full sentiency of dolphins, and makes some frightening suppositions about the repercussions of treating our intellectual equals as beasts.

St. Clair's '40s roots are clearly visible in her style and approach; here is idea fiction, not searching psychological probes.

(If you enjoy her work, we suggest Asimov, Campbell, McCaffrey, or Mitchison.)

PAMELA SARGENT taught philosophy at the university level, but her stories are hardly what one would call academic. She is one of the younger writers whose concerns are character and human behavior. She writes of men and women placed in extreme positions by social or technical changes: an American culture hideously overcrowded, with several rationed medical facilities dispensed by black market doctors, or the effect on the psyche when not-quite-eternal-youth suddenly gives way to senility, or when one is able to visit dead loved ones in the past. Her novel, *Cloned Lives* (despite a title irresistibly reminiscent of a future soap opera), is an extension of this, a study of the first "family" of clones, four male, one female, at various stages of their lives.

(In different ways, McCaffrey and Randall might be enjoyed by Sargent readers.)

JAMES H. SCHMITZ. A salient characteristic of Schmitz' work is the warmth and likability of his characters. This is best illustrated in the novel *Witches of Karres,* in which an interplanetary trader rescues three young ladies from slavery and takes them to their home planet, Karres. The three ladies, Goth, Maleen, and the Leewit (not Leewit, *the* Leewit), and indeed all the natives of Karres, are witches, or at least have powers resembling witchcraft. After leaving the three at home, and then being kicked off his own planet, trader Pausert and stowaway Goth proceed on a grand tour of the Empire, running into vatches, Worm Weather, klatha hooks, and a universe that needs saving.

Witches, and his Vegan novels, *A Tale Of Two Clocks* and *Agent Of Vega*, demonstrate another of his specialties; well developed and detailed use of extra-sensory phenomena. In the Vegan tales especially, ESP is used as a common and necessary aspect of police procedure.

Telzey Amberdon, heroine of *The Universe Against Her,* is typical of all Schmitz' female characters; strong, competent, and fun to be with. An interesting aspect of this is the fact that these stories were written before feminism made it literarily necessary to treat women as people. Telzey runs rampant in two other novels, *The Telzey Toy* and *The Lion Game.*

(If you like Schmitz' work, try reading Edgar Pangborn or Andre Norton.)

THOMAS SCORTIA is primarily a mainstream author who in every few stories uses the science fiction genre. Scortia is a talented writer whose technical skills are finely honed, with intensely well developed characters and situations the result of his facility with words, moods, and ideas.

Artery Of Fire is a tense suspense novel about Norman Bayerd, a man who will give up almost all he has to see a new power source for Earth through to completion. When time is warped, and strange horrifying occurrences begin on Earth, Bayerd must face hostility from the world and doubt within himself. Scortia concocts a taut, complex story of human ambitions and emotions.

His varied skills are even more evident in *Caution Inflammable,* a collection of twenty short and very short storeis on topics ranging from a Phoenix who needs a little help with his pyrotechnics to a woman with the perfect man. The gamut of human emotion and frailty is explored in this collection; there's the happy and humorous "The Icebox Blonde" and the tender and touching "When You Hear The Tone."

Although there's not a great emphasis on the s in Scortia's s-f, the f is very well done, with detailed characterization and high emotional content.

(For those who enjoy skillful writing such as Scortia's, try Theodore Sturgeon or Alfred Bester.)

RICHARD SHAVER was an extraordinary phenomenon, the skeleton in science fiction's closet. In the fragile interface between s-f and UFOology, believers in Atlantis rising again, and chariot-borne extraterrestrial gods, Shaver and his editor (for *Amazing Stories*), Ray Palmer, were alone successful in confusing the two. In the mid-'40s, Palmer published a story by Shaver called "I Remember Lemuria." In a series of following stories, he enlarged on his theme: that Earth had long ago been inhabited by humanoid aliens, who abandoned the planet when the rays of the Sun became poisonous; that in networks of caverns below the surface the machines of these superhumans lay abandoned, but were manipulated by degenerate remnants of their race and evil humans; and that these machines broadcast rays that influenced surface life, i.e. us.

Now this was calculated to appeal to every paranoid who suspected that the guy in the downstaris apartment was doing him in with a death ray. The letters columns of *Amazing* were truly amazing for the length of the "Shaver mystery" (about two years), and circulation for the magazine shot up. But the science fiction community was outraged, and both Palmer and Shaver moved on to other fields.

The stories themselves were quite intriguing; Shaver had created an underground "world" in contact with other worlds of our Solar System that had a great deal of depth (as it were). There were indications that he had read his Burroughs, as in his novel *Gods of Venus* which had some strong plot resemblances to ERB's *Gods of Mars,* but there are worse models for successful pulp writing. And the "mystery's" popularity wasn't hindered by a strongly raunchy element (raunchy, that is, for a pulp magazine of that period) centering around the use of "stim rays" which bore a surprising kinship to current experiments with electrodes feeding pleasure centers in anthropoid brains.

It was fun while it lasted. None of Shaver's work is available at this time; some enterprising editor might just look into it.

BOB SHAW's novels have several odd qualities. One is that in some indiscernable way, they read more like mysteries than s-f. Another is their similarity to the books of Philip K. Dick, except that Shaw's are rational, at least within their own frame of reference.

In *Other Days, Other Eyes,* "slow glass" is inadvertently invented. Slow glass, depending on its thickness and its programming, retains light and slowly transmits it at a delay; on it everything can be replayed. Criminal mischief, delay-sight for the blind, observation of enemies, etc., are some of its dubious uses. The effects of the use of this one-shot gimmick on various and sundry topics provide the impersonal narrative. *A Wreath of Stars* features an antineutrino planet named Thornton's which passes close to Earth and goes away. Yet, something has happened and alien curiosities appear on Earth, ominous portents of disaster to come. When matter and anti-matter meet...

Ground Zero Man is something of a caveat about man's enduring compulsion to be lethal. A man with a device invented expressly for the purpose of destroying all atomic weapons does it, and finds, philosophically, that nonnuclear weapons quickly continue the wars. In the long run Shaw seems to suggest that the plenitude of man makes him disposable in large numbers, and wars will continue.

(As suggested above, those who like Shaw's work might like that of Philip K. Dick.)

ROBERT SHECKLEY is hip and glib as he paints a cynical, comical portrait of the human condition, past, present and future.

Immortality, Inc. (1959) is a trip through Sheckley's future as seen by Thomas Blaine, a 20th-century man snatched from the past as a part of an ad campaign. The world Blaine finds is violent, avaricious and fast paced; he can barely function in it. *Journey Beyond Tomorrow* is similar in style and content, but has even more *Candide*-ish overtones.

Perhaps best known of Sheckley's novels is *The 10th Victim*, where people register in the planet-wide "lottery," alternately being hunter and hunted in a contest of assassination. Anyone who survives ten hunts becomes a grand prize winner. *The 10th Victim* was made into an excellent s-f film.

Sheckley's other novels and all of his short stories expound the same idiosyncratic world view. As a satirist he is unique, but he may not be everyone's cup of tea.

(If you enjoy Sheckley, we also recommend Ron Goulart, Frederic Brown, and Philip Farmer.)

MARY SHELLEY. Hail, Mary, Mother of science fiction, whose pioneering efforts are treated at greater length in "The Spawn of Frankenstein" chapter. Here we are concerned with her work, and can truly say that it, along with Olaf Stapledon, is the *sine qua non* of familiarity with science fiction and its sources. *Frankenstein* is still a marvelously readable book (expect for some rather tedious travel sections) and provides a suitable antidote to the numerous cinematic variations on the theme (excellent films though some of them are).

Ms. Shelley's other works of science fiction, *The Last Man*, suffers from a larger theme that concerns itself with such things as the abolition of the English monarchy as well as the survival of one man in a world stricken by plague in the 21st century. Nonetheless, it too sets a seminal situation that has been used as often as that of the creation of life.

One can't help but wonder what Ms. Shelley would think if confronted with today's science fiction. Faced with Ursula Le Guin and Perry Rhodan, Barsoon and the Foundations, *Star Trek* and *Star Wars*, she might well feel she had helped loose a monster more awesome than Victor's.

ROBERT SILVERBERG has written over twenty-eight s-f novels in less than twenty years, and an uncountable number of short stories. Since the authors of this book are not being paid by the word, no useful purpose would be served by listing the titles. Most of Silverberg's early work (from 1957 to 1965) in good adventurous spaceyarn, marked by a flair for catching characters and making them real. One of his books, *Recalled to Life*, gave notice to the world of what Silverberg would be capable of in later years; it is a complex, moving, and thoughtful book about the discovery of a technique for restoring life to the dead. Silverberg is careful to examine all the implications of such a discovery, and raises questions about life and death which had not been asked before.

In the late '60s his breakneck writing pace slowed to the rate of about one novel a year; the quality of his work benefited considerably. *Nightwings* won a Hugo award and was nominated for a Nebula; it is a sweeping novel which chronicles the future of Earth as seen by an alien race. These beings are first conquered by man, then rise to free themselves and in truth conquer Earth. *Tower of Glass* is a religious parable and social critique: a wealthy man invents androids and the androids make him their god. The androids eventually discover that their god is only human and in their anger and disillusionment revolt against all mankind.

Dying Inside, published in 1972, is the engrossing and sometimes painful story of a telepath. His life is one of voyeurism and cynical opportunism, until his power begins to fade away. Telepathy has been the subject of many an s-f novel, but no one has framed a more powerful work around it.

In *A Time of Changes* Silverberg retells the old totalitarian nightmare, a culture which denigrates and finally denies the individual. In this one though, the changes that occur aren't toward rugged egoism, but to an understanding of the self, and a sharing with others. *The Book of Skulls* is a portrait in microcosm of lust and greed. Four men set out together to seek immortality; in the end they discover that two may possess it, but only if the other two sacrifice their own lives.

Silverberg, a man of seemingly infinite energy, also edits anthologies; more than that, he *crafts* anthologies. He was responsible for the *New Dimensions* series, which has published an astonishing number of stories which subsequently won awards. He also edited the *Science Fiction Hall of Fame*, an anthology of the best (according to the Science Fiction Writers of America) short stories published before 1965.

(If you like Robert Silverberg's work, we suggest Fred Pohl or John Brunner.)

CLIFFORD D. SIMAK was born and raised on a farm in Wisconsin, and the basic life he led there affects almost all of his writing. His characters are generally simple, sure of themselves and of their beliefs, and there is a sense of optimism and love of living beings inherent in his writing.

When Simak's name is mentioned *City* almost immediately springs to mind. A series of short stories published in the magazines *Astounding* and *Fantastic Adventures* from 1943 to 1951, and collected in 1952 as a "novel," it's best dipped into intermittently. The stories are related as fables and ancient legends of the civilization of dogs that has succeeded the race of man on Earth. All of the tales are well told, the feelings ranging from chilling to almost humorous, and "The Huddling Place" is a particularly poignant story of a man unable to leave his familiar surroundings, even to save the life of a friend. *City* won the International Fantasy Award in 1952 for Best Novel.

In 1959 Simak received his first Hugo Award for the novelette "The Big Front Yard," a delightful story about antique dealer and repairman, Hiram Taine, who discovers his front yard is now another planet, due to an alien space warp: Hiram's dealing with the aliens is a lovely picture of the country bumpkin outsmarting the city slickers.

A sense of mysticism is quite prevalent in a lot of Simak's work, sometimes leading to pure fantasy. Leaving these works aside, there are still some borderline stories, such as *Goblin Reservation* in which dwarves, banshees, and trolls abound, but which is also legitimate science fiction. Mysticism is also the basis for *Time And Again,* a complex and well written novel about a man who finds that "nothing is alone" in the universe; that there is something akin to a soul for every man, woman, animal, and android. Time travel, philosophy, and a richness of descriptive detail make it extremely satisfying.

Simak scored another Hugo in 1964 for the novel *Way Station.* A quitely moving and beautiful work, it tells the story of Enoch Wallace, human keeper of an intergalactic depot and stopover for alien travellers. *Way Station* is a simple story, infused with the basic strength of the land, from which its characters and values spring. Ever present is Simak's love of life, be it human or alien.

Simak at his best is among the best in science fiction, skillfully depicting people, places, and ideas, and at the heart of his work an abiding warmth and optimism.

(For those among you who like Simak, the works of Zenna Henderson and Theodore Sturgeon are suggested.)

JOHN SLADEK is an indescribable writer of indecipherably mad stories. His work is that of a prose comic—sometimes grotesque—and his imagination is antic. *The Muller-Fokker Effect* is an insanely complex, fragmentary, fractured story having to do with a man who manipulates a TV soaper, altering its nature completely. Some computer tapes, on which is stored the persona of a character from the soaper, get mislaid and perpetrate a number of grotesque scenes, including one which fouls the military as they try to contain a fascist demonstration in Washington. This is one of those everything-but-the-kitchen-sink affairs, capricious and disjointed, but with a curious sense of interior logic.

In *Mechasm* Sladek's powers as a parodist (he had published a number of mini-parodies of well-known s-f writers in *The Steam Driven-Boy & Other Strangers*) take on some of the more cherished concepts of mankind on the move: a super animated, programmed living body gone haywire, but *then* subdued to serve all of the menial requirements of civilization. Science (in upper case) is the true messiah, and if left to its own device will bring peace and plenty and passivity. The author has fun puncturing such balloons, and he has a field day with style and form, too.

(If the wonderful madness of John Sladek appeals try, obliquely, Thomas M. Disch.)

CLARK ASHTON SMITH might have been startled at his inclusion here. His strongest efforts had been expended toward poetry, and had included translations and paraphrases from Baudelaire, Verlaine and other French symbolists as well as original work which ranged from some of the earliest experiments in English-language *haiku* to the most elaborately phrased lushly-imaged verse ("Bow down: I am the emperor of dreams;/I crown me with the million-colored sun....").

The very elaborateness of his language may have precluded his acceptance as a major poet in a time when the art was turning elsewhere. But it did not detract from the popularity of his stories, most of which—about a hundred—where published in less than a decade (from 1929 to about 1937) in *Weird Tales*. He is another of those writers from that time and that place whose work crossed the boundaries from science fiction to the horrifically fantastic. Smith, H. P. Lovecraft, and Robert Howard were the three great names to emerge from that period; it is generally acknowledged that Smith was the best writer of the three.

Most of the short stories (there were no novels) fall into one of several cycles: of Hyperborea, a pre-ice-age continent; of Poseidonis, "the last isle of foundering Atlantis"; of Zothique, the final continent of a senile Earth, where magic has replaced science. Two take place on the planet

Xiccarph; several on Mars

Only some of the above really qualify as s-f, and expect no hard science here. The future or another world were simply exotic places where Smith could place his highly colored visions, of vampiric flower women preyed upon by intelligent reptiles, of another-dimensional city containing a singing flame which consumes pilgrims from many worlds, of formless masses that repose amid the slime and vapors of a young Earth. It's certainly not to everyone's taste, all very hothouse and opium eaterish and *fin-de-siecle,* but there's nothing else quite like it, and his influence on Lovecraft, Howard, and some of his major contemporary writers in unmistakable.

(If you like Clark Ashton Smith, the closest thing is the early stories of C. L. Moore; also, of course, check out Lovecraft.)

CORDWAINER SMITH. No one else in the science fiction field writes at all like Cordwainer Smith. His tales of a far future when the planets are rules by an "Instrumentality" of Lords and Ladies, while a great religious and social conspiracy of surgically altered half-men takes place in dim, twisted corridors beneath their feet, are as strange, as haunting and often as lovely as the most important myths and fairy tales of our collective heritage. His stories are all connected, a legendary cycle of the future; he has chosen to tell them in the manner of an adult explaining history to a child in terms of fantasies (in the way that our earliest, most magical stories have been passed on to us).

Smith's real name was Paul Linebarger. He was brought up in cities all over the world, spent a good deal of time in China as a young man, and in Australia when he was older. His profession was that of a propagandist, and he was extremely good at it, a fact which may startle readers impressed with the tenderness of his writing.

A very few of Smith's stories have never been published in book form, but most of them are in three volumes, *You Will Never Be the Same, Stardreamer,* and *Space Lords.* In addition there is a novel, *Norstrilia,* which is also, confusingly, published in halves as *The Planet Buyer* and *The Underpeople.* (The one volume edition is the better, telling the story as the author intended it.) Finally, four collected novellas about an adventurer named Casher O'Neill make up *The Quest for Three Worlds.*

People who get hooked on Smith can spend endless hours tracing the interconnected personal histories of the characters of his intensely believable far future, the final and most glorious part of which takes place about A.D. 15,000 at the time of the Rediscovery of Man and the Emancipation of the Underpeople. But ever casual readers can fall for C'mell, the brave and beautiful cat-girl who is the heroine of *Norstrilia* and the short stories "The Ballad of Lost C'mell" and "Alpha-Ralpha Boulevard." The retelling of the Joan of Arc story in "The Dead Lady of Clown Town" is deeply touching, as is the entire saga of the struggle for equality of the "underpeople" or modified human-animals which is threaded through all these later stories. But there is wit and gaiety and lyricism here too.

Just as Smith's plots and worlds and characters don't echo anyone else's, his prose, too, is unique. It uses rhyme, repetition, refrain, alliteration, anything to underline the charmed, legendary quality. If it works for you, you'll go half mad until you can find out what actually happens at the Department Store of Heart's Desire, or what the Abba-Dingo will say to you, or how to pinlight a space dragon or how to make sure a sick sheep will stay just sick enough. What's more, not in Dante nor in the Bible nor the paintings of Bosch will you ever find a description of a believable Hell as truly chilling as that of "A Planet Named Shayol."

(To make the point yet again, there's nobody quite like Cordwainer Smith in s-f. But if intelligence and style appeal to you, try Le Guin and Vance.)

E. E. SMITH, Ph.D. appeared to an astonished world in 1928, when his first book, *The Skylark of Space*, began serialization in *Amazing*. "Doc" Smith is the inventor of Space Opera, and its quintessential practitioner. His books are grandiose, galaxy-spanning, filled to bursting with ideas and inventions, yet have a human touch.

The "Doc" Smith style almost defies description. The world's greatest physicist, a brilliant and highly educated man, is called Blackie, and talks like a refugee from Al Capone's gang. A searching comment on human nature (and alien nature as well) is summed up as "You can't tell how far a flea will jump by looking at him." Smith's heroes whisper endearments to their beloweds like "you square little brick," and break up romantic clinches to discuss the latest inventions.

Smith's heroes and heroines are larger than life, noble to the point of nausea, hard driving, tough brawling, brilliant inventors, and totally unflappable in the face of ther most outre developments. And while Smith's imitators concentrated on the adolescent male's fantasies and left their women to be rescued and admired, Smith himself never denigrated the female. In fact, he went so far as to admit that there were things that women could do that men couldn't possibly manage. Clio Marsden at 19 was more than a match for the evil alien Gharlane.

The vast majority of Smith's books fall into two series, the Skylark books and the Lensmen series. Of the two, the Lensmen group is the largest in scope and concept.

The first in the series, *Triplanetary,* begins with a recap of the collision between our galaxy and another. During this interaction, all of the planets in both were formed, and two races met for the first time. One, inhabitants of the planet Arisia, was composed of disembodied intelligences, civilized, and the good guys. The others, of the planet Eddore, were from another dimension, and were the nastiest, slimiest, most thoroughly rotten beings ever imagined. The Eddorians decided to move into our Galaxy and take over. The Arisians decided that they shouldn't do that; thus battle is met, and continues throughout the entire series.

The Arisians, in their wisdom, cause humanity to be born, and nurture it to the point where Virgil Samms is capable of going to Arisia to receive the Lens, an device which enables him to use his latent ESP. Samms is to form a coterie of Lensmen, drawn from every planet and race in the Galaxy; this group is dedicated to the eradication of all that Eddore represents. And that's just the first book!

The series continues through six more books, until ultimately, in *Children of the Lens,* the five kids (four girls and one boy) of two Second Stage Lensmen are able to defeat Eddore and take over from the Arisians in guiding the course of civilization in two galaxies. In between are such stirring moments as when Kimball Kinneson becomes a junkie to infiltrate an interstellar drug-dealing ring; the time when the Lensmen arranged for two planets to be used as a nutcracker to destroy the enemy's base; and contact with innumerable alien races and cultures. This series is F-U-N, Fun.

The skylark series is smaller in concept but just as far-ranging. The Skylark itself is a spaceship, crewed by four of the greatest minds our race has produced. These four are locked in monumental battle with "Blackie" DuQuesne, the other greatest mind the race has produced, but, alas, inclined to evil, exploitation, and dope-pushing. (Smith really had a thing about drugs.) Surprisingly, Blackie DuQuesne was the one who became the most popular with readers, and in the last book Smith reformed him and inducted him into the Skylark's crew.

Spacehounds of IPC is about a boy and girl marooned on Ganymede, which is populated with man-eating plants, has air and water, and is not all that bad a place. They eventually repair their spaceship and manage to make first contact with the natives of Jupiter. Other novels not connected with any series are *Subspace Explorers* and *The Galaxy Primes.*

After Smith's death in 1965 notes were found which outlined yet another "Doc" Smith series. This was set in a decadent solar system of the future, and was about a circus family, the D'Alemberts, who were also secret agents. The Family D'Alembert series is being written from those notes by Stephen Goldin, and is worth looking in on.

No one in his right mind would call Doc Smith a great writer; he was naive, sloppy, totally innocent of the concept of plot, and caught in the trap of having to top his latest effect in order to maintain the tension of his books. But for sheer gorgeous adventure, and a return to the innocence of another era, Smith can't be beat

(If you enjoy E. E. Smith, we suggest van Vogt, Ed Hamilton, John Rankine, Bill Starr, or Leigh Brackett.)

GEORGE O. SMITH, an author of the "Golden Age" of science fiction, wrote a lot for *Astounding Magazine* under John W. Campbell, and that meant science; detailed and plausible extrapolation of the current state-of-the-art. Drawing on his background as an electronics engineer, Smith was equal to the task, and produced one of the semi-classics of the genre, *Venus Equilateral,* a collection of ten stories that appeared in the magazine from 1942 through 1945. The basis of the stories is the assumption that communication between planets is impossible when the sun is interposed, and the triangle of the title is a communications system set up to overcome this situation. The ten tales concern the science involved in these stations, and the psychology and politics of their operators.

Though all of his stories have a sound scientific base, hard science is not always the central concern. Legal and social implications of educational enhancement are considered in *The Brain Machine* (also titled *The Fourth R),* a suspenseful tale of a child genius tangling with adults in general and the bad guys in particular. *Troubled Star* is the tale of three aliens searching for Earth's leader. The man they settle on as foremost in the population's mind is Dusty Britton of the Space Patrol. What the three don't know is that Dusty is really a TV and film actor and wouldn't know an asteriod if it bit him. It's basic mistaken identity romantic comedy and a lot of fun.

Path Of Unreason, a novel of super-science with a plot comparable to those of A. E. van Vogt (read thoughtfully complex or tremendously confused, depending on your taste), seems to be a simple "The aliens are taking over, why won't anybody believe me?" type thing, but what develops is a thought-provoking consideration of the lengths to which a scientist must go in search of knowledge. If the answer to a problem lies outside the realm of a person's reason and sanity, how does he find that answer? This consideration would seem to apply even more strongly to some of today's theories of modern physics than to the science of the day in which it was written.

Smith is first and foremost a *science* fiction writer with more interest in technology than character, but he supplies plenty of adventure and suspense 'twixt the electrons.

(If you like George O. Smith, try John W. Campbell and A. Bertram Chandler.)

NORMAN SPINRAD is an outrageous writer whose books and short stories have shocked a lot of people. The fact is, he's such a good writer (craftsman, technician, what-have-you) that the violence, sex, and taboo-breaking aren't obtrusive or gratuitous. *The Men in the Jungle* is about futuresque guerilla warfare and what it does to the "civilized" types fighting it. Published in 1967, it is anti-war with a vengeance.

Bug Jack Barron gained its reputation for its sex scenes but should be remembered for its comment on media-hype, a phenomenon with which we are becoming all too familiar. It concerns a TV star who battles and connives his way to the Presidency; Jack Barron is a sheep in wolf's clothing who transforms, and is transformed by, the world he inhabits.

In *The Iron Dream* Spinrad plays with alternate time lines. *The Iron Dream* is a re-titling of *The Lord of the Swastika,* written by that noted American s-f writer Adolf Hilter, whose power fantasies and space opera have entralled a generation of fans. It should be noted that Spinrad did such a good job on this one that people constantly come into the Science Fiction Shop asking for Hitler's other s-f books.

(If you like Spinrad, we suggest Harlan Ellison or Samuel Delany.)

BRIAN STABLEFORD is a slight paradox in science fiction. Most continuing series of novels tend to be lighter reading, with the emphasis on plot and action, and little style or characterization. Stableford, however, in the "Grainger" series offers well developed characters, new concepts, and a well constructed milieu in which they are met. Grainger is shipwrecked in *The Halycyon Drift* and before being rescued is "joined" by a mind parasite. Part of the quality and wonder of this series is Grainger's gradual acceptance of the parasite and the relationship between the two which develops from parasitic to symbiotic. (It's important to read this series in sequence, starting with *The Halycyon Drift* so you know what's going on and where this strange voice keeps coming from.)

Another series by Stableford follows the mission of the laboratory ship *Daedalus*. Set in a future where Earth has sent colonies to space, but then drawn back and abandoned space travel and exploration, the premise of the series is that the human race cannot just go out and live on a planet. Stableford treats the planet as one ecological system and the colony as another; the *Daedalus* is an ecology lab and its mission is to journey to several colonies that were established one hundred years in the past and render help, if necessary, to the colonists. The primary protagonist of this series is Alexis Alexander, ecologist and the narrator of the stories. The interaction of the crew, the problems of political versus scientific expediency, and the personal ideological contrasts, while well developed, are only part of the whole. Stableford is one of the first writers to treat ecology as a viable rational science, and since one of the delights of science fiction is the peripheral knowledge one picks up, his opening up a whole new field of speculation is quite exciting. He details complex interactions between planetary and colony ecosystems, and sets up fascinating problems in need of solution.

Stableford is also the author of a third series (the Dies Irae trilogy), and several novels, all of them characterized by meticulous attention to the details of character development and science, and usually innovative in thought.

(Those who like Stableford's various series might look into those of Piers Anthony.)

OLAF STAPLEDON is the literary and philosophical heir to H. G. Wells. The general opinion of those who know both men's work is that the younger outstripped the older in both fields. Stapledon took the respected English tradition, perfected and popularized by Wells, of using speculative fiction to express philosophical and moral views, and raised it to such dizzyingly transcendent heights, showing us such cosmic visions, that no one has dared to try to outreach him since.

Stapledon was an academic; a Doctor of Philosophy, a lecturer on philosophy and psychology, and a prolific writer, mostly on philosophy and to advance the cause of socialism (another link with Wells). Fairly late in his career, in 1930 when he was forty-four, he published the first of four major works of "science fiction" (for at least two of which the word *novel* is a misnomer); there were also several shorter works that qualify.

Wells had written a "future history," *The Shape of Things to Come*, that took humanity into the 21st century. Stapledon's *Last and First Men* follows man and his descendents for *two billion years* and through eighteen species of mankind. He begins in the early 20th century, and his view of the immediate future is not accurate, of course. Nevertheless, it provides a sort of alternate path to a point that is very likely indeed, the ultimate confrontation of America and China as the two major powers of the Earth. He goes on with the Americanization of the planet, and the fall of the first men (us) through the total depletion of natural resources (this was published in 1930, mind you): second man arises after a dark age of ten million years; he is a vastly superior species, but is almost wiped out in a war with the inhabitants of Mars. (The Martians here are about 100 times as believable as Mr. Wells' work; in fact, they are among the most reasonably created examples of Martians in the entire literature. Stapledon was well up on the scientific theories of his day, as well as having a brilliant talent for extrapolation, that quality so necessary to the s-f writer.)

In the rise and fall of 18 species, the variety and invention never flag. As cosmic catastrophe strikes, man moves first to Venus, then Neptune, each time being crippled as a species by the demands of the transfer. We learn that the book is being dictated to our time by a member of the last species, who have mastered a form of time travel. Last man is facing an inescapable catastrophe; the final pages of *Last and First Men* are almost unbearable tragedy.

Is there any possible way to top this? Yes, as a matter of fact, in *Star Maker* Stapledon charts and chronicles the Universe; the vast span of *Last and First Men* is reduced to a pinpoint on the time scale of *Star Maker*. Approach these two books with care; reading them can give you an individual sense of inferiority that is hard to shake.

The other two major novels are indeed novels; in them Stapledon very specifically adopts that viewpoint that was so generally effective in the "histories," a viewpoint outside of mankind which regards humanity fondly but not very happily. In *Odd John,* the outside view is that of a young Englishman who is in reality the next genetic step beyond man. The novel is a biography of John, who at one point says that living in a world of men is for him like a normal man living in a world of monkeys. We follow him through his awakening to his own being, and his search for others of his kind, sometimes tragic when he finds some who are failed mutations, sometimes successful. In the finale, Stapledon again achieves true tragedy in a classic sense of a being undone by his innate nature.

In *Sirius,* the outside view is this time that of a dog who has been artificially raised to human intelligence. Whether Sirius, with his canine body and senses and human emotions and awareness, or John, with his human and superhuman qualities, is the greater achievement of creation of character is hard to say. But never before and seldom since has science fiction had such memorable "people."

The idea of the next evolutionary step above man has been used again and again, but never with such verismilitude. And the two "histories" have within them the seeds of half the science fictional concepts "invented" since. Ironically, Stapledon apparently did not even know of the existence of s-f as a genre until introduced to it in 1936. But if there is one author, a knowledge of whose works is basic to appreciating the field, it is Olaf Stapledon.

(One hesitates to mention any other author in the same breath with Stapledon, but his philosophical acumen is, of course, akin to Wells. Thematically, one might seek out the variations on the *Odd John* theme by Weinbaum, van Vogt, and Sturgeon, respectively.)

BILL STARR, "They just don't make space opera like that any more." This plaint, which can be heard among veteran science fiction readers, is almost true. But Starr manages to come awfully close to the tried and true formula. Heroic heroes, far-flung adventure, marvels of science, and strange cultures make up the fabric of the classics of this sub-genre and Starr's novels, *The Way to Dawnworld* and *The Treasure of Wonderwhat,* are cut from the same cloth.

The Way to Dawnworld is the story of Dawnboy, brave in the clan MacCochise on the planet Apache Highlands, and his "long-lost" father Ranger Farstar. Farstar and his wife Gayheart, after leaving Dawnboy in the care of his maternal grandmother, hit the star trail in search of adventure and trade. In an accident in space Gayheart is killed and after many years Farstar returns to Apache Highlands to try to convince his son to follow with him the path of an interstellar trader. They set out to find that dream of any space trader, an undiscovered habitable planet, theirs for the selling. Woven into this plot we find the planets Newtonia, seat of scientific discovery, and Capitalia, business capital of the galaxy, political factions, and memorable characters. Starr uses the standard plots but his writing is polished and his characters real. There is a sense of adventure and a sense of humor that make for a few hours of light but enjoyable reading.

The Treasure of Wonderwhat is a sequel and takes Farstar and son on a quest for a fortune in gold and jewels trapped in the tail of the enigmatic comet Wonderwhat.

(If you like Bill Starr, the originators of this type of s-f, E. E. Smith, Jack Williamson, and Edmond Hamilton are recommended.)

CHRISTOPHER STASHEFF. A usually rollicking sub-genre of science fiction is scientific sword-and-sorcery, in which a person of our time or of the future is thrown into a medieval milieu by crossing time space or dimension, and finds there (what else) swords and sorcery, which are given (cleverly or far fetchedly, depending on the author) some sort of scientific rationale. In Stasheff's *The Warlock in Spite of Himself* and its sequel, *King Kobold,* hero Rodney d'Armand and his trusty robot horse find themselves in just this situation on the planet Gramarye, where they have landed in the service of DDT (the Decentralized Democratic Tribunal).

Into this stew are thrown ghosts, elves, witches complete with broomsticks, and enemies from the future. Rollicking is certainly the word.

(If you like Stasheff, try Laumer, some Anderson, the de Camp/Pratt collaborations and one Heinlein—*Glory Road.)*

ARKADI & BORIS STRUGATSKI are, between them, brothers, a space physicist, Soviets, literary translator, and writers of curious s-f tales told with a kind of deliberate confusion and incompletion—done, perhaps, to detour the censors endemic to the kind of political/social system the Strugatskis so openly and lavishly belabor with parodies and satires. They have, in fact, been reprimanded by their government for just such.

Hard to be A God is essentially a political (rather than technological/

cultural, as is usually the case in most s-f speculations about future societal structures) examination of a lord/vassal society on a planet in another system, a planet run by a small number of human operators who are regarded as gods, a regard they find heavy to bear. It sounds familiar, of course; but the emphasis and the wit are atilt, unexpected. *Prisoners of Power* is equally political, and very pointed. A post-holocaust civilization is controlled through the use of radiation applications which make its people mindlessly docile and willing consumers of the outrageous propaganda fed by their fascistic rulers. Some few are immune to the *non compos mentis* effects, and though enlightened they suffer terribly from the radiation, and the powers that be. An outsider appears, a space traveler, and he stays to get involved in the elimination of the unthinkable social conditions. Gradually, as he learns more of this world and the workings of the politics of repression, he finds that he must come to terms with, and even employ, the hate, violence, duplicity, and arrogance of the masters, to deal with and obviate them, and save the eon.

Any exegesis of the other works of the daring Soviet sibling duo would have to continue to focus on their prime concern: politics. Other works displaying this overwhelming but understandable preoccupation are *Monday Begins on Saturday*, about the secret Soviet investigation on a grand scale into paranormal and paraphysical phenomenona, and the mysteriously plotted *Roadside Picnic*. The Strugatskis' work often has much of the antic whimsy and literally mad (in the Lewis Carroll sense) invention found in much post-war Slavic literature, but it is a pointed madness.

(If you find the writing of the Strugatskis fascinating that of Stanislaw Lem will attract you.)

THEODORE STURGEON is the Peck's Bad boy of the science fiction world. Not in the sense of the tantrum-prone endless adolescence of some s-f authors, but as the perpetual maverick, gentle iconoclast, and humanist spokesman in the field. He has worried and infuriated his readers with several long lapses in output (to the extent that after one such hiatus a Sturgeon collection was entitled *Sturgeon is Alive and Well*). He has written articulate critiques for both in-genre and out-of-genre publications (*The New York Times,* for one) whose only problem was that he could hardly bring himself to write a negative word about anyone's work.

In short, he has been a determined individualist. And his writing reflects this very special, indefinable quality. The ratio of his short stories to his novels is large enough so that he might well be considered primarily a short story writer, but the relatively few novels have been so impressive, have remained so much in readers' minds, that no such easy generality is possible.

Since science fiction is a literature of concept ("the idea as hero"), the s-f short story too often reduces the concept to gimmick. Each of Sturgeon's many short stories are all based on a concept, of course, but they never sink to the gimmick level; the ideas are so often startlingly original, the writing style so seemingly effortless, the characters so idiosyncratic, the stories as a whole so fleshed out with detail, that mere gimmickry is transcended.

"It" was Sturgeon's fifth published story, but the first to make a wide-spread impression. And for good reason! It concerns a thing formed around a human skeleton of putrefying material that spontaneously achieves growth and movement, and no horror that science fiction has spawned has ever been quite so real as "It." It is atypical in the sense that most of Sturgeon's alien beings are benign, if not downright lovable. Mewhu, of "Mewhu's Jet," for instance, is an endearing extraterrestrial who arrives among us; even for an alien his behavior seems eccentric until it's realized that he's a lost *baby* alien.

One of Sturgeon's loveliest stories is "The Skills of Xanadu" wherein a representative of the warlike regimented planet Kit Carson meets, is baffled by, and eventually "conquered" by the inhabitants of Xanadu, the most idyllic world ever created. "Thunder and Roses" is literally a love-among-the-ruins tale, set in a devastated and hopeless post-holocaust setting.

Of the novels, *More Than Human* is generally considered the masterpiece. Here is the first really original consideration of the next step for mankind since Stapledon's *Odd John*. Sturgeon hypothesizes a *homo gestalt,* a being of many parts, and whose whole is greater than those parts. The novel, presented in a contemporary setting, tells of the coming together of the strange group of social misfits who unknowingly will make up *homo gestalt,* and in a remarkable feat of stylization, Sturgeon tells the story in a fragmented, kaleidoscopic form that matches and complements the subject matter.

Though Philip Jose Farmer is generally credited with smashing the taboo against sexuality that prevailed in the s-f magazine ghetto until the 1950s, Sturgeon may well be the author who has explored it most often and most variously, in what might seem a determined campaign for tolerance. Here is a master writing on sexually speculative themes—homosexuality in "The World Well Lost," incest in "If All Men Were Brothers, Would You Let Your Sister Marry One?" pre-Le Guin hermaphrodites in the novel *Venue Plus X,* an extraordinary handling of vampirism and sexuality in *Some of Your Blood*—and giving us superlative story telling while stretching our minds. This is science fiction at its very best.

It should be noted that Sturgeon was responsible for one of the few triumphs science fiction scored over mainstream literature until quite recently. His story "Bianca's Hands" won first prize in a contest sponsored by the British *Argosy* in 1946. Who came in second? Graham Greene.

(Sturgeon is unique, but some of his qualities are found in the works of Edgar Pangborn, Thomas Scortia, and Clifford Simak.)

JOHN TAINE was in reality the noted mathematician Eric Temple Bell, born in Scotland, but achieving academic eminence in the United States. The majority of his works were novels; these were published between the late '20s and the '50s and atypically for that period when the magazine was king, some of them saw initial publication as real books.

Taine's work is dated now, or at least out of fashion, but yet has a curious, almost indefinable quality that can still fascinate. Perhaps it was the often bizarre scientific premises he conceived; perhaps the unlikely plots or less plots than situations that he set up as his literary backdrop. For example, *Before the Dawn* hypothesizes a device that can produce visual "records" from the past from rocks; testing it, the technicians watch the hatching of an infant dinosaur. They dub it Belshazzar, and the novel is his biography as seen in this peculiar manner. Accurate or not, few writers have ever evoked a more wonderful picture of the Earth before man.

Taine's subjects were diverse, though many revolved around variations on biological evolution. *The Crystal Horde* tells of the development of cystalline monsters in China; *The Iron Star* and *The .Greatest Adventure* of evolutionary forces run wild; in *The Seeds of Life* we meet Taine's variations on the superman theme; and in *The Time Stream* some very complex speculations on the nature of time and the far future.

These works may not be to everyone's taste. One definite thing can be said about them though; seldom in science fiction has a writer's work evidenced so much science and so little fiction.

(If you like the work of John Taine, try his contemporary, A. Merritt's, or that of Olaf Stapledon.)

STEPHEN TALL has written two books which are essentially collections of short stories about the incidents in the log of the *Stardust,* a scientific survey ship. It's a standard formula for space opera and that is basically what it is, but Tall takes it a little further and in a slightly different direction with development of character and originality of plot elements. One of the stories in *The Stardust Voyages,* "The Bear With The Knot On Its Tail," is an example; Tall creates an alien race and infuses it with a wonderful quiet dignity. This story was nominated for a Hugo Award when it was first published in *Fantasy and Science Fiction.* Details of ecological and other scientific disciplines add to the interest as well as being clues to the puzzle inherent in most of the tales. While *The Stardust Voyages* is all short stories, *The Ramsgate Paradox* contains works of longer length.

(If the ship *Stardust* interests you, the *Daedalus* series by Brian Stableford is something to be looked into.)

WILLIAM TENN is the pseudonym of Phillip Klass, who lives and teaches in Pennsylvania. Although he has written little or nothing since the late sixties (at least in the way of s-f), his stories retain their freshness and relevance. Tenn has a way of getting right at the heart of whatever problem he sets for himself. His stories are witty but barbed comments on the foibles of mankind, which, he is sure, will never change. Tenn's style is literate, and his sense of the incongruous is impeccable.

The bulk of Tenn's work is in his short stories, collected in such books as *The Human Angle* and *The Square Root of Man.* There are two novels; *A Lamp For Medusa,* which is about the day when the Greek gods are resurrected on Earth in all their Olympian splendor, and *Of Men and Monsters,* where the Earth has been invaded (and conquered) by gigantic and inscrutable aliens. Mankind is reduced to the status of vermin, and not surprisingly makes quite a success of it.

It is difficult to describe the flavor of Tenn, but fairly easy to illustrate it. Imagine getting ready to enter your shining spacecraft, on a noble voyage of discovery to the stars; when you trip on the doorway and fall on your face, that's William Tenn laughing in the corner.

(It might also be Frederic Brown; try him if you like Tenn.)

JAMES TIPTREE, JR. is one of the rising stars of the '70s. Brilliant, complex, richly textured, witty...all these words describe Tiptree's style. Tiptree is one of the writers capable of really making chills run up and down your spine, but horror plays no part in the mix. Tiptree is a writer, and, praise be, this writer writes science fiction.

Until very recently, Tiptree wrote only short stories, including the award winning "Houston, Houston Do You Read?" This story is about three astronauts who are caught in a time warp and thrown into the far future. Here they find the space program dominated, to their horror and delight, by women. The characters, so compassionately drawn, so realistic in their drives and manners, so shocked and puzzled at the final revelation, are the heart of the story. Other Tiptree stories have been collected in *Warm Worlds and Otherwise, 10,000 Light Years from Home,* and *Star Songs of an Old Primate.*

Beyond what could be gleaned from the stories themselves, little was known about Tiptree for many years. Rumor had it that Tiptree was a spy, worked for the Pentagon, was a biologist, was old, was young, was black, white or Amerind, was a collaboration; but aside from periodically feeding the rumor mills with contradictory biographies, Tiptree did little to enlighten us. The greatest consensus was that Tiptree was a young, incredibly talented writer with a passion for privacy.

Imagine, then, the surprise and delight which prevailed in 1976 when Tiptree appeared. James Tiptree, Jr., is the pseudonym of a research psychologist and educator who worked for the Pentagon during World War II. Tiptree is over sixty, travels considerably, and lives in Virginia. Her name is Alice Sheldon. She also writes as Racoona Sheldon, which wasn't such a surprise; quite a few people guessed that Racoona might be James, since the style was unmistakable. One has visions of the elusive Tiptree forwarding Racoona's stories with a nice little note about promising young writers.

So what else is there to say? Just this...Tiptree's first novel, *Up the Walls of the World* (1978), is incredible. Plot and counterplot are juggled with great finesse until they fall together, dragging their sub-plots along. The story is set in three locations; Earth, the planet Tyree, and deep space. There are three sets of characters who all reach a state of free mentality that allows them to exchange planets and bodies. Love, hate, envy, and fear appear in many guises here. The novel has a transcendent quality, but also some delightful sketches. Tiptree's description of life in a research facility is brilliant, and the section describing a secret military preserve, with its officious officers and petty security guidelines has no equal in modern fiction.

(If you like Tiptree's work, we suggest Ursula Le Guin or Fritz Leiber.)

E. C TUBB. Earl Dumarest, Earl Dumarest. Will he ever find the home he left as a young boy? Will the evil Cyclan capture him and force from his the secret that will enable them to control the entire universe? These are some of the questions prominent in the books for which Tubb is best known. The *Dumarest Of Terra* series is a long-running space opera that comes close to being "The Perils of Pauline" but is saved and even made first class by Tubb's skillful creation of planet after planet, strange culture after strange culture. Earl Dumarest as a boy stows away on a spaceship that landed on Earth. His travels take him further and further away from his home planet until even the name Terra means nothing and Earth; "Why, Earth is just another name for dirt. Why would anyone name a planet dirt?" As a grown man Dumarest hunts for clues to his birth world from place to place, going where he may have the chance of picking up the slightest hint as to direction or distance. In his travels he has learned the formula for a mind control drug stolen from the Cyclan, a group of persons made artifically emotionless and almost machine-like. The goal of the Cyclan is to be all mankind, to form a mass mind devoid of joy and sorrow, laughter and love, with intellectual achievement the height of accomplishment. So while Earl chases Earth the Cyclan chases Earl. Tubb works with a formula plot and adds a dash of this and a pinch of that. The dash of this is the background for the stories: a well-developed and detailed universe-wide civilization, with attention to the small pieces of information needed by a reader to build on such as modes of travel, historical fact, and scientific knowledge. The pinch of that is the close look that each novel takes at a different planet, culture, or group of people as encountered by Dumarest. Imaginative concepts of possible societal configurations abound and are wellfounded and consistent. Characterization is good and there is adventure and action sufficient for almost any reader's taste. And Dumarest may find Earth.

Tubb has written several other novels, among them *Death Is A Dream,* a use of the suspended-animation-as-time travel theme, and

Moon Base, a suspense detective story of espionage at Luna Station. In *The Space-Born* Tubb has also taken a classic s-f situation, that of the sub-light-speed colony ship that is home to several generations of people on their way to the stars, and has worked out some variations. For one thing, these people *know* they are on a colony ship. (In most of these stories, the ship becomes the world and the "outside" doesn't exist.) What Tubb does here is to study the emotional and political situations that develop when the everyday routine of the ship begins to change, for no known reason.

Tubb is a competent writer whose imagination and attention to detail in character and situation enable him to turn an adventure serial into grand space opera and basic s-f themes into new and fertile ground for speculation.

(If you like Tubb, try Stableford.)

WILSON TUCKER's writing is primarily concerned with either telepathy or time travel or both, and of their effects on the society in which they occur.

The Lincoln Hunters is a novel of a future time traveling society, many of whose members are engaged in "historical research" with a view toward finding crowd-pleasing trivia of the past. Ben Steward is a "Character" for Time Researchers, a time traveler in love with a woman for whose husband's death he feels responsible. The pivotal point in the book and in Steward's life is May 29, 1856 in Bloomington, Illinois, at the delivery of a speech by a tall gangling man named Abraham Lincoln. Tucker vividly recreates the rough frontier atmosphere of the time and most of the novel is a suspenseful race against paradox. *The Year Of The Quiet Sun* is another tale of time traveling in which a visit to the year 2000 AD finds Russia and China at war and the U.S. in a state of savagery after a black revolution.

Tucker's ability to convey emotion, whether it be the confusion and fear felt by telepath Paul Breen in *Wild Talent* or the puzzled awe of a matriarchial society upon discovery of their first virile man, as in *The City In The Sea*, is one of his strongest points.

Tomorrow Plus X, a distant sequel to *Wild Talent*, in which telepathic powers are discovered in humans, combines ESP and time travel in a complex and suspenseful detective novel concerning the search for the perpetrators of a series of bombings that are killing the higher echelon of a new political movement. Good characterization and a well constructed plot line make it one of the few able mysteries in the field of science fiction.

(Those who like Tucker might find Poul Anderson's work, also often dealing with time travel and telepathy, congenial.)

JACK VANCE is one of the most prolific of science fiction writers, and yet one of the most reticent and mysterious. Though by this time he has written scores of books ranging from pure fantasy to reasonably straight s-f, and though he has won two Hugos (for *The Dragon Masters* and *The Last Castle)* and a Nebula (for *The Last Castle*), he remains apart from the main body of science fiction.

This is due in part to a unique (in the field) writing style. It is fanciful, deliberately archaic, decorated with ruffles and flourishes and personal leitmotifs; (some of these are: river journeys, houseboats, masks and masques, arcane theatrical events, music, crafts, old fashioned chivalry, word-play, and a certain humorous air of world-weary sophistication that even creeps into his Burroughsian "Planet of Adventure" series). His language achieves real elegance at times; contrariwise, his plots tend to be simple, or even simple minded, in a deliberate 19th century sense. He has written several series, and will sometimes return to the scene of a much earlier book for a new one.

Aside from the two prize-winning novels, Vance's most popular book may be *The Dying Earth*. In this hybrid s-f/fantasy about the last days of our own Earth under a red and moribund sun, sorcery has come once more into its own. Magicians labor to create a new human strain, adventurers seek the dusty lore of the Museum of Man, relics of ancient technology confound the decadence of the inhabitants. One of the pleasures of *The Dying Earth* is that it can be read as a successor to the lush adventures of C. L. Moore and Henry Kuttner, or even the old master A. Merritt, or as an exquisite takeoff on them, too subtle to be designated as parody. A later book in the same setting, *The Eyes of the Overworld,* though it makes amusing reading, does not attempt to create the same mood.

In another early book, *Big Planet,* Vance gives us one of those adventure treks through the wilds of an unknown planet that were so dear to Golden-Age s-f writers. Typically though, he has twisted the genre to make it his own. Instead of bug-eyed-monsters and other horrors, the little band of adventurers encounters communities with local habits so peculiar that they would fit nicely into Baum's concept of Oz. A much later book, *Showboat World,* takes place on the same world.

This love of human (or humanoid) foible turns up often. *Space Opera* takes an opera company on a tour of wacky planets. *The Languages of Pao* (one of the best novels) explores what happens to a peaceful race when its vocabulary and phonemes are made warlike. *To Live Forever* portrays the last city on Earth and the five eccentric social classes that are the stepping stones to immortality.

Many of the recent novels are pastoral in tone. Sometimes Vance's worlds are forced to be pastoral, as in *Emphyrio,* where Overlords subjugate the populace, but often, as in *The Gray Prince* or the "Alastor" series he has been working on recently, it seems that he prefers them that way. Nevertheless, one of his most successful efforts is an old-fashioned space opera of revenge known as the "Demon Prince" series, in which a hero hunts down a group of the most originally horrid villains (one per book) in some of the best conceived settings in science fiction.

Vance writes short fiction, too, though less frequently. One splendid short story, "The Moon Moth," tackles the problems of a detective on a world where every encounter is complicated by a strict protocol of masks and music.

All in all, Vance is a sensual writer, not in the limited meaning of restrained sexuality, but in the broader mode of appealing to the senses. Every story conjures up vivid pictures, and colors run riot throughout; no writer in the field has thrown such a palette of words at the reader. For those critics who say that science fiction is lacking in style—let them read Vance.

(If Vance appeals, you might try Robert Chilson, Cordwainer Smith, Mark Geston, the lighter works of Ballard and Leiber, or Michael Shea, whose novel, *A Quest for Symbilis,* is set on Vance's Dying Earth.)

SYDNEY VAN SCYOC's writing has the interesting, and admirable, quality of transcending the writer's gender, a problem often afflicting s-f. In her nicely written novels and stories, complex and problematical situations and mysteries are established and resolved, in careful and effective plotting. In *Cloudcry* Verrons (humans) and Tiehl (avian-descended creatures) are quarantined on a planet away from their own when they contact an uncurable and contagious ailment. Exploring the "leper" planet the Verrons and the Tiehl discover lost civilizations and ancient cities, into one of which they establish themselves. The Tiehl despair and revert to birdy savagery while the Verrons are entranced by curious music (a frequent element in Van Scyoc's writing); the marooned outcasts of the two races seem to be at an end. But in graphic and intriguing scenes the author devises both cure and rescue; they are better read than summarized.

The construction of alien, remote, future societies is Van Scyoc's forte, and her *Saltflower* and *Assignment Nor'Dyren* fabricate and explore such societies with thoughtful and evocative detail. In *StarMother* Van Scyoc adds geophysically descriptive material, enriching her social structure with place and sensation. A sort of Peace-Corps person is sent to a muddy nasty planet to care for its mutant children. Her involvement with the mysterious and unpleasant inhabitants and their totems and taboos is evoked with skill and care.

(Admirers of Van Scyoc might enjoy Gerrold, Randall, or McIntyre.)

A. E. VAN VOGT's work can be difficult reading. He says, "Each paragraph—sometimes each sentence—of my brand of science fiction has a gap in it, an unreality condition. In order to make it real, the reader must add the missing parts. He cannot do this from past associations. There *are* no past associations. So he must fill in the gaps himself."

Van Vogt generally advances basic ideas within the complexities of a plot that may be just this side of incomprehensible. An excellent example is one of his best known works, *The World of Null-A* and its sequel, *The Players of Null-A.* (Null-A refers to non-Aristotelian and non-Newtonian systems of thought and/or to the science of General Semantics.) Van Vogt postulates a world of 2560 A.D. in which the majority of the population is trained in Null-A; the protagonist, Gilbert Gosseyne (pronounced, by no coincidence GoSane), finds that he is not really sure who he is, and neither is the reader. Through the novels Gosseyne advances through various selves to the final denouement. The plot is indeed sometimes of a Gordian complexity, but the fascination of the books lies in the creation of a society based on an entirely different system than our own.

In *The Voyage of the Space Beagle,* really a series of short stories made into a novel, we are given the adventures of the crew and technicians of an exploratory survey ship. Again van Vogt uses a "science," this time nexialism, a logical joining and application of all sciences, as a basis for the background and behavior of the characters.

One of van Vogt's strengths is his ability to make the reader understand and even empathize with a totally alien entity, be it an actual member of alien species or an alien member of the human species. This is a major factor in *The War Against the Rull* (again a series of short stories "novelized"). *The Silkie* is a novel about the discovery of merpeople on Earth, and *Supermind* is three connected long short stories which deal with the potential of the human mind, and finally *Slan*, a classic handling of the mutant superman theme which tells the story of Jommy Cross, one of the first of the race of telepathic humans, the slan. Again, concept and convoluted plot are the thing.

Of van Vogt's many other books (he has been writing since 1939 and luckily for his fans, prolifically), *Empire of the Atom* and its sequel, *The Wizard of Linn*, could be called *I, Clane* as they come close to the power-hungry Roman milieu of Graves' Claudius. Set in the post-holocaust world of 12,000 A.D., they describe a civilization that uses atomic power and yet cannot build a gun, an empire that rules the Solar System and yet still struggles against a religion bowing to the several "gods of the atom."

While the short story as a form does not quite give van Vogt the space needed for his accustomed intricacy, he has written more than a few.

All in all, reading van Vogt is at times hard going, at times confusing, but he makes the reader think, and sometimes manages to change that thinking, a rare accomplishment.

(A note about van Vogt: he tends to shuffle and redeal his stories, expanding short ones or connecting and linking them to make a "new" novel. *Caveat emptor.*)

(If you like Van Vogt's layers of reality approach, try Zelazny, E. E. Smith, and some Kuttner.)

JOHN VARLEY's work, though not easily defined, clearly belongs to what might be called the hard-science wing of the genre. Like the work of Larry Niven and Gregory Benford, Varley's fictions grow from present scientific reality and postulates, but they are merely the substance, not the bloom. Varley likes to deal with man off-Earth—ostracized, abandoned, or marooned and adapting. In his novella "In the Hall of the Martian Kings" five skilled techies survive a disaster which kills the rest of a large data-gathering expedition settled on the surface of Mars. When they realize that rescue is impossible they determine to defy reason and survive—and multiply. Martian plantforms which appear to be a basic pvc, and are more mechanical than biological, are found to have abilities of a bewildering variety, all geared to the needs of the stranded Earthpeople. In the end, when a passing spaceship offers them transport back to Earth, they have no interest in leaving. Having multiplied and adapted, having been anticipated all along, they stay to await the return of the Martians who must have created the wondrous plants.

Varley's novel *The Ophiuchi Hotline* also isolates man off-earth; in this case we have been exiled for centuries, and live in apparent satisfaction in fluorescent warrens with complex life-support systems. The story is that of Lilo, a geneticist who has performed forbidden dna-on-human experiments and is to die for her lawbreaking. But Lilo has herself cloned, and with the aid of an old time political boss manages to evade her fate—for a while.

Unlike much s-f, Varley's characters and their environments and the fortuities which shape them are wholly integrated, giving his writing a completeness that is satisfying and sometimes unique. At the end of *The Ophiuchi Hotline* Varley depicts man as finally totally homeless, ejected from the very Solar System. Only Stapledon sees beyond that.

(Those who like Varley's work might check out that of F. M. Busby.)

JULES VERNE was born 23 years before Mary Shelley died, and so far as anyone knows, they never met; if that unlikely event had occurred Mary could have symbolically handed the still barely kindled torch of science fiction on to the young Frenchman.

Verne's place in the history of s-f is covered in the historical chapter and here we are concerned with the question of just how readable Verne's works are today. With the problems of translation, the fact that all his inventions are either commonplace or discovered to be impossible, the 19th century hyberbole of his plots and the lack of character of his characters, is it worth picking up a Jules Verne novel in this day and age?

The answer is a qualified yes, mainly depending on that subjective old bugaboo, historical perpective and how much of it you have.

Given a fair amount of h.p., Verne's books are great fun on the literary level they seem to have found nowadays, that of the boy's adventure novel. Even in the worst translations, Verne communicates an innocent joy in his "*voyages extraordinaires*" that is rather irresistible. How exciting to spend five weeks in a balloon, or be shot by a cannon 'round the moon, or cruise 20,000 leagues under the sea (which, to settle a long-term misunderstanding, means that the *Nautilus* travelled beneath the surface for about 60,000 miles, not that the events of the book take place 60,000 miles down)! Or to be off on a comet to the orbit of Saturn (with ice skating on the way), or go down a volcanic shaft to the center of the Earth, or survive on a mysterious island with only what's in your pockets and end up with electricity!

There are other, more special reasons for reading Verne, too. For instance, Verne was extremely influenced by Edgar Allan Poe, and well into his career, wrote a curiou homage to Poe in a sequel to Poe's *Narrative of Arthur Gordon Pym*, titled *The Sphinx of the Ice-Fields*. Poe-lovers might enjoy tracking that one down. (Just to tie all that into this century, H. P. Lovecraft echoes—literally—Poe's *Narrative* in his Antarctic saga, *At the Mountains of Madness,* by evoking the strange cry heard by Pym, "Tekeli-li, Tekeli-li!"

And certainly anyone wishing a more than superficial knowledge of science fiction should sample Verne—and not just the obvious ones. His later, and somewhat more obscure novels, such as *The Begum's Fortune* and *Master of the World,* reveal a rather startling change of philosophy. The earlier and more halcyon works show an optimistic faith in science and technology unmatched by any s-f writer until Arthur C. Clarke came along, but perhaps significantly, Verne's optimism turned with the century. The world that was already building up to World War I apparently did not seem so sane a place as it had. Verne died in 1905, having seen many of his predicted inventions come to pass and also perhaps, seeing all too clearly the scientific horrors looming ahead.

(Verne's pervasive influence extends through the intoxicated-by-technology works of England and Campbell right through today's "hard science" fiction writers, Larry Niven, Poul Anderson et al.)

VERNOR VINGE, though known mainly as a writer of short stories, published a couple of interesting novels. In 1969 *Grimm's World* told of the arrogant Tatja whose kingdom was hers by deception, and who hoped to dominate the planet as a stepping-stone to the alien intelligence she believed existed in space's vastness. When the confrontation came, when the first alien diplomat arrived, Tatja and her empire learned of their fate.

More recently *The Witling* deals with psychic teleportation, a prince who lacks that power in a kingdom where it is common, a couple of aliens who connive with the prince, using their advanced technical skills

to combat the psychic powers, and clever use of the physics of teleportation to keep the whole thing convincing. Although Vinge uses science as
a supportive basis for his work, the novels have a strong fantasy quality,
probably because of his elaborate and exotic embellishments and use of
a fantasy-like nomenclature.

(Those who enjoy Vinge's work might try that of Tanith Lee and
David J. Lake.)

IAN WALLACE takes things a little further than most writers. Where
one author would mention a sexually triadic species on the planet
Whatever, he takes the reader to the planet Turquoise and makes the
physical and psychological aspects of this relationship an integral part of
a well done s-f detective novel, *The Sign Of The Mute Medusa*. Where
another might skimp on characterization for the sake of plot, Wallace
delves into the psycho-sexual motivations of his characters and the plots
develop naturally.

Wallace mentions in a comment in *Pan Sagittarius* that he has "old,
old concerns with clinical psychology, and these concerns may be showing through..." Nobody who has read Wallace needs to be told of
these concerns. They not only show through but color, to a great extent,
all of his work. To use his own example, though, *Pan Sagittarius* is a collection of stories about Pan, operative for "Operation Second Chance,"
a group within Hell that, using "if nodes," crisis points in a web of
alternate universes, allows some people to replay pivotal situations in
their lives, given the tiniest nudge in the right direction. What happens
after the nudge is up to them. All of the episodes are somewhat
allegorical, some even allegories of known allegory. Perceptive, compassionate writing and the aforementioned psychological approach puts this
novel several cuts above the slick adventure romp it might be.

Wallace is a consistently good writer who combines details in setting
and mood with rich characterization and thought provoking ideas.
Besides that, he's exciting to read.

(Those who have discovered Ian Wallace to be of interest might try
Jack Chalker and Roger Zelazny.)

IAN WATSON is a writer of special knowledge in areas once quite
foreign to s-f. Although van Vogt deals in linguistics, Watson *uses* it as
lingua franca, and empathetic anthropology is his stock in trade. His
novels are oddly structured; rather like classic rondos, they move in

alternating episodes which only gradually relate to each other.

The Embedding tells, spasmodically, of a search for the root language which, if revealed, might provide some ultimate understanding of the nature of reality. Some aliens investigate, and an anthropologist who is hoping to save a remote Brazilian tribe from flood joins in, and a social experimenter who is working with children in a closed environment... he, too, is in on the quest. It is a serious, difficult and fascinating book, one that assumes its reader's intelligence. As does *The Jonah Kit*, which postulates the discovery that Earth, and the universe itself, is merely a kind of after-image or echo of reality, and the metaphor of the man-programmed whale who is sent to the profound ocean to report on his kind. The sections related by the whale are masterful.

Watson returns to Latin America in *The Martian Inca*, in which a Russian ship carrying soil samples from Mars crashes in Bolivia and does in most of the Incas who come in contact with it. This discovery must be communicated to an Earth ship on its way to Mars before contact between man and Mars is made. Intellectual, puzzling, and unsettling, Watson writes for readers who like challenge.

(Readers might also try Michael Bishop.)

STANLEY G. WEINBAUM's first published story appeared in the July, 1934, issue of *Wonder Stories*. He died in December, 1935. With this brief career and a relatively small output (there was a fair amount of work published posthumously), Weinbaum managed to change the face of science fiction. Why and how?

One must be aware of the American magazine s-f scene in the mid-'30s (which was about all there was at that point). New ideas and concepts were to be found in every issue of every magazine. *But*, as stories, most of the fiction was formula-ridden and hackneyed, dominated by cardboard heroes, vapid heroines, mad or kindly (or both) scientists, and aliens, usually wicked, sometimes benificent, but always really just human types in funny rubber suits. (Why else, for heaven's sakes, were they always carrying off the girl when they—literally—had no Earthly use for her?)

Some talented authors worked within the formula and still came up with exciting stories. And the winds of change were blowing people like John W. Campbell into the conviction that s-f could be more than just what the editors allowed it to be. And a young man in Milwaukee began writing stories that played with the formula so outrageously that they did indeed become something else. When the magazines began publishing Weinbaum's work, the readers welcomed it vociferously.

It is part of Weinbaum's misfortune that his innovations were so directly in the line that science fiction *had* to take, so naturally the next step in its evolution, that they are hard to see today, when so many writers have far transcended what he did. Luckily, his works have an individuality which, despite the above mentioned circumstances, makes them still highly readable.

That first story in *Wonder Stories* is the famous *A Martian Odyssey,* maybe the most auspicious debut in the history of s-f. And what set this story apart immediately was one of Weinbaum's major innovations, aliens who were alien. Today that may seem an idiotically simplistic tenet, but then Weinbaum's Martian Tweel, whose reactions to the first human expedition to Mars are sometimes logical, sometimes totally inexplicable, was a revelation. Here was an alien who was *not* just a human done up in a funny suit.

Alien aliens continued to play a large part in Weinbaum's work, but there were other jumps in sophistication, too, since one could only do so much with beings whose main charm was their inexplicability. In three stories featuring a human couple, Ham Hammond and Pat Burlingame, who in their various interplanetary adventures displayed a rapport reminiscent of that other joyous couple of the '30s, Nick and Nora Charles, there was something new to the field in characterization. And in another trio of stories revolving around the inventions of one Professor van Manderpootz, which were superficially of the overdone gimmick invention variety, there was as much philosophical as technical speculation, since the inventions (such as one that showed the user what would have happened if he had followed a course other than what he had in reality) were trickily concerned with matters far beyond simple technology.

So also was his novel, *The New Adam,* which did not see print in his lifetime. It concerns a mutant superman, not of the future but of Weinbaum's present, and his struggles to survive in what to him is a world of primitive intellects. It suffers by comparison to Olaf Stapledon's great novel on the same theme, *Odd John;* what is surprising is that it was certainly written (though not published) before the Stapledon work, when Weinbaum was in his twenties or early thirties, and is a remarkable accomplishment for an American writer of that period.

Weinbaum's other well known novel is *The Black Flame,* really two short novels linked by the titular character, Margot of Urbs. The first part, "Dawn of Flame," is set in a post holocaust America that has reverted to near barbarism. However, a genius scientist has not only rediscovered atomic power, but the secret of immortality. Margot and her brother are among the first immortals, and they set out to reunite America and eventually the world. "Dawn of Flame" concerns a minor conquest of a small town, and an encounter between the devastatingly beautiful Margot and a simple backwoodsman. In "The Black Flame," which takes place several hundred years later, a decadent and bored Margot and her brother do rule the recivilized world, and are confronted with a revolt led by a man from our century, awakened in theirs from suspended animation.

This may sound old hat now, but there were several extraordinary things about these stories. Almost any other writer of the time would have made a blood and thunder epic out of this; by concentrating on Margot and her psychological struggles with deathlessness, Weinbaum brings a new dimension to what was already a hackneyed theme. He also manages to work in some questions, heavy for the period, about freedom and rulership, and he does not load the dice in anyone's favor. The immortals and the rebels of the second section are both represented sympathetically.

Typically, "Dawn of Flame" was rejected when it was first submitted to various magazines because it was too "realistic," not science fictional enough.

Weinbaum's death was announced in *Astounding* with the wildy bathetic (though kindly meant) question: "Did you know that Stanley Weinbaum took off on the Last Great Journey through the galaxies in December?"

(There was, of course, nobody quite like Weinbaum writing in his own time, but later authors who suggest that creative sophistication might be Russel, de Camp, Bester, and Le Guin.)

MANLY WADE WELLMAN has contributed a steady stream of fiction to genre magazines since his debut in the early thirties. A triple-threat man, Wellman is equally at home with s-f, occult fantasy, and crime and suspense stories. His s-f specialty is the bizarre alien, successfully portrayed in such novels as *The Beasts From Beyond* and *Giant From Eternity*. He is a gifted evoker of mood, especially the macabre. His most powerful work is generally acknowledged to be a series of Appalachian stories of the supernatural featuring the strange creatures cobbled out of folktales and his own dark imagination.

Wellman has collaborated recently with his son Wade on a collection of tales entitled *Sherlock Holmes' War of The World's,* a competent pastiche ingeniously weaving the World's Greatest Detective into the events of the H. G. Wells classic.

(If you like Wellman, try H. P. Lovecraft or Clark Ashton Smith.)

H. G. WELLS' importance to the history of science fiction is taken as a matter of course (see "The Spawn of Frankenstein" chapter for that aspect of his career), but aside from that, is there any value in reading Wells today? Unequivocally, yes.

Wells was a superb writer, with that intelligent and knowledgeable British polish so seldom attained by Americans, particularly in s-f. He can also be very witty, another quality in short supply in the field at all points of its history. It is interesting to note that Wells' non-science fiction novels, smash hits at the time of their publication, are very little known today, but many of his "scientific romances" have entered that stage of usually being in print that qualifies them for the adjective "immortal."

Wells denied vehemently that Jules Verne (whose career overlapped his for a considerable period) had any influence on his work (Verne was equally adamant about any connection, accusing Wells of using scientifically shaky concepts), and cited Jonathan Swift as closer to his model. Right there we are made aware of the fact that Wells had Something To Tell Us, and was using s-f as a vehicle by which to do so. This is a pretension that his contemporaries, Haggard, Doyle, and Verne himself, can not be accused of.

The question then arises as to whether Wells made the prime science-fictional mistake of overloading his fiction with messages. Most students of his work seem to agree that in the early period of his writing career he did not, but with *A Modern Utopia,* published in 1905, the socialist replaced the story teller, and the works became top heavy with cautionary concepts.

This is not to deny that the earlier works weren't meant for sociological instruction. The Morlocks and the Eloi of *The Time Machine* are obviously the two British classes whose social functions have become so divided that they have become two different races. However, even if the reader hasn't the vaguest idea of the British class struggle and could care less, the story of a man from our century travelling to a far future where the butterfly Eloi are maintained and preyed upon by the brutish Morlocks is gripping, and there are poetic evocations of that future and an even further one that stay in the reader's mind.

The general concepts of *The Invisible Man, War of the Worlds,* and *The Island of Dr. Moreau* are widely known, if only from the mediocre-to-fine films that have been made from them. They are all cracking good stories; that they also contain warnings about the uses of science doesn't limit their readability a whit. This goes for the less well known *The Food of the Gods,* in which two brilliant but slightly muddle-headed researchers invent a food additive that induces giantism. Due to their sloppy methods, the countryside around their rural lab is soon full of hugh fauna of varous kinds, and one of the great moments of s-f humor occurs when the local vicar's croquet game is invaded by a giant chicken. However, a serious point is made later in the novel when one of the scientists tests the food on his own children; the result is a potential split of humanity into two different races, and the finale is left deliberately ambiguous.

A Modern Utopia has been called "the definitive utopian story"; the novels after that are awash in message but often still of interest. *The War in the Air* was a startling (for 1908) view of aerial combat, and *The Shape of Things to Come,* a "future history" through the 21st century, was inevitably wrong in its general political extrapolations, but sometimes amazingly right on in details, such as the rise of "air piracy," i.e. hijacking, in the late 20th century.

It is hard to believe, now that the ideas are so commonplace, that it was Wells who introduced the concept of the time machine (men had fictionally travelled in time before, but always by occult or "mental" means) and the invasion of the Earth by aliens. He also set the pattern for the use of science fiction as a vehicle for philosophical ideas that was to result in the titanic works of Olaf Stapledon (whom Wells admired, incidentally) and the allegories of Huxley and Orwell, less successful as s-f but undoubtedly influential in their capturing the public's fancy.

H. G. Wells was less "the father of science fiction" than its mentor and guide who brought Mary Shelley's squalling brat to a delayed intellectual maturity, and set a standard of respectability for it that was to help (as well as to intimidate) all the authors following him.

(Wells is another writer whose influence on the field is immeasurable: the contemporary American George Allan England, the Britishers S. Fowler Wright and the great Olaf Stapledon, right up to the modern

Frederik Pohl and Ursula K. Le Guin, all derive something from the polemical Mr. Wells.)

JAMES WHITE has admitted to wanting to be a doctor and his medical bent is evident in some way in almost everything he writes. It shows not only in the plotting of his stories, but in the writing itself; the detail he brings to the physical characteristics of a sick alien enables the reader to *see* the alien, even empathize with it, and his stress of the psychological aspects of any situation leads to naturally well developed characters.

Another prime aspect of White's writing is that he will take an essentially simple plot line and, with extreme care as to detail and characterization, bring life to it, as in his Sector General hospital series. There have probably been medical stories since the first witchdoctor hung a rock outside his cave, but Sector General is a hospital situated on the Galactic Rim. Its patients, doctors, interns, and nurses are a panorama of possible intelligent life backed by science and logic. Ben Casey in this situation is Dr. Conway: intelligent, intuitive, and humorously human. White extrapolates from present day medical apparatus and technique and develops insightful solutions to future problems.

This extrapolation is inherent in almost all of White's work: in *Deadly Litter,* a collection of four novelettes, he proposes a series of basic hazards, physical and mental, man could encounter in space, and proceeds to contemplate the outcome; *Tomorrow Is Too Far* uses the possible *psychological* as well as the physical aspects of faster-than-light travel as regards time dilation, and also turns out to be quite a good mystery novel; *All Judgement Fled* is a novel concerning six astronauts who are sent to investigate an alien craft in orbit far from Earth. Told from the viewpoint of McCullough, psychologist and doctor on the mission, the plot entails not only the difficulties encountered by six men under stress conditions, and those of contact with a hither-to unexpected alien species, but there is also the problem of which alien is the one with which to speak.

White excites the intellect and the emotions, and a sense of compassion is evident throughout his work. Ben Casey wasn't as much fun.

(If White's scientific extrapolation interests you, it is highly reminiscent of Hal Clement's work, and there is a medical kinship with that of Alan Nourse.)

KATE WILHELM is a sound practitioner of the art of story telling; when she has something to say she says it without pyrotechnics or heavy symbolic devices. What she offers is total immersion in her plots and characters. Although she is primarily known for her mastery of the short story (a difficult form) she has written several visionary novels.

Among the best are *Let the Fire Fall* and *Where Late the Sweet Birds Sang*. *Let the Fire Fall* is an ambiguous book, about what happened after the aliens landed on Earth and died of an unknown virus. Evangelical religion, behavioral therapy, and Norman Rockwell just-folks are woven into a tapestry of 21st Century America.

Where Late the Sweet Birds Sang is about clones; their lives, their thoughts, their rituals and limitations. In the face of ecological disaster, an immensely wealthy family seals itself off from the world and brings its population to a viable level through cloning. Eventually the clones take over from the normal humans, and begin the long decline into barbarism.

Othe novels by Wilhelm include *The Clone, The Nevermore Affair,* and *The Abyss.* Her short stories have been collected into several one-author collections, such as *Somerset Dreams and Other Stories.*

(If you enjoy Wilhelm, we suggest Judith Merril, Damon Knight, or Fred Pohl.)

JACK WILLIAMSON. Space opera, the lovely, soaring, wonderous science fiction of the '30s and '40s. And among space operas Williamson's Legion of Space series must rank near the top. The style, steely-eyed and firm jawed, is a delight.

Using a typical ploy of the period, Williamson opens the series with a prologue from a doctor who knew a guy who could see intermittently into the future...you know the one. Seems this guy's descendants are important figures in the Legion of Space, an organization formed when the scientists (read good guys) of the Green Hall Council overthrow the despotic Empire of the Purple Hall. The first novel, *The Legion of Space,* sets the time, the 30th century, and introduces some of the characters that run through the series. Most notable of these is Giles Habibula, a whining, moaning, constantly talking semihero, and one of science fiction's early attempts at characterization. Giles can get irritating, but there are more than two dimensions there. In this first novel we also discover AKKA, the most powerful force in the universe, part physical, part psychical; with it Earth's moon is destroyed. (No mention of tidal waves, but what the heck?)

In the second novel, *The Cometeers,* Williamson has come up with an awe-inspiring concept, which only *begins* with a twelve-million-mile-long spaceship, and ends with destroying Pluto.

In the third of the series, *One Against the Legion,* Williamson unveils the geofractor—two black spheres joined by a metal cylinder ("They are simply holes in the continuum of our universe."). And it works like any self respecting black-hole-matter-transmitter should, too.

Williamson's career is one of the longest in the field; his first story was published in *Amazing Stories* in 1928. And unlike some of his contemporaries who fell by the wayside, he has managed to keep up with the times. His work has always been near the forefront of whatever period he's been writing in.

Among the many novels that have been popular in that long period have been: *Darker Than You Think,* a science fictional treatment of lycanthropy with an uncanny sense of what it is like being a were-animal; *Seetee Ship* and *Seetee Shock* (written under the pseudonym Will Stewart) which deal with contraterrane, or anti-matter matters; *The Humanoids,* who are the ultimate robots, so dedicated to serving man that they go to any lengths to assure happiness of humanity; the "Starchild" trilogy (written with Frederik Pohl) about mankind being forced to deal with the concept and reality of a galaxy-wide civilization.

Though well known in science fiction, Williamson is still probably one of the under-rated authors in the field. His career's longevity, his vast output, his pioneering concepts have certainly earned his place in the s-f pantheon.

(If you enjoy the many faces of Jack Williamson, some are reflected in the works of Poul Anderson, Edmond Hamilton, Frederik Pohl, and Bill Starr.)

GENE WOLFE. Best known and most widely read of the works of this fugitive writer is the three-part *The Fifth Head of Cerberus.* It is composed of the novellas, "The Fifth Head of Cerberus"; "'A Story' by John V. Marsch"; and "V. R. T.", telling overall the story of two symbiotic planets, Saint Anne and Saint Croix, originally settled by Frenchmen from Earth. In *Fifth Head* a scientist operates a brothel so that he may afford eternal life via cloning. His possible son (perhaps he isn't) undergoes youthquest pangs and kills his "father." "A Story" tells of Marsch's effort to rediscover the aboriginal life on the inter-circling planets; and "V. R. T." confronts him horrifyingly with the system that uncaringly destroyed the beauty and wonder of this distant double world and its inhabitants.

Operation Ares more conventionally tells of an America degenerating into a barbaric past, relinquishing its technology, and finally hoping that an impending invasion from Mars (where America has forfeited its colonies) may save the crumbling world. *The Devil in a Forest* is a fantasy regarding the ambiguities of good and evil and one man's difficulty in seeing black and white when gray is the only true color. *Peace* is an un-science-fictional but distinctly speculative inquiry into the inner mind.

Wolfe's books truly defy description: both plot and prose weave complexities and subtleties into magical and often more than elusive tales. Gene Wolfe is clearly a writer for the careful and patient reader.

(Those who admire Wolfe's work might try that of Ian Watson or Jack Vance.)

S. FOWLER WRIGHT was English, much influenced by H. G. Wells, and writing in his tradition. He never achieved Wells' fame nor did he reach the level of accomplishment of Wells' only real heir, Olaf Stapledon. Nevertheless, Wright's work is still most interesting; science-fictional ideas novelized in the solid, satisfying form that was an inheritance from the Victorian.

Deluge is an account of the flooding of the Earth through a shifting of its surface; the struggles of the survivors are solid adventure. The sequel, *Dawn*, is an equally solid narrative concerning the rebuilding of society. Wright, like so many Englishmen of his generation—that which had seen so much of itself destroyed in WWI—seemed preoccupied with global destruction. *The Adventures of Wyndham Smith* is another post-catastrophe story, the catastrophe in this case being the highly original one of racial suicide by the humanity of the future.

His masterpiece, however, is the two novels, *The Amphibians* and *The World Below*, often published as one under the latter title. Here he practically takes Wells' *The Time Machine* theme intact, but extends it into a much more complex future. Most of what Wright's time traveller sees is practically incomprehensible to him and to the reader, but somehow the author engages us in this strange and beautiful world nevertheless, a world of intelligences alien to man, and perils far more mysterious than those of our age would be to a Cro-Magnon. Wright's reputation can rest on this extraordinary work if no other.

(Those who like Wright might try Hodgson, England, or, of course, Wells.)

PHILIP WYLIE was a culture hero before the term was invented; he was well known for such books as *Opus 21* and *A Generation of Vipers,* which scandalized America by daring to attack its most sacred sacred cow, Mom and motherhood. Throughout his career however, Wylie kept returning to speculative themes, using science fiction as the most congenial medium for the expression of his opinions and theories. Unlike most mainstream writers who do this, Wylie managed to write some interesting s-f which was not overloaded with message.

His first novel that could be considered s-f was *Gladiator,* the story of an artificially bred "superman." This was followed by *When Worlds Collide* and *After Worlds Collide* (written with Edward Balmer); if somehow the novels and the movie have escaped your notice, the titles tell it all.

Tomorrow! is a harrowing account of a nuclear attack on the U.S. written to promulgate Wylie's strong pro-civil defense stand, it's a bit dated now; *Triumph* brings the same theme closer to the present.

The Disappearance might technically be considered a fantasy, since it gave no explanation for the vanishing of each sex from the other's ken for four years. The realistic handling of the situation, however, brings it close to s-f, and it had a good deal to say about the sexes and sexual roles long before they became a matter of public interest. His last novel, *The End of the Dream,* was another cautionary tale, this time of ecological disaster. He died in 1971.

JOHN WYNDHAM is really John Wyndham Parkes Lucas Beynon Harris. With all those names to spare, Wyndham wrote under a number of pseudonyms during his long career, at least two of which established firm separate identities in the public mind. Readers are still surprised to hear that the John Beynon of *The Secret People* published in 1935 was the same person as the John Wyndham of *The Day of the Triffids* published in 1951 in the pop prestigious magazine *Collier's,* during the first science fiction "boom."

Wyndham as Wyndham emerged in the post-World War II renaissance of English science fiction with Christopher, Ballard, and Aldiss— the world destroyers, as they might well be called. Wyndham's contribution to the devastation was world-wide blindness combined with killer plants (*Triffids*, destined through its initial publication in *Collier's* and the not-so-hot film to be one of the best known novels ever to emerge from *within* the genre) and alien invaders who bed down in the ocean bottoms and proceed to melt the ice caps and flood the Earth *(The Kraken Wakes*, published in the U.S. as *Out of the Deeps).*

One of the qualities that the world destroyers brought to their catastrophe s-f, and this applies particularly to Wyndham, was a kind of non-melodramatic *verismo,* a typically British common sense approach which made for an enormously realistic feel to the horrific situations conjured up.

This quality certainly contributed to the success of Wyndham's *The Midwich Cuckoos,* in which the women of some English villages are impregnated during a day-long "blackout" of the community. Wyndham nicely captures the horror of the inhabitants when months later the women are all found to be pregnant, and the subsequent reactions to the very curious children who are born from this event. It is, of course, the basis for one of the very best science fiction films, *Village of the Damned.*

In his exceptionally long writing career, Wyndham (or John Beynon or John Beynon Harris or Lucas Parkes) produced a number of novels of high quality and many short stories that are equally distinguished. It might be noted that with one exception, he was the only Englishman to have made a name (or names, as it were) for himself in the heyday of the American science fiction magazines. (The other is, of course, Arthur C. Clarke, who made it just under the wire in the late '40s.) John Wyndham died in 1969.

(If you like Wyndham's no nonsense approach, try the early Christopher and the early Ballard.)

GEORGE ZEBROWSKI is a young writer and activist in s-f officialdom. Editor of such respectable collections as *Tommorrow Today, Human Machines* (with Tom Scortia), and *Faster Than Light* (with Jack Dann), Zebrowski also emits weighty short stories and novels.

His first novel, *Omega Point,* won Zebrowski a following and from it grows the Omega Point Trilogy. In *Ashes and Stars* which takes place some forty-five centuries hence, a father-son team from the defeated Herculean Empire connive to reopen the war with Earth, the war that devastated their civilization centuries before and scattered their surviving people. Seriously, if not ponderously, the author takes us through their labors: "All through his first watch, the younger Gorgias was irritated by the shroud of hyperspace covering the known universe, hiding the diamond hard stars, abolishing the black void's comfort, leaving only the ash-white continuum dotted with the obsidian analogs of objects in normal space-time." And there will be more to come. *The Monadic Universe* gathers some of Zebrowski's stories and *Macrolife* concerns itself with the sociological interface found in space colonies. (If you like Zebrowski, try George R. R. Martin.)

ROGER ZELAZNY. Yes, but which Roger Zelazny? The author of the rich and mythically resonant *This Immortal* and *Lord of Light* and *The Dream Master,* who copped s-f's most prestigious awards in the '60s. Or the author of bang 'em up action stuff such as *Today We Choose Faces* or *Damnation Alley?* Or the fantasist of the Amber series? Those with a taste for the complex, many-leveled and mercurial tales of the early Delany should delve into the first group. *Lord of Light* tells of a Hindu culture brought to a remote planet. Incarnation is a reality and is used cybernetically, and with created intelligence. A sort of Buddha-Messiah painfully eliminates the corrupted self-appointed god-rulers and restores human progress. As always, Zelazny's unusual command of the material—here, his knowledge of Hindu mythology—provides substance and food for thought.

For action tastes, and Keith Laumer fans, the second group of Zelaznys are on the mark. *Damnation Alley,* for instance, is non-stop slam-bang gut-busting adventure, with its cross-country odyssey beset by giant crawlies, murderous tornados, barbaric Kansans, and cosmic lightning. And *Doorways in the Sand* is a truly funny novel of silly aliens, interstellar blackmail and idiotic espionage.

Readers into the "realist magic" tradition descending from *Unknown* magazine, de Camp, and Pratt will find happiness in the Amber series, Zelazny's third face.

Few authors in s-f move as freely among the established sub-genres as Zelazny has done, and it makes things confusing for his readers. "Do you like Zelazny?" is a question that won't elicit an informative response because the only constant in his work is its unrelenting narrative action. Sometimes the writing seems to exist only for the sake of that action, while at other times the narrative just keeps chugging away while Zelazny takes up what seems to matter more; in *Isle of the Dead,* for example, the experience of near-divine power is given a texture and solidity that remains long after the wide-screen stereophonic climax is gone.

Though none of Zelazny's books are uninteresting, it may need a second try if the first doesn't take. There are, in a sense, three writers subsumed under that formidable name; one of them is certain to please.

(If you like the works of Zelazny, try those of Jack Chalker, David Lake, and Richard Lupoff.)

Part Two

Last and First Books
A Guide to Major
Science Fiction Series

The reader new to science fiction, sooner than later, makes the discovery that the field is riddled (literally and figuratively) with series. Here you've found this intriguing book that you're enjoying no end, but around 50 pages in, it begins to dawn on you that it is the latest in multi-volume saga. And it is often nigh impossible to even find out what the other books in the series are, much less find the books.

Those publishers that are dead set on immediate sales will often not indicate on the cover that the book is part of a series for fear of scaring off the potential buyer that has not read the earlier volumes. And at The Science Fiction Shop, it has become lore that if #2 or #3 of a series is published, #1 or #2 will immediately become unavailable from the publisher. While this is not strictly true, it happens often enough to make you wonder.

Why is s-f so series prone? Unlike other genres, where a series is usually built around a charismatic character (Mr. Holmes, for instance), in science fiction, it may often be built around an environment, a created world, or a future universe—after all, the author has taken all the trouble to construct this milieu, why waste it on just one book?

There are various ways of handling this. The series can be loosely knit, as in Heinlein's "Future History" where a number of novels and short stories take place in the same future, but seldom overlap in plot or even characters. It can be almost one continuous narrative, such as Jack Vance's "Planet of Adventure" series where a single character fights his way through four volumes of assorted obstacles. Or it can be somewhere in between: Marion Bradley's Darkover novels are a collection of episodes in the biography of the planet Darkover.

There *are* the charismatic characters, too. Poul Anderson's Flandry of Terra, Alexei Panshin's Anthony Villiers, and, of course, the indefatigable Perry Rhodan, whose adventures now number in the thousands in Europe and well over a hundred in translation into English. (You won't find a list of Perry Rhodan books here; they are turned out assembly line fashion by several authors and are generally known by number rather than title.)

Some of the series you will find here are complete, others are ongoing. As we implied, all of a series will not necessarily be available at any one time. If your bookseller tells you that all or part of a series is out of print, there are two things to do: keep an eye on all the used book stores, and write a letter to the publisher. If they get enough requests, it will occur to them that it might pay to republish.

In this section, generally, we've tried to cover a lot of questions that we've been asked over the years about series. We know you will find it useful.

ALAN BURT AKERS

Dray Prescott Series
1. *Transit to Scorpio*
2. *The Suns of Scorpio*
3. *Warrior of Scorpio*
4. *Swordships of Scorpio*
5. *Prince of Scorpio*
6. *Manhounds of Antares*
7. *Arena of Antares*
8. *Fliers of Antares*
9. *Bladesman of Antares*
10. *Avenger of Antares*
11. *Armada of Antares*
12. *The Tides of Kregen*
13. *Renegade of Kregen*
14. *Krozair of Kregen*
15. *Secret Scorpio*
16. *Savage Scorpio*
17. *Captive Scorpio*
18. *Golden Scorpio*
19. *A Life for Kregen*
20. *A Sword for Kregen*
21. *A Fortune for Kregen*

The "Battle Circle" Series
1. *Sos*
2. *Var*
3. *Neq*

(These three novels have been combined in one volume entitled *Battle Circle.*)

The Cluster Series
1. *Cluster*
2. *Chaining The Lady*
3. *Kirlian Quest*
4. *Thousandstar*

The Planet Tarot Trilogy
1. *God of Tarot*
2. *Vision of Tarot*
3. *Faith of Tarot*

ISAAC ASIMOV

The Foundation Trilogy
1. *Foundation*
2. *Foundation and Empire*
3. *Second Foundation*

(The trick here is to remember that *Second Foundation* is the *third* book.)

LLOYD BIGGLE, JR.

The Jan Darzek Series
1. *All The Colors of Darkness*
2. *Watchers of The Dark*
3. *This Darkening Universe*
4. *Silence Is Deadly*
5. *The Whirligig of Time*

POUL ANDERSON

Polesotechnic League Series (Van Rijn, or Trader, Series)
1. *The Man Who Counts* (Also titled *War of the Wing-Men*)
2. *The Trouble Twisters*
3. *Trader to the Stars*
4. *Satan's World*
5. *Mirkheim*
6. *The Earth Book of Stormgate* (contains short stories which fall chronologically between the novels)

Flandry Series
1. *Ensign Flandry*
2. *A Circus of Hells*
3. *The Rebel Worlds*
4. *Mayday Orbit (A Message in Secret)*
5. *Earthman, Go Home (A Plague of Masters)*
6. *We Claim These Stars (A Handful of Stars)*
7. *A Knight of Ghosts and Shadows*
8. *A Stone in Heaven*

(Flandry short stories available in *Agent of the Terran Empire* and *Flandry of Terra*)

Associated Novels (These books are set in the same universe but do not include van Rijn or Flandry)
1. *The People of the Wind*
2. *The Day of Their Return*

PIERS ANTHONY

The Omnivore Series
1. *Omnivore*
2. *Orn*
3. *Ox*

JAMES BLISH

Cities in Flight
1. *They Shall Have Stars*
2. *A Life for the Stars*
3. *Earthman, Come Home*
4. *The Triumph of Time*

After Such Knowledge
(This series does not have an order as such, but does have a linking theme.)
1. *Doctor Mirabilis*
2. *Black Easter*
3. *The Day After Judgement*
4. *A Case of Conscience*

LEIGH BRACKETT

The Skaith Series
1. *The Ginger Star*
2. *The House of Skaith*
3. *The Reavers of Skaith*

MARION ZIMMER BRADLEY

The Darkover Novels
1. *Darkover Landfall*
2. *Stormqueen*
3. *The Spell Sword*
4. *The Forbidden Tower*
5. *The Shattered Chain*
6. *Star of Danger*
7. *Winds of Darkover*
8. *The Bloody Sun*
9. *The Heritage of Hastur*
10. *The Planet Savers*

11. *The Sword of Aldones*
12. *The World Wreckers*

(We call these the Darkover *novels* rather than the Darkover *series* because they are not a continuing narrative, but sometimes overlapping pieces in the jigsaw puzzle of the history of the planet Darkover. In other words, they can be read in any order. In fact, we suggest reading the first novel, *Darkover Landfall*, after reading some of the others; familiarity with what Darkover is to become adds to the enjoyment of discovering the sources.)

EDGAR RICE BURROUGHS

The Mars Series
1. *A Princess of Mars*
2. *The Gods of Mars*
3. *The Warlord of Mars*
4. *Thuvia, Maid of Mars*
5. *The Chessmen of Mars*
6. *The Mastermind of Mars*
7. *A Fighting Man of Mars*
8. *Swords of Mars*
9. *Synthetic Men of Mars*
10. *John Carter of Mars*
11. *Llana of Gathol*

The Venus Series
1. *Pirates of Venus*
2. *Lost on Venus*
3. *Carson of Venus*
4. *Escape on Venus*
5. *The Wizard of Venus*

The Pellucidar Series
1. *At the Earth's Core*
2. *Pellucidar*
3. *Tanar of Pellucidar*
4. *Tarzan at the Earth's Core*

5. *Back to the Stone Age*
6. *Land of Terror*
7. *Savage Pellucidar*

The Caprona Series
1. *The Land That Time Forgot*
2. *The People That Time Forgot*
3. *Out of Time's Abyss*

LIN CARTER

The Green Star Series
1. *Under the Green Star*
2. *When the Green Star Calls*
3. *By the Light of the Green Star*
4. *As the Green Star Rises*
5. *In the Green Star's Glow*

The Callisto Series
1. *Jandar of Callisto*
2. *The Black Legion of Callisto*
3. *Sky Pirates of Callisto*
4. *The Mad Empress of Callisto*
5. *Mind Wizards of Callisto*
6. *Lankar of Callisto*
7. *Ylana of Callisto*

JACK CHALKER

The Saga of the Well World
1. *Midnight At The Well of Souls*
2. *Exiles At The Well of Souls*
3. *Quest For The Well of Souls*
4. *The Return of Nathan Brazil*
5. *The Legacy of Nathan Brazil*

A. BERTRAM CHANDLER

John Grimes and the Rim Worlds
1. *Into the Alternate Univese*
2. *Contraband from Otherspace*
3. *The Road to the Rim*
4. *Spartan Planet*
5. *The Rim Gods*
6. *Alternate Orbits*
7. *The Dark Dimensions*
8. *To Prime the Pump*
9. *The Inheritors*
10. *The Gateway to Never*
11. *The Hard Way Up*
12. *The Big Black Mark*
13. *Star Courier*
14. *The Way Back*
15. *To Keep the Ship*

The Rimworlds
1. *The Rim of Space*
2. *Rendezvous on a Lost World*
3. *Beyond the Galactic Rim*
4. *The Ship from Outside*
5. *Catch the Winds*

C. J. CHERRYH

The Quest of Morgaine
1. *Gate of Ivrel*
2. *Well of Shiuan*
3. *Fires of Azeroth*

The Faded Sun
1. *The Faded Sun: Kesrith*
2. *The Faded Sun: Shonjir*
3. *The Faded Sun: Kutath*

JOHN CHRISTOPHER

The White Mountains Trilogy
1. *The White Mountains*
2. *The City of Gold and Lead*
3. *The Pool of Fire*

The Prince in Waiting Trilogy
1. *The Prince in Waiting*
2. *Beyond the Burning Lands*
3. *The Sword of the Spirits*

L. SPRAGUE DE CAMP & FLETCHER PRATT

The Harold Shea Series
1. *The Incomplete Enchanter*
2. *The Castle of Iron*
3. *The Wall of Serpents*
4. *The Green Magician*

(This series has a most confusing publishing history. The first—which to compound confusion is a combination of two novelettes, "The Roaring Trumpet" and "The Mathematics of Magic"—and the second have been later published as *The Compleat Enchanter,* an obviously misleading title. The third and the fourth, which are also technically only novelettes, have been published in a very small hard cover edition called *The Wall of Serpents,* now a collector's item. The third has also appeared in a collection, *Great Short Novels of Adult Fantasy,* Vol. 1. *The Wall of Serpents,* containing both, has been recently republished.)

GORDON R. DICKSON

The Childe Cycle
1. (Unpublished, and possibly unwritten, the first book is projected as an historical novel set in the 1300s)
2. *The Necromancer* (also published as *No Room for Man*)
3. *The Tactics of Mistake*

4. *Dorsai!* (originally *The Genetic General*)
5. *Soldier, Ask Not*
6. *The Spirit of Dorsai*

GEORGE ALLAN ENGLAND

Darkness and Dawn
(3 volume version)
1. *Darnkness and Dawn*
2. *Beyond the Great Oblivion*
3. *The Afterglow*

(5 volume version)
1. *Darkness and Dawn*
2. *Beyond the Great Oblivion*
3. *The People of the Abyss*
4. *Out of the Abyss*
5. *The Afterglow*

PHILIP JOSE FARMER

Riverworld
1. *To Your Scattered Bodies Go*
2. *The Fabulous Riverboat*
3. *The Dark Design*
4. *The Magic Labyrinth* (provisional title)

The World of Tiers
1. *Maker of Universes*
2. *The Gates of Creation*
3. *A Private Cosmos*
4. *Behind the Walls of Terra*
5. *Lavalight World*

MIKE FARREN

Trilogy
1. *Quest of the DNA Cowboys*
2. *Synaptic Manhunt*
3. *The Neural Atrocity*

ALAN DEAN FORSTER

The Humanx Commonwealth Series
1. *Bloodhype*
2. *The Tar-Aiym Krang*
3. *Orphan Star*
4. *The End Of The Matter*
5. *Midworld*
6. *Icerigger*
7. *Mission to Moulokin*

(The last three novels, although connected with the series, do not follow the exploits of Flinx and Pip, heroes of the first four.)

EDMOND HAMILTON

The Starwolf Series
1. *The Weapon From Beyond*
2. *The Closed Worlds*
3. *World of the Starwolves*

HARRY HARRISON

The Deathworld Series
1. *Deathworld 1*
2. *Deathworld 2*
3. *Deathworld 3*

The Stainless Steel Rat Series
1. *The Stainless Steel Rat*
2. *The Stainless Steel Rat's Revenge*
3. *The Stainless Steel Rat Saves The World*
4. *The Stainless Steel Rat Wants You!*

FRANK HERBERT

Dune Series
1. *Dune*
2. *Dune Messiah*
3. *Children of Dune*
4. *?*

NEIL R. JONES

The Professor Jameson Stories
1. *The Planet of the Double Sun*
2. *The Sunless World*
3. *Space War*
4. *Twin Worlds*
5. *Doomsday on Ajiat*

D. F. JONES

The Colossus Series
1. *Colossus*
2. *The Fall of Colossus*
3. *Colossus and the Crab*

KEITH LAUMER

Lafayette O'Leary Series
1. *Time Bender*
2. *Shape Changer*
3. *World Shuffler*

Retief Series
1. *Retief Unbound*
2. *Envoy To New Worlds*
3. *Galactic Diplomat*
4. *Retief's War*
5. *Retief and The Warlords*
6. *Retief of the CDT*
7. *Retief At Large* (Contains material available in other collections.)

URSULA K. LE GUIN

The Earthsea Trilogy
1. *The Wizard of Earthsea*
2. *The Tombs of Atuan*
3. *The Farthest Shore*

MURRAY LEINSTER

The Joe Kenmore Series
1. *Space Platform*
2. *Space Tug*
3. *City on the Moon*

The Med Service Series

1. *SOS From Three Worlds*
2. *Mutant Weapon*
3. *Doctor to the Stars*
4. *This World is Taboo*

C. S. LEWIS

The Perelandra Trilogy
1. *Out of the Silent Planet*
2. *Perelandra*
3. *That Hideous Strength*

ANNE McCAFFREY

Lessa of Pern
1. *Dragonflight*
2. *Dragonquest*
3. *The White Dragon*

Menolly the Singer
1. *Dragonsong*
2. *Dragonsinger*
3. *Dragondrums*

MICHAEL MOORCOCK

Elric
1. *Elric of Melnibone (The Dreaming City)*
2. *A Sailor on the Seas of Fate*
3. *The Weird of the White Wolf (Stealer of Souls)*
4. *The Vanishing Tower (The Sleeping Sorceress)*
5. *The Bane of the Black Sword*
6. *Stormbringer*

Runestaff
1. *The Jewel in the Skull*
2. *The Mad God's Amulet*
3. *The Sword of the Dawn*
4. *The Runestaff*

Count Brass
  1. *Count Brass*
  2. *Champion of Garathorm*
  3. *Quest for Tanelorn*

Corum
  1. *The Knight of Swords*
  2. *The Queen of Swords*
  3. *The King of Swords*
  4. *The Bull and The Spear*
  5. *The Oak and the Ram*
  6. *The Sword and the Stallion*

John Daker
  1. *The Eternal Champion*
  2. *The Silver Warriors (Phoenix in Obsidian)*

Michael Kane
  1. *City of the Beast (Warriors of Mars)*
  2. *Lord of the Spiders (Blades of Mars)*
  3. *Master of the Pit (Barbarians of Mars)*

Cornelius
  1. *The Final Programme*
  2. *A Cure for Cancer*
  3. *The English Assassin*
  4. *The Condition of Muzak*

(These have been published in one volume as the *Cornelius Chronicles*.)

The Dancers at the End of Time
  1. *An Alien Heat*
  2. *The Hollow Lands*
  3. *The End of All Songs*

(*Legends from the End of Time* and *Messiah at the End of Time* are satellite volumes to this series.)

(Note: Moorcock's series tend to interlock, to a point where it would take a three dimensional grid to work them out. This is the best we can do in two dimensions.)

LARRY NIVEN

The Known Space Series
1. *Tales of Known Space* (Short story collection)
2. *World Of Ptavvs*
3. *The Long ARM Of Gil Hamilton* (Short story collection)
4. *Protector*
5. *A Gift From Earth*
6. *Neutron Star* (Short story collection)
7. *Ringworld*

JOHN NORMAN

The Gor Series
1. *Tarnsman Of Gor*
2. *Outlaw of Gor*
3. *Priest-Kings Of Gor*
4. *Nomads Of Gor*
5. *Assassin Of Gor*
6. *Raiders Of Gor*
7. *Captive Of Gor*
8. *Hunters Of Gor*
9. *Marauders Of Gor*
10. *Tribesmen Of Gor*
11. *Slave Girl Of Gor*
12. *Beasts Of Gor*
13. *Explorers Of Gor*
14. *Fighting Slave Of Gor*

ANDRE NORTON

The Ross Murdock Series
1. *The Time Traders*
2. *Galactic Derelict*
3. *The Defiant Agents*
4. *Key Out Of Time*

The Solor Queen Series
1. *Sargasso Of Space*
2. *Plague Ship*
3. *Voodoo Planet*
4. *Postmarked The Stars*

The Forerunner Series
1. *Storm Over Warlock*
2. *Ordeal In Otherwhere*
3. *Forerunner Foray*

The Witch World Series
1. *Witch World*
2. *Web of the Witch World*
3. *Year of The Unicorn*
4. *Three Against the Witch World*
5. *Warlock of the Witch World*
6. *Sorceress of the Witch World*
7. *Spell of the Witch World* (Short story collection)
8. *The Crystal Gryphon*
9. *The Jargoon Pard*
10. *Trey of Swords*
11. *Zarsthor's Bane*

ALEXEI PANSHIN

The Anthony Villiers Novels
1. *Star Well*
2. *The Thurb Revolution*
3. *Masque World*

MACK REYNOLDS

The Joe Mauser Series
1. *Mercenary From Tomorrow*
2. *The Earth War*
3. *Time Gladiator*
4. *Fracas Factor*

The United Planets Series
1. *Section G: United Planets*
2. *Code Duello*
3. *Planetary Agent X*
4. *Rival Rigelians*
5. *Amazon Planet*
6. *Dawnman Planet*
7. *Brain World*

The North Africa Series
1. *Black Man's Burden*
2. *Border, Breed, Nor Birth*
3. *The Best Ye Breed*

JAMES H. SCHMITZ

The Telzey Amberdon Series
1. *The Universe Against Her*
2. *The Telzey Toy*
3. *The Lion Game*

E. E. "DOC" SMITH

The Lensmen Series
1. *Triplanetary*
2. *First Lensman*
3. *Galactic Patrol*
4. *Gray Lensman*
5. *Second Stage Lensman*

6. *Children of the Lens*
7. *Masters of the Vortex*

The Skylark Series
1. *The Skylark of Space*
2. *Skylark Three*
3. *Skylark of Valeron*
4. *Skylark DuQuesne*

The Family D'Alembert (with Stephen Goldin)
1. *Imperial Stars*
2. *Strangler's Moon*
3. *The Clockwork Traitor*
4. *Getaway World*
5. *Appointment at Bloodstar*

BRIAN M. STABLEFORD

The Star Pilot Grainger Series
1. *Halcyon Drift*
2. *Rhapsody In Black*
3. *Promised Land*
4. *Paradise Game*
5. *The Fenris Device*
6. *Swan Song*

The Dies Irae Series
1. *Days Of Glory*
2. *In The Kingdom Of The Beasts*
3. *Day of Wrath*

The "Daedalus" Mission Series
1. *The Florians*
2. *Critical Threshold*
3. *Wildeblood's Empire*
4. *City Of The Sun*
5. *Balance Of Power*
6. *The Paradox of the Sets*

OLAF STAPLEDON

The Last and First Men Trilogy
1. *Last and First Men*
2. *Last Men in London*
3. *Star Maker*

E. C. TUBB

The Dumarest of Terra Series
1. *Winds of Gath*
2. *Derai*
3. *Toy Man*
4. *Kalin*
5. *Jester At Scar*
6. *Lallia*
7. *Technos*
8. *Veruchia*
9. *Mayenne*
10. *Jondelle*
11. *Zenya*
12. *Eloise*
13. *Eye Of The Zodiac*
14. *Jack Of Swords*
15. *Spectrum Of A Forgotten Sun*
16. *Haven Of Darkness*
17. *Prison Of Night*
18. *Incident On Ath*
19. *Quillian Sector*
20. *Web of Sand*
21. *Iduna's Universe*

JACK VANCE

The Alastor Series
1. *Marune: Alastor 933*

2. *Trullion: Alastor 2262*
3. *Wyst: Alastor 1716*

(Note: the Alastor books are connected only by their being set in the same star cluster. There is no connection in plot or character.)

The Durdane Series
   1. *The Anome* (AKA *The Faceless Man*)
   2. *The Brave Free Men*
   3. *The Asutra*

The Planet of Adventure Series
   1. *City of the Chasch*
   2. *Servants of the Wankh*
   3. *The Dirdir*
   4. *The Pnume*

The Demon Prince Series
   1. *Star King*
   2. *The Killing Machine*
   3. *The Palace of Love*
   4. *The Face*
   5. *The Book of Dreams* (tentative title)

IAN WALLACE

The Adventures of Minds-In-Bodies Series
   1. *Every Crazy Wind*
   2. *The World Asunder*
   3. *Pan Sagittarius*

The Croyd Spacetime Maneuvers Series
   1. *Croyd*
   2. *Dr. Orpheus*
   3. *A Voyage to Dari*
   4. *Heller's Leap*

The St. Cyr Interplanetary Detective Mysteries
1. *The Purloined Prince*
2. *Deathstar Voyage*
3. *The Sign Of The Mute Medusa*
4. *Heller's Leap*

JAMES WHITE

The Sector General Series
1. *Hospital Station*
2. *Star Surgeon*
3. *Major Operation*
4. *Ambulance Ship*

(Although the first two and the fourth are connected short stories, the third is essentially a novel.)

JACK WILLIAMSON

The Legion Of Space Series
1. *Legion Of Space*
2. *The Cometeers*
3. *One Against The Legion*

ROGER ZELAZNY

The Amber Series
1. *Nine Princes in Amber*
2. *The Guns of Avalon*
3. *The Sign of the Unicorn*
4. *The Hand of Oberon*
5. *The Courts of Chaos*

Part Three

The Space Academy Awards
What Won What?

A perfectly valid way to test out a class group of science fiction authors is to read through the winners of the major awards in the field, most of which (with a few baffling exceptions) are usually available. Just remember that, like any awards in any area, there are factors brought to bear besides sheer quality.

Keep in mind that the *Hugos* (named for Hugo Gernsback, one of the several "fathers of science fiction") are to a degree a popular award, since they are voted by the membership of the annual World Science Fiction Convention, a membership that anyone can join, even those not planning to attend the convention itself. Those that do join are usually the "active fans," a small but vociferous percentage of the total science fiction readership. Winners here tend toward the obvious, the big book of the year by an established author; not that this necessarily precludes quality, nor does it sometimes preclude surprises (see the novel winners for 1970 and 1977).

The *Nebulas* are awarded by the membership of the Science Fiction Writers of America which, obviously, *not* just anybody can join. Here the award is more likely to be for craft and quality in writing; nevertheless, the SFWA is still a relatively small and sometimes incestuous group, and subject to the sentiments and feuds of any such.

THE HUGO AWARDS

(Voted on and awarded by members of the annual World Science Fiction Convention.)

1953
Novel: The Demolished Man (Alfred Bester)

1954
No Awards Given

1955
Novel: They'd Rather Be Right (Mark Clifton & Frank Riley)
Novelette: The Darfsteller (Walter M. Miller, Jr.)
Short Story: Allamagoosa (Eric Frank Russell)

1956
Novel: Double Star (Robert A. Heinlein)
Novelette: Exploration Team (Murray Leinster)
Short Story: The Star (Arthur C. Clarke)

1957
No Awards Given

1958
Novel: The Big Time (Fritz Leiber)
Short Story: Or All the Seas With Oysters (Avram Davidson)

1959
Novel: A Case of Conscience (James Blish)
Novelette: The Big Front Yard (Clifford D. Simak)
Short Story: The Hell-Bound Train (Robert Bloch)

1960
Novel: Starship Troopers (Robert A. Heinlein)
Short Fiction: Flowers for Algernon (Daniel Keyes)

1961
Novel: A Canticle for Leibowitz (Walter M. Miller, Jr.)
Short Story: The Longest Voyage (Poul Anderson)

1962
Novel: Stranger in a Strange Land (Robert A. Heinlein)
Short Fiction: The Hothouse Series (Brian Aldiss)

1963
Novel: The Man in the High Castle (Philip K. Dick)
Short Fiction: The Dragon Masters (Jack Vance)

1964
Novel: Way Station (Clifford Simak)
Short Fiction: No Truce With Kings (Poul Anderson)

1965
Novel: The Wanderer (Fritz Leiber)
Short Fiction: Soldier, Ask Not (Gordon R. Dickson)

1966
Novel: And Call Me Conrad—AKA *This Immortal* (Roger Zelazny) tied with *Dune* (Frank Herbert)
Short Fiction: 'Repent, Harlequin' Said the Ticktockman (Harlan Ellison)

1967
Novel: The Moon is a Harsh Mistress (Robert A. Heinlein)
Novelette: The Last Castle (Jack Vance)
Short Story: Neutron Star (Larry Niven)

1968
Novel: Lord of Light (Roger Zelazny)
Novella: Riders of the Purple Wage (Philip J. Farmer)
         Weyr Search (Anne McCaffrey)
Novelette: Gonna Roll the Bones (Fritz Leiber)
Short Story: I Have No Mouth and I Must Scream (Harlan Ellison)

1969
Novel: Stand on Zanzibar (John Brunner)

Novella: Nightwings (Robert Silverberg)
Novelette: The Sharing of Flesh (Poul Anderson)
Short Story: The Beast that Shouted Love at the Heart of the World (Harlan Ellison)

1970
Novel: The Left Hand of Darkness (Ursula K. Le Guin)
Novella: Ship of Shadows (Fritz Leiber)
Short Story: Time Considered as a Helix of Semi-Precious Stones (Samuel R. Delany)

1971
Novel: Ringworld (Larry Niven)
Novella: Ill Met in Lankhmar (Fritz Leiber)
Short Story: Slow Sculpture (Theodore Sturgeon)

1972
Novel: To Your Scattered Bodies Go (Phillip J. Farmer)
Novella: The Queen of Air and Darkness (Poul Anderson)
Short Story: Inconstant Moon (Larry Niven)

1973
Novel: The Gods Themselves (Isaac Asimov)
Novella: The Word for World is Forest (Ursula K. Le Guin)
Novelette: Goat Song (Poul Anderson)
Short Story: The Meeting (Pohl & Kornbluth) tied with Eurema's Dam (R. A. Lafferty)

1974
Novel: Rendezvous With Rama (Arthur C. Clarke)
Novella: The Deathbird (Harlan Ellison)
Novelette: The Girl Who Was Plugged In (James Tiptree, Jr.)
Short Story: The Ones Who Walked Away from Omelas (Ursula K. Le Guin)

1975
Novel: The Dispossessed (Ursula K. Le Guin)
Novella: Adrift Just off the Islets of Langerhans (Harlan Ellison)

Novelette: A Song for Lya (George R. R. Martin)
Short Story: The Hole Man (Larry Niven)

1976
Novel: The Forever War (Joe Haldeman)
Novella: Home is the Hangman (Roger Zelazny)
Novelette: Borderland of Sol (Larry Niven)
Short Story: Catch That Zeppelin (Fritz Leiber)

1977
Novel: Where Late the Sweet Birds Sang (Kate Wilhelm)
Novella: By Any Other Name (Spider Robinson)
Novelette: The Bicentennial Man (Isaac Asimov)
Short Story: Tricentennial (Joe Haldeman)

1978
Novel: Gateway (Fred Pohl)
Novella: Stardance (Spider and Jeanne Robinson)
Novelette: Eyes of Amber (Joan Vinge)
Short Story: Jefty Is Five (Harlan Ellison)

THE NEBULA AWARD

(Awarded annually by the membership of the Science Fiction Writers of America.)

1965
Novel: Dune (Frank Herbert)
Novella: The Saliva Tree (Brian W. Aldiss)
       He Who Shapes (Roger Zelazny) (tie)
Novelette: The Doors of His Face, The Lamps of His Mouth (Roger Zelazny)
Short Story: "Repent, Harlequin," Said the Ticktockman (Harlan Ellison)

1966
Novel: Flowers For Algernon (Daniel Keyes)
       Babel-17 (Samuel R. Delany) (tie)

Novella: The Last Castle (Jack Vance)
Novelette: Call Him Lord (Gordon R. Dickson)
Short Story: The Secret Place (Richard McKenna)

1967
Novel: The Einstein Intersection (Samuel R. Delany)
Novella: Behold The Man (Michael Moorcock)
Novelette: Gonna Roll The Bones (Fritz Leiber)
Short Story: Aye, and Gomorrah (Samuel R. Delany)

1968
Novel: Rite of Passage (Alexei Panshin)
Novella: Dragonrider (Anne McCaffrey)
Novelette: Mother to the World (Richard Wilson)
Short Story: The Planners (Kate Wilhelm)

1969
Novel: The Left Hand of Darkness (Ursula K. Le Guin)
Novella: A Boy and His Dog (Harlan Ellison)
Novelette: Time Considered as a Helix of Semi-Precious Stones (Samuel R. Delany)
Short Story: Passengers (Robert Silverberg)

1970
Novel: Ringworld (Larry Niven)
Novella: Ill Met in Lankhmar (Fritz Leiber)
Novelette: Slow Sculpture (Theodore Sturgeon)
Short Story: NONE

1971
Novel: A Time of Changes (Robert Silverberg)
Novella: The Missing Men (Katherine MacLean)
Novelette: The Queen of Air and Darkness (Poul Anderson)
Short Story: Good News From the Vatican (Robert Silverberg)

1972
Novel: The Gods Themselves (Isaac Asimov)
Novella: A Meeting With Medusa (Arthur C. Clarke)

Novelette: Goat Song (Poul Andersen)
Short Story: When It Changed (Joanne Russ)

1973
Novel: Rendezvous With Rama (Arthur C. Clarke)
Novella: The Death of Dr. Island (Gene Wolfe)
Novelette: Of Mist, and Grass, and Sand (Vonda K. McIntyre)
Short Story: Love is the Plan, The Plan is Death (James Tiptree, Jr.)

1974
Novel: The Dispossessed (Ursula K. Le Guin)
Novella: Born With the Dead (Robert Silverberg)
Novelette: If the Stars Are Gods (Gordon Eklund & Gregory Benford)
Short Story: The Day Before the Revolution (Ursula K. Le Guin)

1975
Novel: The Forever War (Joe Haldeman)
Novella: Home is the Hangman (Roger Zelazny)
Novelette: San Diego Lightfoot Sue (Tom Reamy)
Short Story: Catch That Zeppelin (Fritz Leiber)

1976
Novel: Man Plus (Frederik Pohl)
Novella: Houston, Houston Do You Read? (James Tiptree, Jr.)
Novelette: Bicentennial Man (Isaac Asimov)
Short Story: A Crowd of Shadows (C. L. Grant)

1977
Novel: Gateway (Frederik Pohl)
Novella: Stardance (Spider & Jeanne Robinson)
Novelette: The Screwfly Solution (Raccoona Sheldon)
Short Story: Jefty Is Five (Harlan Ellison)

1978
Novel: Dreamsnake (Vonda N. McIntyre)
Novella: The Persistence of Vision (John Varley)
Novelette: A Glow of Candles, A Unicorn's Eye (Charles L. Grant)
Short Story: Stone (Edward Bryant)

Part Four

The 5 Parsec Shelf
A Suggested Basic Library
and/or
Reading List in Science Fiction

Of course any such "basic" list is inevitably subjective. In this case, many knowledgeable science fiction readers will scream, yell, and have an attack of the vapors because such-and-such masterpiece was excluded, and this-and-that turkey was included. To stave off some such attacks, let us give you a bit of background as to how this list was arrived at.

As noted earlier in this volume, the four authors have widely divergent, but generally complementary, tastes. We each prepared our own list of 50 books, bearing in mind that we were treading a fine line between recommending those books that were to us must-reads—those we have pressed on to our friends and customers—and the necessity of including those works that we may not personally like but know to be important to the field.

As it turned out, the books that received two or more "votes" all became part of the combined list, leaving a few spaces for authors with a split vote of one each for two works. The choice there was left up to the senior member of the team, who included the titles that would seem to broaden the list's perspective most.

To clarify several of the individual entries:

Asimov's Foundation Trilogy has been published several times in one volume, which is how we considered it.

Anthologies, no matter how excellent, have seldom had enough impact to be "classics." But the first *Dangerous Visions*, edited by Ellison, was not only a wonderful sampling of the writers working in the exciting late '60s, it revolutionized science fiction in the matter of attacking more controversial subject matter.

C.S. Lewis' Perelandra Trilogy, to our knowledge, has never been published in one volume, but is in essence such an integrated, on-going story that it would have been silly to list only the first one.

Michael Moorcock's four Jerry Cornelius novels have been published as one under the *Cornelius Chronicles* title; for individual titles, see the

"Last and First Books" section.

We had a problem with Doc Smith. One vote was cast for the first of the Lensman series, one for the last, on the theory that this particular series improved markedly as it went along. We compromised on *First Lensman* as an acceptable, accessible beginning to the series.

If you manage to get these 50 volumes under your belt, we feel that you will have had a good smorgasbord of every kind of science fiction. The reader already familiar with s-f might give himself a little test as to how many of the 50 he's read. Twenty or under might indicate that you've restricted your reading within too narrow limits.

But where ever you may stand in knowing science fiction, we think that these titles are the cream of the crop, and that you, the potential reader, stand very little chance of going wrong with any of them. They are all extraordinary in one way or another.

(A final note on availability. All of these books, with a very few exceptions, are so well regarded that they are almost constantly in print. So there should be little difficulty in finding them at any well stocked book store.)

Brian Aldiss—*The Long Afternoon of Earth* (AKA *Hothouse*)
Poul Anderson—*Tau Zero*
Isaac Asimov—*The Foundation Trilogy*
J. G. Ballard—*Vermilion Sands*
Alfred Bester—*The Stars My Destination*
James Blish—*A Case of Conscience*
Ray Bradbury—*The Martian Chronicles*
John Brunner—*Stand on Zanzibar*
Edgar Rice Burroughs—*A Princess of Mars*
Arthur C. Clarke—*Childhood's End*
Arthur C. Clarke—*The City and the Stars*
Hal Clement—*Needle*
Samuel Delany—*Dhalgren*
Philip K. Dick—*The Man in the High Castle*
Gordon Dickson—*Dorsai!*
Thomas M. Disch—*334*
Harlan Ellison, Ed.—*Dangerous Visions*
M. John Harrison—*The Centauri Device*
Robert A. Heinlein—*Citizen of the Galaxy*
Robert A. Heinlein—*The Moon is a Harsh Mistress*

Frank Herbert—*Dune*
William Hope Hodgson—*The Night Land*
Henry Kuttner—*The Dark World*
Henry Kuttner and C. L. Moore—*Earth's Last Citadel*
Ursula K. Le Guin—*The Left Hand of Darkness*
Fritz Leiber—*The Big Time*
C. S. Lewis—*The Perelandra Trilogy*
H. P. Lovecraft—*At the Mountains of Madness*
A. Merritt—*The Moon Pool*
Walter M. Miller—*A Canticle for Leibowitz*
Michael Moorcock—*The Cornelius Chronicles*
Larry Niven—*Ringworld*
H. Beam Piper—*Little Fuzzy*
Frederik Pohl and C. M. Kornbluth—*The Space Merchants*
Joanna Russ—*And Chaos Died*
Mary Shelley—*Frankenstein*
Cordwainer Smith—*Norstrilia*
E. E. Smith—*First Lensman*
Olaf Stapledon—*Last and First Men*
Olaf Stapledon—*Odd John*
Theodore Sturgeon—*More Than Human*
A. E. van Vogt—*The World of Null-A*
Jack Vance—*The Dying Earth*
Jules Verne—*From the Earth to the Moon*
Stanley Weinbaum—*A Martian Odyssey and Others*
H. G. Wells—*The Time Machine*
Jack Williamson—*The Humanoids*
S. Fowler Wright—*The World Below*
John Wyndham—*The Midwich Cuckoos*
Roger Zelazny—*Lord of Light*

Part Five

The Spawn of Frankenstein
A Painless History
of Science Fiction

'I shall not be supposed as according to the remotest degree of serious faith to such an imagination; yet, assuming it as the basis of a work of fancy, I have not considered myself as merely weaving a series of supernatural terrors. The event on which the interest of the story depends is exempt from the disadvantages of a mere tale of spectres or enchantment. It was recommended by the novelty of the situations which it develops; and, however possible as a physical fact, affords a point of view to the imagination for the delineating of human passions more comprehensive and commanding than any which the ordinary relations of existing events can yield.''
—Mary Shelley, Preface to *Frankenstein*

That paragraph by Ms. Shelley is an absolute wonder (to use that word for the first of many times). In those few lines lies not only a beginning for our history of science fiction, but some very strong hints toward a definition—endlessly argued, never settled; maybe by looking at its past we can define its present. And aspiring s-f writers can pick up a few pointers from Ms. Shelley in the above, to boot.

Science fiction is fantasy, but fantasy of a particular sort. And of course fantasy has been with us since the first wondering quasi-intelligence made up a story to explain the thunder. As to where fantasy becomes entangled with myth, that we will leave to anthropologists and theologians. How to sort out fantasy from plain old fiction is a more complicated matter—*all* fiction is fantasy in a way (there wasn't really a family named Rostov living in Moscow in 1812, after all), and here's a beginning to the semantic nit-picking one must do in this sort of matter.

Let's say that fantasy is fiction where things occur that are unlikely at least, and downright impossible at most. This immediately brings up fantastic literature such as allogory, satire, and surrealism, which seem to be somewhere else. The difference here is that the author is in no way trying to make you believe what he's writing about or, to use an overworked phrase, to suspend your disbelief. He is communicating on a different level, and reality (or believability) is expendable. Orwell's

Animal Farm is an edifying fable, but I doubt if many readers really believe in the world of talking animals that Orwell has set up.

In true fantasy (including science fiction), part of the author's skill is spent in convincing you, if only for the duration of the reading, that the wonders that you are being told are real, and part of this is making the milieu where the fantastic events are taking place as logical, convincing, and consistent as possible.

So now we've boiled it down to a large lump of fiction which we might as well call "realistic fantasy," an appealing contradiction in terms. (From another direction, "speculative fiction" also does nicely, though a term not in favor with semantically snobbish s-f fans.)

Now back to Mary Shelley, who with prescient genius, if rather condescendingly, forecast the three major divisions into which "realistic fantasy' would split. Her story "is exempt from the disadvantages of a mere tale of spectres or enchantment." Spectres, or the supernatural tale in which the impossible is invoked primarily to frighten, both by playing on the universal fears of "things that go bump in the night" and, more subtly, to convince us, if only temporarily, that the safely natural order of the universe can break down at any moment.

Enchantment, or magic, elves and "A Midsummer Night's Dream": perhaps the major tale of enchantment, of "pure fantasy" of our day is Tolkien's *Lord of the Rings,* in which magic is presented as an operable premise, and the world is recognizably our world and not some other planet.

So what of Mary Shelley's own tale? What was it? She herself had no handy label to apply to it even while making sure that it would not be considered merely a ghost story or a frivolous fantasy.

Frankenstein was published in 1818; for two centuries already the Enlightenment has been substituting the application of reason for faith and superstition, and the Industrial Revolution was well on its way in England. Science and progress were coming to be viewed as the moving forces of civilized man.

It is ironic and perhaps indicative that the first major science fiction novel is essentially an anti-science anti-progress science fiction novel. Mary Shelley was obviously feeling the hot breath of the winds of change, and felt someone should hold up a warning sign to the effect that Science and Progress weren't necessarily going to result in the best of everything.

However, don't mistake Mary's novel for a cautionary tract disguised as fiction (which describes a lot of later pseudo-science fiction. Orwell's *1984*, for instance.) She's a story teller with a story to tell, and she's come up with a fascinating concept which, she implies, will be *wonderful* (literally—full of wonder) for the reader, but more convincing than a mere ghost story or fairy tale.

There has always been that appreciable percentage of humanity who enjoyed hearing of wonders. Up until recently this need was filled by myths, legends, and other such folk literature, and travel tales, either true or false.

Now Mary Shelley was at the right time and the right place (and, of course, possessing the requisite talent and intelligence) to make a discovery that only a very few had done previously. And that was to enlist the mysteries of science and progress to make her wonders more convincing. Already, as we have noted, the population was becoming aware of changes in their lives wrought by science and progress, were confounded again and again by new genies from these strange bottles, and were ready, with a little help, to believe that anything was possible. The little help, of course, came from the author. Throw in science as a cause, either legitimately and knowledgeably, or with convincing scientific double talk, and the effect on the reader is conviction.

So there it was. The old wonders, marvels, impossibles, newly and convincingly based in progressive science and scientific progress.

It is indicative that one begins to talk of science fiction in terms of its concepts and concerns, or more loosely, its content, as opposed to its style. There's no denying that science fiction is a form of literature, but it you try judging it in literary terms, you might as well forget a great deal of its past in addition to a healthy chunk of its present. This will be no apologia for science fiction's frequent lack of literary values; like any genre, its values lie elsewhere.

But to simply set this genesis of science fiction into a literary context, one might call it a mutant child of the Gothic novel. One could go on at some length about the Gothic ancestry, and a great many have. *Frankenstein*, indeed, has been called the epitomal Gothic novel. But for our purposes, what was new in it was much more important than what was used.

Now that we've settled all that, let us sink Mary Shelley into the west (with much gratitude), shelve our conclusions temporarily and proceed further into the 19th century. For, curiously, that virgin spring that is to be a major tributary to contemporary science fiction ran almost unnoticed for a while. But other streams, some similar, some from left field, were rising also. Let's ford a few of the more obvious.

One of these where we need not get our feet too wet is Edgar Allan Poe, America's one claim to a science fictional progenitor. And a pretty shaky one it is. Some anonymous idiot called him "the father of science fiction" around the turn of the century, and people have been wondering why ever since. Whoever he was, he either didn't know much about Poe, or didn't know much about science fiction. True, a minority of Poe's stories could be considered science fiction in the loosest sense, having to do with the destruction of the Earth, viewing the past, or even going to the moon, but they are also so involved with such matters as mesmerism, survival after death and other such matters that his quoted dictum, "that everything should be scientifically logical," while valid, seems more preaching than practice.

On the other hand, the French in the mid-19th century were going through a period of typcial Gallic overenthusiasm about Science and Progress. This resulted in Jules Verne.

Verne wrote most of the works that got *him* dubbed "the father of science fiction" during the first part of his career. They were optimistic and enthusiastic about that visible manifestation of Science and Progress that could loosely be described as technology. Everything could and would be solved by technology, and we have here the beginning of what has come to be known as the "nuts and bolts" school of science fiction. In *The Mysterious Island*, castaways on a deserted island manage all the amenities with more or less what they have in their pockets. This may seem more like Robinson Crusoe than science fiction, but when you realize that one of the amenities is electricity and that the book was published in 1875, it comes a bit closer to fantasy. Here we have the direct antecedent of all those heroes of the pulps who saved the universe with only what they had in *their* pockets.

Our castaways also run into Captain Nemo, hero of the earlier *20,000 Leagues Under the Sea*. *Human* hero, we might note; the real hero is the *Nautilus*. Verne often would suggest one technological invention, and weave the story about what could be done with it.

Though later in his life, he would speculate further about the morality of science and progress, it is the earlier works that are perennially popular.

Despite these Franco-American side trips, the major well-spring of science fiction was to be England. Another factor in England in the 19th century, besides Science and Progress and all that, was The Empire. Merchants and military returned from all corners of the globe with wonderful travel stories which were, for the most part, true. But it was an easy step from there to the tale of wonders that just *might* be still to be found in some yet untrodden area.

This sets the stage for the entrance of the redoubtable H. Rider Haggard, pith helmet and all. His turf was Africa, and his first great success was the novel *King Solomon's Mines,* which set a discernible pattern: a "realistic" African setting in which, beyond the bounds of explored territory, is found something extraordinary. Perhaps epitomal is *She,* in which the found object is an immortal lady ruling over the decadent remnants of a great ruined civilization. She's powers are not simply magical; there are hints of rational explanations for them though often couched in mystical terms.

It is certainly arguable that what Haggard was writing was *true* science fiction in the sense that *Frankenstein* was. Nevertheless, if the older novel were speculation in biology and chemistry. Haggard's works were equally validly speculation in anthropology, geography, and archeology. And while Haggard, for a change, was *not* dubbed "the father of science fiction" by anybody, he may well have been the greatest influence of all on the soon-to-emerge American school, as we shall see.

Another Englishman out of left field who was to be a factor was William Morris, a Renaissance man of the arts. At least one of his novels, *News from Nowhere,* would certainly be considered science fiction today; it is a tale of the future with a strong social reform theme. But perhaps even more important were his "fantasies," dreamlike romances laid in vaguely Medieval mythical worlds. Here was a start in creating the "created world" which was going to be of great value when science fiction writers started creating their own worlds in space. (Dunsany and Tolkien, Morris' two great successors in fantasy, were equally adept at creating worlds themselves, and were of great influence in that area of science fiction.)

Now, another "father of science fiction" (did ever a baby literary field *have* so many fathers?) and probably more deserving of that paternal cognomen than anyone, was the amazing Mr. H. G. Wells.

In essence, Wells' role was as much synthesizer as innovator. He brought together all the strains so far; the adventure of exotic places, the potential of new inventions, the awareness of the future and social change, the speculative imagination; and he put them together with enormous intelligence and literary grace and wit.

Wells' work might be called a culmination, in a way, of the work not only of those authors we have mentioned, but of many others whose names have not worn so well, but whose forgotten novel or story might have added an iota of inspiration to that finished product. And writing at the same time as Wells were others who would, along with him, offer a basic form to be played with. Certainly deserving of mention are Conan Doyle, who in his Professor Challenger stories was attempting to do with the new genre what he'd done in the detective story with Sherlock Holmes; the strange genius William Hope Hodgson, whose lengthy novel of the future, *The Night Land,* can still inspire awe by the originality of its concept as well as the monumentality of its length; and the wonderful Edith Nesbit, whose fantasies for children (supposedly) were models of consistency and logic that many a future science fiction writer might envy.

And there was one Englishman to follow Wells that even that egotist admired, who took the Wellsian model of a scientifically valid speculation with philosophical overtones and so transcended the model that no one yet has matched the breadth of his works. He was Olaf Stapledon.

But before this, during the midpoint of Wells' writing career, whatever strange winds that rule cultural change, quietly and unnoticed at the time, began stirring to the west across the Atlantic and whatever creative impulse that gives rise to the writing and reading of science fiction began to wane in England and to wax, ever so slowly, in America. The first major spark was named Edgar Rice Burroughs.

Before we take a closer look at Burroughs' wild talent, though, just a few speculations on why the science fictional muse might have decided on a (for the time being) one way ticket to the still barely civilized United States.

Science fiction seems to flourish best in a cultural climate of optimism and self assurance, and a belief in a (or the) future. It also needs, of course, a literate readership. With the growth of literacy in the U.S., which also enjoyed the cultural climate mentioned above, there came a demand for more and more fiction, a cheap escape for a reading public with jobs that were often tedious and dreary. At this point, the demand was not for anything sophisticated or subtle. Action/adventure was the thing, and the need was supplied by mountains of penny dreadful and dime novel magazines.

There were more or less four categories of fiction to be found in these magazines. There was romance, where the adventure was mostly wildly emotional and the appeal was to the female; their remote descendants are the contemporary Gothics. For the male, adventure came *au naturel* in the great outdoors, which for Americans generally meant the West; these developed into the Western. Urbanized adventure became the crime-detective-murder mystery. Very rarely at first, there appeared adventure in exotic lost civilizations a la Haggard or even more rarely, on other planets.

The emphasis on adventure meant the elimination of the British ideas of philosophical content or scientific validity.

Certainly nothing could be more illustrative of the American approach than Edgar Rice Burrough's first effort, published in *All Story* magazine with the still romantic title of *Under the Moons of Mars*. Here we meet for the first time the all-American hero, John Carter, the beautiful Princess of Mars, the incomparable Dejah Thoris, and Mars itself, a world of dead sea bottoms, ancient cities, lost cultures, and startling flora and fauna, known to its inhabitants as Barsoom.

The Tarzan stories, to be begun later, more than anything else showed the Haggard influence directly. The ape man Lord of the Realm was always stumbling across secret corners of Africa that served as home to extant dinosaurs, lost Roman legions, and other wondrous phenomena. Since so far as anyone knows, Burroughs never set foot in Africa, the locale of the Tarzan stories was just about as mythical as Barsoon.

It is indicative of the very earliest American s-f that John Carter gets to Mars initially by some unexplained sort of astral projection. Burroughs, however, shaped up and got his other heroes to their exotic destinations by more sensible means. His science was always the popular theoretical concepts of the time: Mars had canals, Venus was a watery world, and almost everything technical was activated by undefined "rays." It must be noted however, that intentionally or not, he stumbled upon a very sophisticated concept in Pellucidar, the inner world that has no night or other time divisions. In Pellucidar, he tells us, time was relative; what was for one character a lunch break was for another days of fighting sabre tooth tigers.

The action never flags, and most of what is considered literary values are sacrificed to it; a modern adult coming to Burroughs for the first time might find reading him a painful experience. This set a pattern for American science fiction. Over the years, it has been most subject to attack for its lack of literary values. "Pulp trash" it was called, and trash it was—as literature. Until recently the excitement of the field lay in the ideas and concepts, not in the style.

Here began the nearly half century of science fiction's confinement to magazines. Any s-f published between hard covers (paperbacks were uncommon to the point of nonexistence), aside from out-of-genre attempts such as *Brave New World,* was such an exception as to prove the rule that the public was not willing to spend more than a dime on such "literature."

The only real change that came about until the middle of the century was in the 1920s, when the daring step was taken of publishing specialized magazines, rather than the "all-story" type that included many varieties of fiction. This was an almost immediate success; apparently then as now, s-f readers were seldom concerned with other genres, and adventure of any sort was far less the attraction than the particular excitement of science fictional mind-stretching.

The first of these specialized magazines was *Weird Tales* (1923) and its "specialization" points out an interesting and on-going confusion between true science fiction and its fellow sub-genre, the supernatural story. *Weird Tales,* during the first part of its history, published both, on the theory that anything from "beyond," either ghost or extraterrestrial, was menacing, weird, and scarey.

This developed a sort of hybrid fiction, of which the best exemplars were H. P. Lovecraft and Clark Ashton Smith, both of whose writings were certainly calculated to inspire horror, and both of whom often used pseudo-scientific rationales for the taking-off points of their eldritch creatures, such as "other dimensions." (This combination, of course, goes as far back as dear old *Frankenstein* and is as recent a manifestation as the "science fiction" film, almost every one of which continued the popular confusion between s-f and horror.)

The pure, unadulterated stuff, in the meantime, was taking off in every direction (except literary). In a score of years, Burroughs' tentative exploration of our closest neighbor planets had been expanded by fellow writers into expeditions throughout the galaxy and beyond in search of adventure and imaginative conceptualizing. Such truly specialized magazines as *Amazing, Astounding* and *Science Wonder* (two of which were founded by that pioneer Luxembourgois, Hugo Gernsback, after whom the annual s-f award, the Hugo, is named) were by the '30s tossing worlds around like confetti, and writers as diverse as the formula-setting E. E. Smith and the quirkily experimental (for the time) Stanley

G. Weinbaum were broadening the story concepts by leaps and bounds, each not only inventing new ideas but building on those of other writers.

At this felicitous point, let's break off from chronological history to point out an important dichotomy that had now developed in science fiction. On the one hand the basically English school, using imaginative and speculative ideas to point out a moral or a warning or to illuminate some part of the contemporary culture, and sometimes coming close to satire. On the other, the unquenchable American school (*cum* Verne), with an action-adventure background using science fictional ideas for their own sakes; it could be considered science fiction for the fun of it. Science fiction had arrived at the place that almost every field of the arts comes to, the division into "classic" and "romantic" schools, as it were; or intellectual and emotional; or Apollonian and Dionysian; or stuff and nonsense, if you will. Brian Aldiss makes the authorial distinction between "the thinkers" and "the dreamers" (and being English, had fewer kind words for the dreamers). These are by no means to be regarded as absolute or mutually exclusive; they are the far ends of a spectrum with many areas of intermixture.

The pulp magazines were so named because of the kind of paper on which they were printed. There were all kinds—Western, detective, jungle tales and even Spicy This-or-Thats, which in reality were about as spicy as a slice of white bread. The pulps were regarded as just short of pornography by the majority of the public (especially parents), but aside from the busty ladies on the covers they were literally as pure as the driven snow. And since science fiction was for forty years to be confined to their pages, it too avoided sexuality and controversy—the average reader of the s-f pulp was regarded as an intelligent but socially retarded late adolescent, a view that was not all that inaccurate then and still manifests itself today in science fiction "fandom."

Despite the vitality of the field in its American magazine aspect, by the mid-'30s the energy began to flag. Concepts were getting more and more fanciful, with less and less grounding in scientific possibility, and were therefore becoming less and less believable. Literary quality was not improving; in fact with certain major exceptions the stories were becoming formula ridden and cliched.

In 1937 a very simple event changed the face of science fiction. A young writer became the editor of *Astounding Stories*. His name was John W. Campbell; under that name he had written a good deal of formula s-f for various magazines. He had also, under the pseudonym of Don A. Stuart, published other stories that were more thoughtful, more questioning of the tenets that other authors had taken for granted, such as the innate superiority of humanity.

As editor, Campbell's requirements did not seem all that revolutionary. Basically, he demanded more valid grounding for the scientific speculation inherent to science fiction. As a corollary to this, he developed and encouraged (and *edited*, a rare talent these days) young authors who were not only logical in their use of speculation, but just more downright intelligent in their approach to everything.

The list of major writers that emerged from the Campbell stable is staggering; their influence on the field immeasurable. And even though "literary" quality was not the major quality Campbell looked for, it came because the Campbell writers were for the most part inherently above the hack level. Far from alienating the reader who was regarded so condescendingly by the magazine publishers, the Campbell revolution was greeted with widespread acceptance.

Even today, the backbone of the field consists primarily of Campbell writers from the late '30s and the '40s, and their works are the basic, "classic" literature of the genre. Asimov, de Camp, del Rey, Bester, Heinlein, Sturgeon, Leiber, and van Vogt are but some of those he introduced and/or nurtured in the pages of *Astounding*.

Later, Campbell was to turn off some readers because of opinionated conservative views expressed in editorials and his support of such questionable causes as Dianetics, but he continued to maintain *Astounding's* top position in the field until his death in 1971.

Willy or nilly, the "new" science fiction spread to the other magazines and flourished with new vitality, despite World War II—or perhaps because of it, since seldom before had fantasy been so needed. Some authors such as Heinlein were inactive during the war because of military duty, and several worthy magazines were forced to discontinue publication because of paper shortages, but s-f as a whole emerged from the war in good health, and in no way harmed by the use of such a "science ficitional" device as the atomic bomb. (A well-known piece of science fiction folklore concerns an investigation for security leaks that was launched against *Astounding* during the war because of one author's speculations about atomic power.)

If you had decided to be a science fiction reader in 1946, what would you have found? Primarily, nothing but magazines; you would almost never have needed to enter a bookstore—the corner magazine stand would have been your haunt.

And what would those magazines have been? First, you would have probably discovered *Planet Stories,* as the most overtly science fictional pulp on the stands, still dedicated to the old fashioned space opera and proclaiming it every issue with the *de rigueur* romantic-action trio of guy, girl, and BEM (bug-eyed monster) on the cover.

Twin magazines called *Amazing Stories* and *Fantastic Adventures* might next have caught your eye; supposedly *Amazing* was dedicated to science fiction, *Fantastic* to fantasy, but since they also were keeping alive the pre-Campbell tradition, that particular distinction between s-f and fantasy was fairly dim. *Amazing* had survived for over two decades (it was one of the first true s-f magazines) on the publication of new stories by the seemingly everlasting Edgar Rice Burroughs, but he had made his last contribution there several years earlier. The editor at that time, Ray Palmer, had in 1946 however, just stumbled on something that he felt would restore circulation. It did indeed; it would go down in the annals of science fiction as the Shaver Mystery, based on stories by one Richard Shaver (in the author section), and would be one of the prime embarrassing moments in the history of the field.

With equally raunchy covers, but far different interiors, were two other "sister" magazines, *Startling Stories* and *Thrilling Wonder Stories.* They had just come under the editorship of Samuel Merwin in 1945; until then they had been sturdy practitioners of the formula pre-Campbell school, but under Merwin's aegis they would soon challenge *Astounding* and Campbell with authors such as Jack Vance, Ray Bradbury (in a switch from his earliest stories which were in the supernatural horror vein), and the young Englishman, Authur C. Clarke (in a couple of years, Clarke's novel *Against the Fall of Night*—to be rewritten as *The City and the Stars*—would appear in *Startling Stories,* with typically, an illustrative cover featuring a scantily-clad lady whose relationship to the novel was dim to say the least).

Those were the core magazines, with one exception: a magazine you would probably take a while to find, since it looked different. Digest-sized, with better paper and nary a naked lady to be found on its covers ever, John Campbell's *Astounding* was undeniably the class act of the science fiction world. It was at this point going through a rather trying period for any reader uninitiated into *Astounding* esoterica. A. E. van Vogt had just published the first of his novels, complex as anything built by Daedalus, based on non-Aristotelian logic and semantics (this is, in four decades, a long, long way from Burroughs' Martian princesses). Called *The World of Null-A,* it has become a classic, but is certainly not recommended for the novice reader even now.

The versatile Henry Kuttner almost one upped van Vogt with *The Fairy Chessmen,* and intricacy was the name of the game at *Astounding* during this period. But there were simpler rewards to be found there too. Readers were begging for another Foundation story from Isaac Asimov, who was then right about in the middle of those short stories and novelettes that were to become the great Foundation trilogy, perhaps epitomal of '40s science fiction; and they were also begging for more "City" stories from Clifford Simak, and more *anything* from Robert Heinlein. One can see why this post war era is considered the Golden Age of science fiction.

If our hypothetical novice searched farther afield in the magazine stand, he would have come up with two more related magazines. *Famous Fantastic Mysteries* reprinted in every issue a book-length novel from the past, in any of the three sub-genres of fantasy. Here was the only real opportunity a younger reader would have of becoming acquainted with the works of the past, such as those of John Taine, A. Merritt, or H. P. Lovecraft. They were usually unavailable in any other form.

And there was still *Weird Tales,* the oldest of them all, now sticking entirely to tales of the supernatural.

The magazine period of s-f is so important an era in its history that several other aspects of it need be mentioned. It had a great influence on form, for one thing; the short story was king. Even those works announced on the covers as "novels" were barely novelette length, and only *Astounding* dared print a true novel as a serial. Here was the basis for that form almost unique to s-f, the series of interconnected but complete-unto-themselves short works that would later become a "novel" hopefully greater than the sum of its parts. The above-mentioned Foundation trilogy is the perfect example.

All this had led academicians to the belief that the best form for science fiction is the short story. This is highly debatable indeed; since the magazine era, the science fiction novel has more than proved itself a viable form. There is also the inevitable problem of the short story in science fiction, "where the idea is King," becoming nothing *more* than an idea, a gimmick story, to be exact.

Another aspect of the magazine scene was the art. Every magazine had illustrations, at least one per story, and over the years the pulps developed some fine craftsmen indeed. Among the earliest was Frank R. Paul, whose covers and interior illustrations are redolent of the '20s but nevertheless show endless ingenuity and imagination. Of the later masters, Virgil Finlay displayed incomparable draughtsmanship in his more-beautiful-than-life figures, embellished with the stuff of fantasy, stars, bubbles and lightning flashes; Hannes Bok, a disciple of Maxfield Parrish, who carried that fine artist's art nouveau style to strange and wonderful heights; and Edd Cartier, with a basically cartoonist style with which he portrayed delicious aliens and robots.

Science fiction readers nostalgic for the "golden age" often long as much for the monthly or bimonthly thrill of finding new works by these artists as they do for the literary material of that period.

And finally some mention must be made of science fiction fandom, which was reaching a sort of crest in the late '40s. All of the magazines had letters columns, and through these a vociferous minority of readers made their opinions known in no uncertain terms. The results were sometimes informative (the readers were constantly mentioning classics; one of the few ways the novice reader could learn what *were* the classics in the field, since at that point almost nothing had been written *about* science fiction) but mostly social. Readers would contact each other through these columns for correspondence; since there would only be one or two "active fans" per area, a loose network was set up across the entire country.

From these fans came many of the professionals of today. Any given issue of *Startling Stories* in the late '40s might well have contained a letter from Lin Carter, Marion Bradley, Arthur Clarke (though he already published professionally), Poul Anderson, or one of us.

Alas, all this was to end in the early '50s. The pulp magazines per se vanished for a variety of reasons, two of the major ones being the skyrocketing costs of publishing and the increasing popularity of the paperback book. *Astounding* kept going; it had already adopted the practical shape of the future, which was digest sized and on better paper. It was eventually to change its name to *Analog*, under which it still exists. *Amazing* and *Fantastic* also reduced their size and kept going with an almost total lack of distinction. The rest disappeared, to be replaced by two newcomers which were to make their mark on the field. These were *The Magazine of Fantasy and Science Fiction*, which eclectically published across the board fantasy, supernatural, and science fiction stories, and *Galaxy,* which concentrated on science fiction. Both were to have long and distinguished careers, but the era of magazine supremacy in the genre was over.

There were several peripheral results of this. One was that science fiction art fell into a decline from which it has not yet recovered; the cover of a paperback book was a poor substitute for the myriad illustrations of the pulps, and only recently has attention been paid to them as an art form. (Luckily, some dedicated aficionados of pulp art have determined that these artists will not be relegated to forgotten crumbling magazines, and several collections of covers and interior illustrations have recently been made available.)

And more attention began being paid to the science fiction novel. The major magazines all began to publish the long form as serials, which would then be published as full length paperback books. Because of this, out of sheer necessity, literary quality began to rise slowly but surely, and such matters as characterization and form began to be important.

During the 1950s and the early 1960s, new and talented authors emerged such as Poul Anderson, Marion Bradley, the Roberts Shaw, Sheckley and Silverberg, and the unique Cordwainer Smith. The older generation met this competition with some mighty works of their own: Alfred Bester's two blockbuster novels, *The Demolished Man* and *The Stars My Destination;* Arthur Clarke's reworked *The City and the Stars* and *Childhood's End;* a host of Heinleins, including "juvenile" novels that would be so influential to an upcoming generation; and the Theodore Sturgeon masterpiece, *More Than Human.*

Hard cover publication was still rare for the field, despite the valiant efforts of smaller specialty publishers, whose books are now collectors' items. But the paperback market flourished, particularly a new line called Ballatine Books which was backed by the near-impeccable taste of Ian and Betty Ballantine.

And the readership grew. The annual world conventions, begun in 1939 by hard core active fans, became major events, and more and more regional conventions were held. As in any marketplace, even literary marketplaces, there were booms and busts, but slowly and surely more people were reading science fiction.

But there was still this curious, almost indefinable gap between the genre and the mainstream culture. This can be best illustrated by the fact that the venerable *Saturday Evening Post* for a short time ran quite a bit of science fiction (and not just mainstream copies—several stories by Heinlein first appeared there), but soon gave it up. There was still that stigma attached to "that Buck Rogers stuff" that literally divided the world into two sorts of people—those that appreciated science fiction and those who felt it to be an intellectual eccentricity at best, a contemptible sub-literature at worst, and with almost no viewpoint in between. Which is why, particularly in the older generation of both readers and professionals, there is often a defensiveness close to hostility towards outsiders.

Despite the activity mentioned above, the talented authors old and new, and the major works, the only really perceptible change in science fiction was a shift away from the "romantic," space-operatic, Burroughsian stuff toward more "classical," Meaningful, Socially Significant work. The major force here was *Galaxy* magazine, but the tendency was evident almost everywhere in the genre.

This was probably the inevitable result of the Campbellian revolution of two decades earlier, and certainly widened the scope of American s-f. The results ranged from the near satire of Robert Sheckley and the team of Frederik Pohl and C. M. Kornbluth (whose *Space Merchants,* reflecting the mid-century's intellectual distrust of Madison Avenue, portrayed a future dominated by advertising) through the subtle Stapledonian humanism of Arthur Clarke's *Childhood's End* to the growing philosophical didacticism of Robert Heinlein.

The other interior event during this period was what might be called a Renaissance of British science fiction writing which for many years had been moribund (with the exception of Clarke and one or two others who published primarily in American magazines). Curiously, they reversed the American trend of the period; they tended more toward the romantic school, concentrating on ending the world, or at least civilization, in various engaging ways. There was still the element of the cautionary tale, given the subject, but the emphasis was on concept and action, overlaid with typical British common sense and *verismo* writing, making the end result all the more convincing and horrendous.

This "twilight of Empire" group included such names as J. G. Ballard, John Christopher, John Wyndham (who had been writing for years under various names, but only now began to receive major attention), and Brian Aldiss, who was less destructive than the others (his *Long Afternoon of Earth,* as the title implies, ended our planet not with a bang but with a vegetation/insect dominated whimper).

The most important development however was, of course, American youth and in the mid-60s, they created a cultural revolution whose reverberations are still being felt. And it seems that most of these young people had at least a nodding acquaintance with science fiction, and many had grown up on the adolescently-oriented books of Robert Heinlein, Andre Norton, and others. More than a few knew *Childhood's End,* and Heinlein's *Stranger in a Strange Land* and Frank Herbert's *Dune,* and those that didn't soon would; these three became the cult books of a generation (as did Tolkien's *The Lord of the Rings,* a pure fantasy that was to play its part in reshaping s-f).

The effect of this on the field was felt with amazing rapidity. Perhaps the most surprising was that science fiction, for the first time in its history, developed an *avant-garde.* Other fields of the arts had to a degree become used to the cycle of the establishment of an Establishment, and then a determined attack on its conventions by a rebellious and original youth. But this had never really happened before in science fiction and the resulting unpleasantness was perhaps the more acrimonious for that reason. Somehow typically the field could find no original term for its young Turks, and so resorted to the cinematic "new wave." The issues were so conventional for this sort of situation as to be almost comical: most of the established writers were aghast at what they felt to be a concentration on sex and obscenity in content, and downright sloppiness and/or incomprehensibility in style. Most of the "new wave" felt science fiction was in a rut, avoided sex to the point of Puritanism, was concerned with only safe issues, had no style whatsoever, and in general felt that the science fiction Establishment consisted of a bunch of fuddy duddies who were hypocritical, fascistic and militaristic.

As usual, there was a bit of truth on each side. Science fiction was still almost as pure as the driven snow when it came to sex, and the magazines were still being edited for the hypothetical, socially retarded adolescent with the watch-dog mother. And there had been a certain concentration on militarism in the field, mostly because it was a part of s-f's action-adventure heritage.

On the other hand, much of what was produced by the avant-garde, as with *any* avant-garde, was experimental garbage, but that's the only way to find out what of the new will work. And typical of their generation, the younger writers were for the most part a good deal more sophisticated than their elders in many areas.

The English, befitting their general position of having started the broad cultural brouhaha with the Beatles and all that, came in swinging and for a while centered the new wave around a magazine called *New Worlds,* edited by the young, imaginative, prolific writer Michael Moorcock. For a change, here was an English magazine publishing the hottest young American writers—Thomas M. Disch, Samuel R. Delany, and Norman Spinrad, among others.

There was no equivalent magazine in the U.S.; there were only three major ones left now and, while holding their own, they were not about to jeopardize their position with their faithful readers, many of whom lived in areas of the country that were notoriously unsympathetic to the greening of America or any of its concomitants.

This paved the way for a revolutionary book that almost singlehandedly revived the moribund science fiction short story as a form. Harlan Ellison, the hotspur of the younger writers, edited an anthology called *Dangerous Visions,* which essentially contained stories considered unpublishable by the American magazines. It was a brilliant success, artistically and with the readers. And, curiously enough, was an early step toward reconciling the factions in the field, since Ellison had the good sense to use stories from every section of science fiction—almost all writers, whatever generation, had stories that had been refused by the magazines for reasons other than quality.

In fact, the whole squabble was resolved to a large degree with surprising speed. As is almost always the case in this kind of esthetic split, the field benefited immensely from new ideas and new blood. The conservatives recognized, accepted, and sometimes emulated the new areas of endeavor; the "avant-garde" found that there was room for anybody with talent. This is not to imply that science fiction has been since then one happy little family. It's still a surprisingly small world (though for how long is questionable). There is still a familial intermingling of writers and readers, and almost everyone beyond a certain level of professionalism knows a good percentage of everybody else at that level. This situation has advantages and disadvantages: excellent lines of communication and interchange with few obstacles, human or bureaucratic, but also the usual incestuousness, cliques, feuds, and small community pettiness and unsophisticated provinciality.

As with society overall, the ripples of the '60s in science fiction are still felt. And they are almost entirely positive. The near infinite potentials of the field became apparent, and it has been taking off in innumerable directions ever since. Readership has grown steadily. Events and developments of the past decade are beyond the scope and scholarship of this particular volume, but a few of them might be noted before an open ended conclusion:

The magazines, particularly *The Magazine of Fantasy and Science Fiction,* broadened their spectrum of material considerably.

The quality of writing (as opposed to conceptual quality) has finally become a major factor in science fiction.

The stigma attached to "that Buck Rogers stuff" is disintegrating fast; among most literate people, even nonaficionados, that particular prejudice has come to seem quaintly old fashioned.

The romantic, Burroughsian strain of science fiction has made a strong comeback. Here was one point where the science fictional revolution went contrary to the cultural one. Where the larger was vastly *more* concerned with issues of social significance, science fiction, which had in a way contributed to that area of consciousness, now became linked with the drug culture, fantasy, and escapism. An immediate result was a revival of interest in Burroughs' works; certainly linked was the popularity of Tolkien's epic fantasy. So another shift occurred, and more and more s-f leaned toward the fantastical and exotic.

A brief-lived rock group called itself "H. P. Lovecraft" and other rock groups in titles and lyrics showed an awareness of various aspects of science fiction.

There was an all-too-belated impact by women on science fiction. Long viewed as only of interest to the male for the inane reason that women weren't interested in science and technology (a view, it must be pointed out, that many women themselves promulgated), science fiction, until the last decade, had had only a handful of women writers. (But what a handful—C. L. Moore, Leigh Brackett, Margaret St. Clair, Judith Merril, and, of course, Mary Shelley.) The roster of names now is long and impressive, and they have found, as a side effect, that science fiction can serve as powerful propaganda (at least to the literate) for a cause.

While there is no room in this chapter to name even a few of the exciting and varied stories and novels that have enlarged and enhanced the science fictional universe in the last ten years, one demands to be mentioned, and it is indeed by a woman. There have been few writers in the genre that have in one or a few works figuratively goosed s-f into a quantum leap in quality and sophistication; Weinbaum and Bester spring to mind as examples. When a reviewer's copy of Ursula Le Guin's *The Left*

Hand of Darkness, hot off the press, had been read to the extent of some fifty pages, one knowledgeable addict remembers thinking, "Science fiction will never be the same." And it wasn't.

Sex has finally come more or less of age in science fiction, both as realistic detail and speculative subject matter. (For those who haven't read it, *The Left Hand of Darkness* is set on a planet whose inhabitants are physically bisexual—male at one time, female at another—or asexual; from this Le Guin extrapolates an extraordinary culture without the sexual dichotomy of our own.) And Le Guin's novel is a symbol of that event, where a brilliant but hardly experimental writing style set off beautifully a subject that was daring for the field.

More and more science fiction has been reprinted; publishers are slowly realizing that, being fantasy of a sort, s-f doesn't date except for style.

Isaac Asimov and Arthur C. Clarke became well known outside the science fiction world; both men, nevertheless, kept up their ties in the field. Robert A. Heinlein also gained fame, but almost entirely for his work as a science fiction writer, which is a unique achievement. (Clarke, Asimov, and Heinlein have entries in the recent *Random House Encyclopedia,* as does Tolkien.)

So what have we ended up with? What *is* science fiction, after all that? Well, let's settle on a definition that emerged some ways back in this article: "Science fiction is a form of realistic fantasy whose wonders are explained by a scientific or pseudo-scientific rationale." It doesn't fall trippingly off the tongue but it's still simpler than most we've heard. And if you like pictures or diagrams, you can visualize the past of science fiction as a tree, with some sturdy and powerful roots (the 19th century "fathers and mother"), one stem (the American magazine period ca. 1920-1950), and after that such a branching and leafing and flowering as has seldom been seen in any form of art or literature.

We can admittedly be accused of a certain chauvinism here for not mentioning any foreign language s-f. What *has* been translated is either humorlessly satirically Meaningful—the middle Europeans—or light to the point of being ephemeral—the French. There may well be hundreds of masterpieces out there waiting to be translated; until they are, we will confine our admiration to the Anglo-American authors.

And why read science fiction? Well, the most valid and simple answer to that is because one enjoys it. But if pressed by a classic pedant that must have an answer based on values beyond enjoyment, one can always fall back on wonderful Mary Shelley and her magic paragraph.

It gives us another point of view; that our minds are stretched to either seeing humanity from an outside position, or at least an alternate. Through science fiction, we are given different facets of reality, and we are trained to extrapolate not only A, but B and C from current reality. We can even venture to say that if the majority of Americans had been science fiction readers fifty years ago, we would not be in the ecological mess we're in now, since it might have been more readily seen by more people able to do more about it.

But mostly, science fiction is the play of and on reality; it is the thinking man's escape, and we'd have it no different.

As long as there is an unexplored corner of this universe, there will be some form of science fiction to speculate on what's in it; as long as there is youth, there will be young minds speculating.

Worlds without end. Amen.

Index